IN MY OWN NAME

MAUREEN McTEER

A MEMOIR

Random House Canada

www.randomhouse.ca

NATIONAL LIBRARY OF CANADA CATALOGUING IN PUBLICATION

McTeer, Maureen, 1952–
In my own name : a memoir / Maureen McTeer.

Includes index.
ISBN 0-679-31231-5

1. McTeer, Maureen, 1952– 2. Prime ministers' spouses—Canada—Biography.
3. Lawyers—Canada—Biography. 4. Ottawa (Ont.)—Biography. I. Title.

KE416.M38A35 2003   340'.092   C2003-903055-5
KF345.Z9M38 2003

Jacket and text design: CS Richardson

Photographs are from the author's collection.

PRINTED IN THE UNITED STATES OF AMERICA

10 9 8 7 6 5 4 3 2 1

To Joe, Catherine, Chad and Mom,
and my family near and far. Thank you for your love
and for a half-lifetime of memories.

INTRODUCTION

TODAY, JUNE 8, 2002, IS CATHERINE'S wedding day. Beautiful and poised, my daughter glides into the National Gallery's Great Hall with her new husband, Chad Schella. Behind them, the Parliament Buildings are bathed in the June evening light. She has chosen this magnificent place for her wedding dinner to remind people of our love of art and to have "Daddy's office" (as she used to call the Parliament Buildings) in the background. Their stately presence reminds us of the political dramas that have formed our lives. I watch my precious daughter, standing between her father and husband, and am filled with happiness. Turning slightly, I see the tiny island to the west in the river nearby. Just over a century ago, my Irish ancestors would have been quarantined there for fear they carried deadly, contagious diseases. Today, four generations later, the island's buildings are in ruins; my family is a proud part of Canada's capital city, my husband one of our country's leading statesmen. What would they have thought had they been able to see us now, such a fortunate family, blessed with good friends, surrounded by people of affluence and influence.

Above the celebration, I hear my husband's distinctive laugh and glance back as he greets Jean Charest, a friend whose decision to step down as leader of the Progressive Conservative

Party of Canada in 1998 so dramatically altered my own life. It was during the leadership campaign which followed that Catherine met Chad and they fell in love. I watch the two of them greet the crowd and I wonder if the lessons that politics at its best can teach—those of commitment and loyalty—will bind them together as they have Joe and me these past thirty years.

I laugh as I spy my closest girlfriends gather in a circle around Catherine. They support her today as they have always supported me. I have known them for decades, and our lives are bound by stories of happiness and pain, of good times and bad. As each one hugs my only child, I thank them quietly for their presence with me today, and pray that Catherine will be as lucky in her friendships as I have been in mine.

In a whirl, my mother enters the huge windowed hall, ushered along by my youngest sister, Jane, who is Catherine's godmother. In a minute they will join me and Chad's mother, Charmaine, to pose for family pictures. My mother is bursting with pride. Friendly and warm, she greets old friends and makes Chad's family feel at home. As I watch her, I feel a sudden stab of sadness. I wish my father were here. He has been gone for twenty-four years now, almost all of Catherine's life, yet I know he would have been proud of this sight. The room below is filled with people from politics, business and sports, friends from all walks of life who have touched Catherine's and Chad's lives over the years and who are joined by their love for this young couple. I become aware that my name is being called, and I turn to see my new family waiting. For twenty-five years, Joe, Catherine and I have been a close-knit trio. Now, as I welcome Chad with a hug, I realize that we are four. I kiss them all and we smile for the camera. A new stage of our lives begins.

—

In every life there are moments like these—events that mark passages and require reflection. Catherine's wedding is one such moment in a year that has been filled with passages. In February 2002, I turned fifty. It has been a busy year—a wedding, two moves, Joe's decision to step down as party leader and my own to take a sabbatical year in England. Even by the standards of my hectic life, this has been a pivotal year for us personally and professionally.

And, of course, I decided to write this book, allowing me to share some of my own stories of the first half of my life's journey, as lived by a very private person in a very public way. My life has been fascinating and full, with its share of happiness and of pain. No lesson could have prepared me for the public life I have led and the prominent role I have assumed. I have challenged social conventions: I kept my name when it was unpopular; became a feminist before it was fashionable; and joined the first wave of women professionals who sought to balance family and work, refusing to choose one over the other. I ran for Parliament in a federal election—as part of the first husband-and-wife team to ever do this—to show by my own example that politics is a profession that needs women. Through all of this I have sought to carve a different role for myself as a political wife and an independent woman. It has rarely been easy, but it has always been worthwhile—a life of opportunity and hope, of birth and death, of public duty and personal commitment.

I am about to enter a new stage of my life. But before I do, I need to retrace some of my steps. I have spent the past three decades at high speed, taking care of my family, pushing forward in my career and fighting to keep a private life while charting new waters in a public one. Unnoticed, the passing years have brought me to middle age. The retirement years are supposed to lie ahead, and yet I feel energized and restless for new adventures. I belong to a lucky generation—the first generation of women to taste equality, enjoy higher education and compete professionally in all fields. I have been in the vanguard of social changes so profound that they have yet to be digested fully and understood. I am a woman of my generation—a feminist and mother, a professional and volunteer. I am an empty-nester and a chronically worried parent. I want to abandon well-travelled paths in favour of others yet unknown. I am in transition. Joe and I both are, and this both excites and frightens me. So I have stopped here for a moment to reflect, to look back so I can move forward. This, then, is my story, which I share, as always, in my own name.

1

IN THE SPRING OF 2001, CARROLL O'CONNOR, the actor who played the character Archie Bunker in a long-running television series, died. I was surprised at the flood of memories his death evoked. For Carroll O'Connor and my father looked like identical twins. When we were young we thought that maybe he was a long-lost uncle and watched his show diligently for a mention of Canadian cousins. Now it seems to me that the Archie Bunker character summed up my father's generation. He belonged to a generation that lived through massive social change over which he had no control, and which he bitterly resented and resisted. In the days following O'Connor's death, I caught some old episodes of *All in the Family*. I was appalled at Archie's behaviour, and yet it reminded me of a time not so long ago, when men regularly treated women with disrespect, and it was acceptable to portray women as stupid, mindless domestic servants in their own homes. Racial and sexual discrimination were endemic, and domestic violence and verbal abuse were all too often part of the family picture. I thought a lot about the memories of my father these episodes evoked and realized for the first time that despite the physical similarities, the characters of Archie and our "Archie" (as we called our father in his later years) were very different. Yes, my father was a great defender of the status quo in matters of family life. He was the father and expected my mother, his five daughters and his son to accept his decisions on all matters that affected the family. Yet despite this, he also tried to understand what was going on in the world into which he was propelling his six children. He sought an education for his daughters and always urged us to achieve—be it in school or sports or public speaking. Though he saw the home front as women's work, he supported my mother by doing the shopping and even cooking on the weekends to give her a break. He had one foot in the past and one in the future and was, as a result, a bundle of both certainty and contradiction.

My father was an Ottawa native and an all-round athlete in his youth. In the 1930s, he played football with St. Patrick's College in Ottawa and paddled with the Rideau Canoe Club. But his passion was hockey and, in 1938, he was recruited to the North Bay Trappers to play defence on the strongest junior team in northern Ontario. While there, he attended Scollard Hall high school and played for their rugby team. During this period, Dad was on the reserve list for the Detroit Red Wings, and was to set sail for Scotland upon graduation in 1939 to play hockey for the Edinburgh Rockets. The outbreak of war in Europe forced him to join the Washington Eagles of the Eastern Hockey League from 1939 to 1941, after which he joined the Canadian army.

My parents met in Hamilton, Ontario, introduced by my mother's older sister, who was a colleague of my father's. They courted against the objections of both their families—hers, farming Irish-Canadian Protestants, and his, urban Irish-Canadian Catholics. Only two of her six sisters attended the wedding in the Catholic church in Hamilton on Thanksgiving weekend in 1949, and her conversion to Roman Catholicism would be a family dividing line for years to come. Until I was in school, I rarely saw my maternal grandparents, although one day, shortly after my brother's birth in 1961, my grandmother called a truce and visited us at home.

They had been long and lonely years for my mother. A beautiful and fun-loving young woman, she had her first child in 1951, followed by me and the twins in the next twenty-seven months. My older sister, Colleen, was just under a year when I was born in 1952, and I was a mere fifteen months when the twins, Patricia and Pamela, were born the following June. My sister Jane was born five years later and my only brother, John, three years after that in 1961. Women rarely had recourse to contraception in those days, and after the twins were born, my mother was in despair. She once told me of her reaction at the twins' birth. At that time there was no ultrasound, and women were anesthetized while giving birth. When she awoke after the delivery, she was so shocked at the news that she started to cry. She asked the nurse how she would cope. "No problem," said her nurse. "I've been trying for years to get pregnant and I'll take them both for you." My mother stopped crying and took my twin sisters home.

My father's sales job kept him away most of the week, and in the early years of her marriage my mother was left to fend for herself on a small acreage thirty miles east of Ottawa. Always a pragmatist, she decided to use her farming experience to add to our family's meagre income. She raised everything from pigs to turkeys until she finally took a clerical job with an insurance company in Ottawa in 1965, when my brother was four years old. My clearest memory of my mother is as a peacemaker. She rarely challenged my father's decisions, even though she was a determined and intelligent woman with views of her own. They often spoke of building a new home, but it was always a dream "for the future." Finally, fed up with the plumbing and other problems of our old farmhouse, my mother put her foot down. In 1967, on a salary of about fifteen thousand dollars a year, Mom decided to borrow the money from an elderly and wealthy family friend to build a new home—a bungalow that became our Centennial project and in which she still lives today.

Most weeks when I am in Ottawa now I drive the thirty kilometres or so to my childhood home on the Ottawa River near Cumberland, Ontario, to have supper with my mother. The neighbourhood has been changing this past decade, and it won't be long before all the small farms around hers give way to subdivisions. When I was growing up, though, before Ottawa started moving east and homes replaced hayfields, the landscape and lifestyle of rural eastern Ontario revolved around a simple way of life. Ours was a quiet existence that included school, play, church, domestic chores, Brownies, 4-H and horseback riding. It was an existence that bred a strong sense of self-reliance in all of us.

I had no inkling of the shape my life would take, yet from the earliest days, my parents pushed me to master my shyness and my fear of crowds and public speaking. Until high school, I was overcome by panic and nausea every time I had to speak in public. I remember pleading with my mother one night when, as the leader of my Brownie pack, I had to say the grace at our annual mother-daughter dinner. "Just read your notes," she said soothingly, and held my hand all the way into town. I am not sure when I stopped being sick before speaking in public, but I do know that my father's insistence that my older sister and I compete in local public-speaking contests and join the high school debating team made a real difference. All that practice finally forced me to overcome my fear. I sometimes laugh to think of the first time I told my father that I charged a fee to speak. "They pay *you* to talk!" Then, ever my booster, he added: "Well, I told you years ago that you were a good speaker."

From the time Colleen started grade one in 1957, we were all taught the importance of education. My father worked as a salesman for a national moving company then, and knew that his future prospects were hampered by his lack of a university education. Dad was always a keen observer of social trends, and his growing up in Ottawa as a Roman Catholic had meant he had many French-speaking friends at school and in sports. He watched the changing political and social landscape around the capital and decided that in the future, bilingualism would be essential. I can remember his predicting, during the 1965 election campaign, that John Diefenbaker, his political hero, would be the last unilingual national political leader. He also predicted that bilingualism would soon be required for jobs and promotions in the federal government. And so, when it came time for us to start school, he enrolled us in the local separate school that was, given the rules in Ontario at the time, really a French Roman Catholic school. My father was a difficult man with a personality set in stone. He could be charming, but generally he lacked subtlety and had no intention of learning any. He was a pugilist who fought until he was either defeated or had won. Years later, he told me the story of how he had stared down the local school board members who objected to a unilingual English-speaking family attending "their" French school. My father was setting a precedent; no English family had ever gone there before. We were Roman Catholic, my father told them, and were entitled to attend the separate school. They disagreed, and used the fact that my mother had been raised an Anglican against him—to accept English-speaking children with a Protestant mother was really asking too much. "She's Catholic now," my father assured them, showing the reluctant board members her baptismal certificate and ours. "They will slow down our children, as they speak no French," a board member claimed. My father called their bluff. He struck a deal with them. We would all start grade one and if any of us did not come first in our class, he would withdraw us voluntarily. So that he could help us, he sat at the head of the dining-room table during the school year while we all did our homework around him, and he taught himself French by memorizing ten words a day from an English-French dictionary.

Recently, I drove by the little one-room school on my way from my mother's to my sister Jane's horse farm nearby and stopped to take a closer look at the place that had been my daily destination for the first eight years of my school life. It is someone's country home now, but it brought back vividly my first day of school. My older sister, Colleen, was six when I started, and entering grade two. She had blazed the trail for me the year before, walking the two miles to class all alone each morning and then again in the afternoon. My mother left the twins with a neighbour the day I started grade one, and walked with Colleen and me to school. As Colleen skipped along, she taught me a few basic words of French so I could greet the teacher and sound as if I was "bilingual" (as she put it). I was terribly upset about starting school and my mother could sense it. Colleen, the extrovert and pioneer, had insisted that there was nothing to it, but I was not reassured. As we drew closer to the school, Colleen told me quickly that I had to stick up for myself. "Don't cry," she warned me, "they hate cry-babies." She was already running ahead to greet her friends, and had no intention of being seen with her little sister.

Even today, my mother can speak only a few words of French. She can greet and thank people politely, and in a show of national pride in 1967, she memorized the words to "O Canada" in French. But that morning, as she introduced me to my new teacher, Madame Dubeau, neither of us knew a word of French. Madame Dubeau was a middle-aged woman who never smiled. But she was a brilliant teacher and a consummate disciplinarian and she filled me with a love of learning.

Our one-room school had only thirty students and all the classes were small. There was only one other student in grade one. Jacques Roy was the last child of a large family who had all attended this school. I thought he was so lucky, as he had an older brother and two sisters in higher grades to defend him, and I had only Colleen. His oldest sister, though, took me under her protective wing, clucking over the two of us and calling us *les petits*. Jacques and I were to experience all the passages of grade school together and then, at the end of grade eight, I went off to Notre Dame, a Catholic girls' school in Ottawa, and he went to the local French high school. We said our goodbyes and never saw each other again.

When that exhausting first day of school was finally over, Colleen and I started the long walk home. Only after the last of our schoolmates left us along the way did she take my hand and carry my bag. More than anything, I wanted my mother, who had promised me that she would pick us up at the halfway mark in the buggy with our Shetland pony. And there she was, holding our pony with my four-year-old twin sisters beside her, cheering us on, as if we were exhausted marathon runners nearing the finish line. Seeing her waiting for me that day remains one of the happiest pictures of my childhood. I crawled up onto the buggy seat beside her, hugged her tightly and then, suddenly conscious of my new status, proudly told my little sisters all about school.

From that first day, I began to learn the traditions of my French-Canadian friends. At school we prayed three times a day. In the morning, we said routine prayers before our first class; after lunch we all kneeled on the seat of our desks, our arms extended in a cross, and recited the rosary; and when classes ended, we said a prayer to keep us safe on our return home. We had catechism each day, and I started a collection of holy pictures of Christ and the saints, which we received when we had a perfect mark in class. By Christmas of that first year, I had mastered all the required prayers in French, and could pray more easily in French than English—a habit I maintain to this day. Until grade three all lessons were in French only. From then on, we learned everything in both languages. We saw Canadian history through the eyes of our French-speaking friends, and it had its own twists. I remember telling my mother confidently that the French had won the Battle of the Plains of Abraham. When she called to ask the teacher what was going on, she was told that the British had cheated!

While my father had trumped the local school board, the truth was that our presence was not always welcome. I was conscious of being an outsider. For all of our assimilation into the dominant culture at school, we were the only family who spoke English at home. We did not watch the popular French television serials, like *Les belles histoires du pays d'en haut*, and we cheered for the Toronto Maple Leafs rather than the Montreal Canadiens. We went to the English-language church most of the time, although after my father had a run-in with the local priest, we did move to the French church instead. We badgered our mother to make us *tourtières* and *ragoût de pattes de cochon* and to mark New Year's Day as our friends did. We did not fit in fully in either group—English or French. At school, we were the only English family. At home and in our family's circle, we were the only English kids who spoke and studied in French.

My family was always slightly different from the others, and that experience can make a person either a total conformist or a confirmed individualist. I tried both as I grew up, but found conforming too exhausting. Yet my sisters and I managed remarkably well despite the strangeness of our lives in the context of the time, when the French and English rarely met as equals. We learned early the excitement of a new culture as well as its language. The experiences of that one-room school shaped my perception of diversity in Canada, and made me sensitive to those who must start from scratch in a new environment. They also provided me with a depth of understanding about the cause of Quebec nationalism. During those eight pivotal years, I became fluently bilingual, and my sisters and I all kept our father's commitment to stand first in our grade. Yet in the end, we were still an English family in an all-French school, a kind of oddity, made more so by my father's insistence that we go to university. Only one other person in that school's forty-five-year history joined Colleen and me at university. As my very best friend in grade school, Suzanne Lalonde, confided to me one day as we walked the long road home from our school: "In the end, Maureen, you must remember, you are really English, not French, even though you sound just like me."

My father had two passions outside our family—hockey and politics. He taught us all to skate and stickhandle. There were no girls' hockey teams in our area, so we played with the neighbourhood boys on the Ottawa River behind our home and on the open rink in the village of Cumberland nearby, and I dreamed of a future in the National Hockey League.

My first brush with feminism came as a result of this when I was about twelve, during a game between the Toronto Maple Leafs and the Montreal Canadiens. My father and I were in the living room enjoying our well-established Saturday-night ritual of *Hockey Night in Canada*. We were debating the pros and cons of yet another penalty for Eddie Shack on the Toronto team. "When I am in the NHL," I proclaimed, "I will be like Gordie Howe." I waited for my father's words of praise. Nothing. Turning from the black-and-white screen I looked at him and repeated myself. He didn't meet my eyes when he finally spoke, but his reply will always be clear in my mind. "Look at that team, Maureen," he said. "How many girls do you see? Girls don't play in the NHL."

He was right, of course. How had I missed the obvious? His answer affected both of us, challenging, as it did, everything he had ever taught me. It made no sense. Was he telling me that I could not play because of my skill as a hockey player or because I was a girl? All my short life he had pushed me to succeed, to try harder, to be first. I could skate and stickhandle and score. What else did I need for the NHL? Now he was telling me something very different. All night and the next day I tried to figure out the lessons here. What should I do? How could I resolve this new and seemingly ridiculous dilemma? What did being a girl have to do with my chances in the NHL? Was this the only dream I would have to leave behind? Were there other activities and fun that girls were excluded from, and how would I find out?

On that cold wintry night in the 1960s, as I watched our national sport through a new lens of exclusion based on sex, I faced for the first time in my life the reality of being a girl. I had just been told by the very man who kept urging me to push myself that intelligence and ability were not enough for a woman. Up until then, my father had insisted that we could do whatever we wanted to do in life, provided we were willing to work for it. The sky was not a limit but a goal. He was wrong, of course. I would learn time and time again that there are different rules for girls and boys, for women and men, often explained away as natural and justifiable practices, based on our different physiology.

But the damage of this lesson was both subtle and serious. It taught me that the limiting of dreams for girls and for women goes beyond the question of careers and capabilities. Its corrosive effect runs deep, diminishing our sense of who we are and sapping our self-esteem. For many months, this new truth eroded my youthful self-confidence and struck at the heart of my ambition. The message was clear. Girls should conform. They should be happy to cheer rather than to play; to focus on the conventional and the convenient; to see security as the goal and risk as a threat. Before that, I had been looking forward to my independence in high school the following year, and assumed independence was part of all of our lives as adults. I wanted to be in charge of my own life. Wasn't that why my parents had encouraged me to study and excel at sports? Yet after this episode, I was not sure I would be.

I did recover from the initial shock of this bitter lesson. I came to see that I had two choices. I could give in and accept the core of my father's proposal—that girls could not achieve their dreams—or I could fight. I chose to fight. Since then, I have always stood for women's equality. I knew the stance would condemn me to being an outsider in a world and a society that prefers the status quo. And it would be a lie for me to pretend that I have not paid a price, both personally and professionally, for fighting for women's equality and for refusing to toe the line. Many times, I have comforted myself with one of my father's oft-repeated lines—"Remember that each morning when you look in the mirror, it is the person in front of you with whom you will have to live."

Years after that night in our living room, I was approached by the organizers of the nascent women's hockey association in Canada to speak at their awards banquet in Spruce Grove, Alberta. These women played for the Hoffman Cup, in recognition of Abby Hoffman, who had disguised herself as a boy to play hockey as a child. I provided a second one, the McTeer Cup, for the runner-up team. I knew my late father would have seen the irony.

While I could no longer aspire to a career as a hockey player, no one could stand in the way of me indulging my growing interest in politics. My father urged me along into political activity, perhaps to lessen the blow that had been inflicted on my ego by his hockey announcement. When I was twelve, he decided to run for reeve of our municipal district, promising to clean up welfare abuse and reduce local taxes. He lost miserably, and would never again run for public office. His experience convinced him that his place was behind the scenes, as a political strategist and organizer. His unsuccessful municipal campaign was my first taste of politics, and while I was devastated at his defeat, the campaign was one of the most exciting things I had ever experienced. My mother hated politics and refused to participate. She thought it mean and brutal, and was upset by the heated arguments that are always part of any debate about issues. Politics was a sore point between my parents during my adolescence, but that did not stop me from sharing my father's passion for political strategy and campaigning. Like him, I saw politics as the tool with which changes to our lives could be accomplished. He was insistent that giving in this kind of way was essential to our democracy. I did not then fully understand how right he was, but was enthused by his commitment and shared it.

By the time I started high school in 1965, he was the regional organizer for the provincial Progressive Conservative Party. He had always worked for the federal PC party at election time. I remember coming home from school one Friday night when I was fifteen and in grade eleven, to be told by my father that I was the new president of the party's provincial youth wing in our constituency. "You will second the nomination of Albert Bélanger, our provincial candidate in Prescott-Russell," he told me. "He is a good man." I was still having trouble speaking in public without being sick to my stomach, and I protested: "I'll go, but I can't give the speech." My protests made no difference; nor did my mother's pleading on my behalf. Colleen and I were involved; she was one of the riding's youth vice-presidents. Still, Mom did not want either of us to have anything to do with politics and told my father so. The next weekend, though, after days of anxious memorizing, I went before a large and partisan crowd in Hawkesbury, Ontario, and dutifully delivered the speech he had prepared for me. Our candidate, Albert Bélanger, went on to win that provincial election. It was an exciting campaign, and by the end of it, I was hooked. Six months later, Colleen and I took the bus to Toronto and were Albert's guests at Queen's Park. We met Premier John Robarts and saw question period. Thus began my lifelong commitment to political activity and the PC Party.

When I graduated from grade eight, my parents decided to send Colleen and me to Notre Dame, a Catholic high school for girls in Ottawa. I had been looking forward to the independence I assumed high school offered and had wanted to attend the local public high school. But that year, to everyone's astonishment, Colleen failed grade ten and my fate was sealed. No amount of complaining would change my father's mind. His daughters would be educated, and there would be no distractions. Obviously, my very bright sister had been distracted (I assumed he meant by boys). That would not happen again if we went to a Catholic girls' school. The two of us would stay with my father's mother and maiden sister in Ottawa during the week and come home with him on the weekend. I railed about the unfairness of it all, and protested being punished for Colleen's actions—all to no avail. That September I began high school at Notre Dame.

There is considerable debate in the literature these days about the value and purpose of girls-only schools. I have heard the argument that it is harmful for adolescent girls, as it deprives them of the experience of socializing and competing with boys as peers in the classroom. But from my own experience, I believe that having time during adolescence for athletic and academic challenges without the distraction of the opposite sex around constantly is a real advantage for young women. Even though I was increasingly self-confident, I came from a family dominated by girls, and I doubt I would have pushed myself or shown qualities of leadership at such a young age had I been surrounded by boys. I also saw how the boys were favoured by certain teachers in later co-ed classes, and I resented the change in the class dynamic that resulted. I particularly noticed how my female friends reacted. A climate of competition reigned and we vied for the attention of the boys rather than helping each other as we did when they weren't with us. Over those five years, I built strong friendships with my classmates, some of which last to this day. It was also the first time in my life that I fully realized women could be educated and independent. The nuns seemed to me to be the first feminists I had ever met, and several inspired me to higher education and future achievement. They also encouraged me to consider a religious vocation, and I admit to thinking seriously of it for a time. But by grade thirteen, I could see that the religious life was not really for me. There was a limit to my capacity to follow strict rules, and by then I had a boyfriend and was looking forward to the excitement of university.

In grade twelve, I decided that I would like to study for a career in law. I was on the Ontario PC Youth Executive, and as a young, bilingual woman, I was asked regularly to thank Premier John Robarts at fundraising dinners around the province. Many of my young political friends were planning to study law and I, too, felt that it was the best training for politics. My father urged me along in this choice, but my mother, ever the pragmatist, was aware that there was no money in the budget for a university education. Six years of study seemed a long and expensive time, and student loans would leave me burdened before I even started work. She wanted me to consider nursing instead. She encouraged Colleen to go first to teachers' college, work a few years and then to go on to university for an education degree. As a woman who had long ago abandoned the hope of an easy life, she wanted us to have a practical education. We always knew that if we wanted to go to university we had to pay our own way; and there were precious few well-paying summer jobs available to us. A nursing degree in the early 1970s came at minimum cost and with a guarantee of a life-long job (or so said the popular wisdom of the time). Nursing students received their education "free," and then paid the hospital back by working on the wards—good training for them and low-cost labour for the hospitals. This seemed a perfect solution to my mother. "Start at the bottom and work up," she suggested. "You can go back and get a university degree later when you've saved up some money. A nurse (and a teacher) can always get a job." But when you are eighteen, thirty looks ancient, and I did not want to be old and grey before finally reaching my goal. "No," I told her, "I plan to study law."

Over the Christmas holiday at the end of 1968, my father and I took one of our long walks along the old road in front of our home. As we walked along in the dark, I could tell that he was upset about something. In a quiet voice, he finally said: "I'm really sorry to have pushed you all these years to get a good education and to now be unable to pay for your university." It was the only time my father ever apologized to me, and I was so startled I was not sure what I could say to make him feel better. "That's what scholarships are for," I told him. I was finishing high school on a scholarship and knew this was an option for university. A city-wide high school debating tournament was coming up in February and I had been asked to debate for Notre Dame's team. As my father and I walked, I realized that this tournament was my main hope for university—the top prize was an entrance scholarship to the University of Ottawa. I decided to register and asked Colleen to be my debating partner. She was a top athlete and was to be the valedictorian at her grade thirteen graduation later that year. She was an Ontario Scholar and planned to study for a degree in physical education and French at university. After some cajoling, she agreed and we immediately set our minds to the task, assisted by Sister Pauline Jutras, the debating coach at Notre Dame. We both wanted to win, for we knew that a scholarship would be the answer to our prayers.

The day of the event was snowy and miserable, and we worried that we might not make it into town on time for the early morning debate. When we got there, though, we were confident and well practiced and won the key morning debate and the impromptu one during the noon hour. As the day drew to its climax, our names were called and we jumped up excitedly from the audience to join in the final debate. We gave it all we had, helped along by our family and classmates who cheered us from the front seats. I was almost too excited to hear the judge announce that Colleen and I were the winning team and that I was the tournament's best speaker. We were rushed by our friends, and I could see my parents out of the corner of my eye, beaming at our victory. I knew then that I really could pursue a career in law. I had won a scholarship and the chance to attend university.

—

Of course, no one ever promised that life would be a straight line, and it soon became clear that unless manna came from heaven or we won the Irish Sweepstakes, Colleen would not be able to save enough money from her summer job to attend university that fall. She planned to take out a student loan if she could, but my parents were reluctant to have her start her life in debt. We all talked about options, but none seemed to work. One day, amid all this discussion of Colleen's future, it occurred to me that one solution to this problem would be for me to give her my scholarship. I felt panicky at the thought, not particularly generous or heroic. If anything, I felt resigned and depressed. But Colleen was my older sister; she was intelligent and she deserved this. My parents knew how much I wanted to study law, and they refused to let me make the sacrifice at first. Yet they knew as I did that Colleen had to go to university first and so, that June, they accepted my decision to give her my entrance scholarship.

The process seemed straightforward to me, but convincing the university was another story. I argued that Colleen had been my debating partner, that she had been runner-up for the prize, that she needed it right now and I did not. When this failed, I told the university officials that I would be stepping aside, knowing that were I to do this, the scholarship would automatically go to her. And so, in 1969, Colleen went to university and I entered grade thirteen, not the happiest person in the world, but comforted by the feeling that comes when you make a sacrifice for someone you love.

2

GRADE THIRTEEN WAS A DIFFICULT YEAR. All my life, my father and I had been close, but as I neared my eighteenth birthday and became more independent and self-confident, our relationship deteriorated. I was no longer willing to accept everything he said at face value, and my aggressive style, so important in debating, often turned our discussions into fights. He did not like my boyfriend, George Johnstone, who was two years older than I was and had started university in Ottawa that fall. I wanted more freedom to attend college events with him; my father insisted on a strict curfew of 11 P.M. on the weekends. I still lived with my grandmother and aunt during the week and felt as if I was under house arrest, unable to make any phone calls or go out in the evening. It became a year of contradictions. I was too young to be really independent and yet too old to follow blindly the rules set by my parents and teachers. I felt trapped, treated like a child at home and only a high school student at the university events I attended with Colleen or with George.

It was during this time that I decided I would go to university the next year no matter what. I saw university life as a promise of freedom and fun, and I was ready to flee my structured home life and set out on my own. Somehow I had to fund this decision, and I began in earnest to work through the options. I could always take out a student loan and hold a job while studying, but I worried that my grades would suffer if I tried to work and study at the same time. Around Christmas, as Sister Jutras was canvassing the class for recruits once again for the annual *Ottawa Journal*–University of Ottawa debating tournament, I hit upon a possible solution. If I could win a debating tournament one year, why couldn't I win it again? Sister Jutras wasn't sure about the rules, but after a little digging, she discovered that nothing prevented one year's winner from debating (or even winning) again. The rules had always assumed that most of the competing students would be in grade thirteen. Without telling my parents, I asked a friend and classmate, Rosemarie Boyle, to debate with me and we registered. We prepared like fiends and Sister Jutras drilled us mercilessly. By the time the big day arrived in February, we could argue both sides with equal passion.

Then, as if I did not know that my university career hung in the balance, I nearly blew my chances before the debate even took place.

In early January 1969, on a lark, a group of girls in my class decided to try out for a contest sponsored by a popular local radio station. The dubious prize was a year as Miss CFRA. We all changed out of our school uniforms and went down after school one day to be interviewed by a panel of radio personalities and to answer such skill-testing questions as "What do you want to do when you grow up?" and "What is your favourite radio station?" My classmate Mary Carol Gilmore and I were among the three finalists, and the winner was to be announced at a big dance the night before the debating tournament. As finalists, we were required to attend and make a little speech explaining why we would be the best choice for this glorious title and a full year of unpaid smiling duties at local events. When I told my father he was furious, but I flatly refused his order to skip the dance and focus on the next day's debate. I was convinced I could do both and thought the party would be great fun. My father did not talk to me the entire week before the dance, but he did drive me there and pick me up after it was over. Fortunately, I came in second and was saved the year of smiling. To break the ice as we drove home, I declared: "Tomorrow, I will come first." He held his tongue.

It was tough slogging the next morning. I was tired from my late night, aggravating my regular nervousness. A migraine lurked behind my right eye all day, and I vowed never again to take on two major commitments at once—a promise I have never kept. Rosemarie and I started off slowly that morning, but Sister Jutras' coaching paid off, and we won all three of the required debates, advancing to the final round. Sister Jutras joined my father and mother, Colleen, Rosemarie's parents and some of our other classmates in the centre row. After all our years of public speaking, my father knew how important it was to have supporters near the front to allow us friendly eye contact, and he always sat where I could see him. Even though we were warring at home at the time, he watched me intently that afternoon and nodded encouragingly each time I scored a point for our team. I tried not to remember that my university career depended on winning, in case I panicked. After we finished, the judges left the room and conferred for a long time. I was terribly nervous when they finally returned and the lead judge rose to make the announcements. He seemed to go on forever about the quality of the debates and how hard it was to choose a winner. My stomach felt sick from all the adrenaline, and Colleen and my parents did not look much calmer than I did. Suddenly it occurred to me that all this talk meant something was wrong—maybe there was some rule we had missed that disqualified me from winning a second time. As this thought jumped into my mind, the judge turned dramatically to Rosemarie and me and congratulated us on winning the tournament. He praised

Rosemarie for her debating skills and my heart sank. Then, he handed her an envelope and told her that she had won the runner-up prize. Turning towards me, he offered his hand and said: "We have an unusual situation this year, but after a long discussion we have decided that despite her win last year, Miss McTeer must, on her merits, be awarded the top prize as best speaker of the tournament." I thought I would faint. My father beamed and hugged Sister Jutras, Colleen and Mom were jumping up and down, and I just sat there, relieved and exhausted. I had won the coveted prize, an entrance scholarship to the University of Ottawa.

No one had ever done this before; and after my second win the university promptly changed the rules so a student could win the entrance scholarship only once. I studied hard the rest of the term, and it was a wonderful moment when I graduated that June and discovered that I was an Ontario Scholar, just as Colleen had been. My application to the bachelor of arts program at the University of Ottawa had been accepted that May, and as I said goodbye to friends and teachers at the party on my high school graduation day, I could hardly wait for the summer to be over. Finally, I would be free of the constraints of my family and high school. I was off to university.

When I started university in September 1970, I was full of enthusiasm and energy. I decided not to waste a minute and joined the English debating team and the Progressive Conservative Campus Club. During initiation week, I walked past the Student Union building and saw an ad for writers for the English-language newspaper, *The Fulcrum*. Intrigued, I went in and met with the student editor, Ian Green (now a deputy minister in the federal government). Six people had volunteered to staff the paper, he told me, but there was one position open if I wanted it. I could be the features editor. Flattered, I agreed to my first assignment, due the following week. Without any previous experience, I was to write a feature-length article on a lay professor who taught theology and claimed his classes were being blacklisted because of his anti–Roman Catholic views. After a week of investigation, I agreed with his claim and said so in my article. No sooner had the paper hit the halls of the university than the rector's office called to demand a retraction.

Two weeks on campus and already I was in hot water. Ian called the "staff" together to discuss the issue, and in a show of solidarity, they stood by me and refused to retract. I was called to the office of the rector, Father Roger Guindon, to explain myself. He listened attentively, but to my surprise he offered no rebuttal. Instead, he congratulated me on winning the debating scholarship and noted positively that I was a Catholic and had been Notre Dame's youth representative on the special committee on Vatican II—the major international reform initiative within the Roman Catholic Church undertaken by Pope John XXIII in the 1960s. He said that he hoped I would focus on my studies in the future and not spend too much time on extracurricular activities like the student paper. We parted on a conciliatory note and the whole matter was dropped. I felt vindicated but worried that no matter how subtle and diplomatic the rector had been, I had been told to toe the line. Maybe life was not as free at university as I had thought.

Although I took the rector's words as a warning to avoid controversy, I did not feel I needed to become a hermit. As a young and energetic student away from home and family restraints, I was delighted to be at university. The University of Ottawa is situated in the heart of Canada's capital, and is a dynamic and political place. Its bilingual campus and location just across the Laurier Bridge from the Parliament Buildings have always made it a hub of political debate.

The fall of 1970 was no exception. The topic was Quebec. The political mood was tense as a new political movement, the

Parti Québécois (PQ), led by former provincial Liberal cabinet minister René Lévesque, was gaining strength and supporters to the cause of Quebec's independence from Canada. At the same time another group, the Front de libération du Québec (FLQ), advocated the use of force to achieve an independent Quebec and had been conducting a campaign of terror in that province, mainly through bombs in mailboxes. Hundreds of Quebec students were enrolled at the University of Ottawa, many of whom supported the Quebec nationalist cause and opposed Prime Minister Pierre Trudeau's centralist views. I could feel the tension whenever I entered the Student Union Building, the local coffee house or student pub. Everyone had an opinion on the matter, and I often joined in these discussions as much to learn what others felt as to offer my opinion on violence and democracy.

I admit that sometimes I was unnerved by all the rhetoric and surprised by the anger against English-speaking Canadians among many of the Quebec students. I was proud that I could speak French and argued with them in their own language. In my first month at university, as I struggled with the historic relationship between English and French Canadians, I thought often of the remark of my grade-school friend who had insisted that my bilingualism did not make me a French Canadian.

October 5, 1970, began as just another ordinary day for me. I awoke, had coffee and turned on my radio to listen to the morning news. I don't remember much else about that day, other than a feeling of nausea and panic. British trade commissioner James Cross had just been kidnapped from his Montreal home by members of a cell of the FLQ. The theory of Quebec independence that had been at the heart of so many discussions on campus had become a brutal fact. Five days later, in the early evening, another FLQ cell kidnapped Quebec's labour and immigration minister, Pierre Laporte, from his home in the Montreal suburb of St-Lambert. Like all my university friends, I was stunned. Hysteria and confusion dominated the public,

Parliament and the press. The kidnappers had several demands, including gold, the release of "political" prisoners and safe passage out of the country in return for the two men's release. Quebec Premier Robert Bourassa, supported by Montreal mayor Jean Drapeau, asked the federal government for troops, and some seventy-five hundred soldiers were deployed in Montreal, Quebec City and Ottawa. While even the Prime Minister agreed in his remarks to the nation that the kidnappers were "a few misguided persons," he was considering extraordinary action. When asked by journalist Tim Ralfe how far he was willing to go to meet the threat, he replied with the now famous phrase: "Well, just watch me!"

On October 16, he invoked the War Measures Act, which gave his government sweeping powers and suspended individual liberties and civil rights. This law had never before been used in peacetime, nor has it since. The FLQ, its members and supporters were declared illegal, and within forty-eight hours, 250 people had been arrested, including entertainers and writers. Thirty-six of those arrested were members of the PQ. René Lévesque wrote a newspaper article calling for "solidarity and calm democratic strength to prevent this dangerous climate from degenerating into blind repression." On Saturday, October 17, Pierre Laporte's dead body was found in the trunk of a car at a municipal airport near Montreal.

In that one week, our quiet campus in the heart of the capital changed from a place of free expression and heated debate to an armed camp. On every corner in downtown Ottawa, soldiers with machine guns stood guard against terrorists. The Parliament Buildings were closed and surrounded by troops. We were under siege. It was as if the Canada I had known—sleepy, solid, secure—had somehow morphed into a monster. I was frightened by the kidnappings and the violence, but felt that the Prime Minister's decision to invoke the War Measures Act was wrong. I applauded Opposition leader Robert Stanfield and

New Democrat Tommy Douglas for expressing reservations about the law, and agreed with Douglas that the government had used "a sledgehammer to crack a peanut." I understood that a senior politician had been murdered and that the situation was serious. But I could not accept that suspending my citizens' legal rights would help the government catch the killers. I supported more money and personnel for the police to do their job, but the suspension of our rights merely gave the police carte blanche to attack the federal government's political enemies. Students who had expressed support for Quebec's independence on campus went into hiding.

I remember one night when a friend was driving me home and we were stopped at a red light on campus. Like a flash, a classmate raced out from behind a building, jumped into the back of our car and flung herself on the floor out of view. She was terrified of being arrested. Suddenly, all of this chaos had a human face.

During those difficult days, my views on democracy and freedom were put to the test. Gone were the innocent times when we had all debated and disagreed about Quebec nationalism and separatism. I believed then, as I do now, that there can be no freedom without the basic legal right of free expression. Until the October Crisis, I had assumed that as a Canadian, I had freedom of expression as my birthright. I could voice my opinions and opposition to government policy, and I often did so. But after the War Measures Act was declared that October, the chill of fear silenced me. I saw a spy in every classroom and feared arrest if I was bold enough to object to the government's draconian methods.

The War Measures Act did more than give the police unlimited power to search without a warrant, to arrest without an immediate charge and to refuse bail without cause. It set the precedent for the removal of our fundamental rights by a simple vote in Parliament. The October Crisis ended my political innocence. I saw how easily public opinion could be whipped up to rally the majority against the minority and the ease with which a charismatic leader could turn us to his plans. I prayed for the soul of Pierre Laporte and for the safe return of James Cross but I grieved for my country and what it had become. The events of that autumn taught me a difficult lesson. My rights are no more guaranteed here than in any other democracy. I would never again blindly trust the Parliament of Canada to protect my rights. I saw that democracy was not just precious but precarious, and I vowed to be vigilant against its abuse. In those bleak fall days in 1970, Canada was under martial law. I lived in a country that was at peace and yet at war with itself. It is a memory I can never forget. It became one of the defining moments of my life and made my political involvement and commitment more than a youthful distraction. It made it my life's focus.

—

During the winter of 1971, the PC Party of Ontario held its leadership convention in Toronto to replace John Robarts, who was stepping down. Still reeling from the October Crisis, I felt that the frivolity of such a convention, with all its parties and hoopla, was irrelevant to the larger questions of the day. I considered not attending, but under pressure from my father joined the campaign team of Ottawa provincial member A.B.R. (Bert) Lawrence. My father had been his riding campaign manager and was his organizational chairman for our area. While it was a long shot, Dad felt a leadership run would position Bert for a top cabinet post in the next Ontario government. I went to Toronto as a youth delegate and was glad that I did. Working with my father again helped me to bridge some of the distance that had grown between us during my last year of high school. The arrangement was good for him, too, as once again he could be my political mentor. But most important for the long term, working with my father that week taught me how a leadership campaign was run. Dad had been right about Bert's chances, and the former education minister, Bill Davis, won the race and became Premier. Returning to Ottawa at the end of the week, I realized that I had enjoyed the distraction of the leadership race and had made lasting political friendships. This was to be the last time, however, that I ever attended a provincial leadership campaign. After all the drama of politics on Parliament Hill that year, I found the lure of the federal scene much more enticing and compelling. The issues at the provincial level seemed mundane by comparison.

That spring, my relationship with my boyfriend needed attention, too. He did not like politics at all, and I knew our relationship would end if I ignored his concern that I was too caught up in it. He was an only child and his parents treated me like their daughter. I loved them all dearly and did not want politics to end our connection. But the truth was that political activity was an integral part of my life. Nor was this commitment merely to partisan party politics. I had been raised to believe in community service and the importance of political commitment as a citizen living in a free society. I had been shaken to my roots by the previous autumn's crisis, and was more decided than ever to become a lawyer and to work for our basic rights and freedoms. I no longer hesitated about being involved in all kinds of causes and was increasingly interested in issues of women's equality, such as access to education and equal pay. I often felt pulled in two directions—one towards a quiet existence beyond politics and public service, the other towards even greater commitment to both. It was a problem that would not go away.

After the provincial leadership convention, I began to look for a summer job. Ian Green, my editor at the student paper, and Hugh Segal, president of the student union, had jobs lined up as staffers with PC members of Parliament and agreed to look around the Hill on my behalf. Aware of my plans for a legal career, they found me a job with the legal officer in the PC parliamentary research office. My job was to draft private members' bills and to undertake legislative and policy research for Robert Stanfield and his caucus. My new boss, Robert Batt, was a brilliant legislative lawyer, but he was overwhelmed and his office showed it. I cleaned up his office and set up a filing system for him before I tackled anything else. During that summer, I confided to Bob my growing interest in women's equality, and he asked the director to assign me the briefing note on women's issues for the party's policy conference that year. I could not believe my good fortune.

I began to think of running for Parliament. I discussed it with my father, noting that other friends my age, including Sean O'Sullivan, president of the Ontario Youth Association, Perrin Beatty, whom I had met during Bert Lawrence's leadership campaign, and my university friend Hugh Segal, would run in the coming election. Dad was adamantly against my running at that time, insisting that I was too young and urging me to finish university before taking on such a huge responsibility. He reminded me of how hard I had tried to win a scholarship to university and told me not to waste this chance to start a career in law. I had to concede that he was right.

After an intense summer of working directly with the PC caucus, I decided to step back a bit from politics that semester and focus on my studies and debating commitments. I agreed to debate for the university in a major international tournament that fall at Wesleyan University in Connecticut and worked hard to prepare. Ian Green was also on the team, and we made it to the semifinals, only to be defeated by an American team. It was my first big trip to the United States, and I was fascinated by the dynamic contrast among the American university students at the tournament. They were full of opinions and not shy about sharing them. At the social event the night before the debate, I joined a group of American students who were hotly contesting whether the U.S. and the Soviet Union would sign a strategic-arms-control agreement. Moving on to another room at the fraternity house where the party was taking place, I joined a group that was adamant that America's invasion of Laos earlier that year had not succeeded in giving them the edge in the Vietnam War. They agreed that there had to be an end to the Vietnam War, but there was no agreement about President Richard Nixon's chances of re-election the following November.

Our own coach was a philosophy professor from the University of Ottawa who hailed from Massachusetts, and all the way home I grilled him on American politics. My head was spinning from all the discussions, and I wished that I had enough money to study in the United States for a year. The trip awakened in me the desire to travel and learn more about American history. It also convinced me that I should take a year off after completing my undergraduate degree in 1973 to travel before going to law school.

At the end of March 1972, I was offered a summer job at the PC research office again. With an election expected that fall, and the polls indicating that Robert Stanfield stood an excellent chance of winning, my job description was tailored to meet the needs of the national campaign. My boyfriend had to be away that summer and I decided that I would accept the job offer. Although I started again in the research office, it wasn't long before I became a part of the campaign team and was asked to handle the issue advance for the leader in Ontario and Quebec. This required me to provide a briefing on all the issues of concern in each of the constituencies that he visited—no small task that summer, as he criss-crossed the country, speaking at candidate nomination meetings and preparing for the election campaign. I was chosen for this specific job in part because I was bilingual, but more for my experience in political organization—two necessary skills in any national tour.

It was an exciting summer. I travelled around Ontario and Quebec advancing the leader's visits to constituencies. I was too young to rent a car, so Murray Coolican, Stanfield's executive assistant, lent me his old Volvo with an equally old battery that needed to be boosted each morning. I finally abandoned the car and took the bus after the ignition key broke in half and left me stranded in southwestern Ontario one rainy evening. The Quebec portion of the tour was an eye-opener for me. It allowed me to see first-hand a province I had only visited in 1967. Like so many other Canadians, I had been to Expo that year. That summer before the 1972 election offered me many challenges. One was unique. I was only twenty, and most of my meetings in Quebec that year were in bars! Fortunately I looked older than I was, but my parents were clearly worried about me, and Dad even offered to drive me whenever I had to travel that summer. I still think he just wanted to be part of the action.

I am not sure why I did not run for Parliament myself that year. Three close friends, Perrin Beatty, Sean O'Sullivan and Hugh Segal, had thrown their hats in the ring. Perrin and Sean were elected and began successful political careers (although Sean would leave Parliament in 1977 to become a priest; he died at a young age of leukemia in 1989). There were no secure seats open in 1972 in Ottawa that I could run in, although for a while I thought it would be a good start to take on Justice Minister John Turner in Ottawa-Carleton; I had worked as a youth volunteer with Ken Binks's campaign when he ran unsuccessfully against Turner in 1968. I also knew the riding well, as my family home was situated within it. Dad had worked hard for Ken and I knew he could help me organize effectively.

My father had discouraged me when I first raised the idea of running, but had I really insisted I am sure I could have persuaded him. I knew he was right to be concerned about my future career in law. In my time as a political staffer, I had seen members of Parliament who had been defeated after serving their ridings for many years and knew how precarious and short-lived a political career could be. I knew that I had to build other options for myself, just in case future constituents decided they didn't need or want me anymore. But in hindsight, I wish I had taken the plunge in 1972, while I was young and without other personal responsibilities. It would be fifteen years before I would have another chance.

In spite of my entrance scholarship, I had to work to make ends meet throughout my three years as an arts undergraduate. After Robert Stanfield lost by a whisker in October 1972, I was without a job at the PC research office. I was running short of money when a friend rescued me with a tip about a new MP from Alberta who was looking for a bilingual constituency assistant. The only Albertan I had ever known up to that point was Jack Horner, and I had not been impressed. "Don't judge the whole province by one man," my father insisted, and several friends reminded me that this new, young member of Parliament for the riding of Rocky Mountain was energetic and intelligent, and had worked for Robert Stanfield before running. I made an appointment to meet with him in his office and went off to Parliament Hill for the interview.

Joe Clark was young and bursting with energy that morning. He could barely sit still. By the time I left an hour later, I had filled six pages of notes of things he wanted to do within the first month of being elected. He wanted an office set up, furniture for the apartment he had just rented nearby and staff. He was entitled to two secretaries in Ottawa and one in the riding, and he wanted to be sworn in as a member and give his maiden speech in Parliament before Christmas. I was exhausted listening to him. Here was a man who knew what he wanted and was willing to work to get it. He was astute and knew that his parliamentary position was precarious. He was in a minority Parliament, had defeated a popular Liberal member who still had considerable local support and another election could come at any time.

So that there would be no misunderstanding, I told him I could work only until the following September, when I planned to take a year off to travel, probably around Europe, before going to law school. At that point in early November 1972, I was finishing the four undergraduate arts courses I needed to graduate. While I had to work my schedule around my classes, I assured him that I would get all the work done. He sounded a little dubious and told me he had two more people to interview and would call me the next day. He insisted that he would have to offer the better-paying position to a full-time secretary, "who can type." Without much subtlety I reminded him that I had excellent references and that while I could not type, I could think.

That evening I asked Marjory LeBreton, who was Stanfield's scheduling assistant, what she knew about him. "Well," she started, "he can dictate more on one tape than any other person I have ever met." She told me how Joe and another political assistant, Lowell Murray from Cape Breton, Nova Scotia, had lived together while they worked on the leader's staff for three years. "They gave me their salary cheques each week and their laundry each morning. I arranged for a cleaning woman for them and paid all their bills each month. They work like fiends and know more about political strategy and organization than almost anyone I know. One thing, though—neither cares much about the ordinary details of life." She then told me the story of Lowell's car. When they moved out of their apartment the year before, Lowell had left his car in the basement parking garage, claiming it was broken and offering it to her husband, who restored vintage vehicles. "I couldn't take it," she said. "All it needed was air in the tires!"

After speaking with Marjory, I asked Bob Laing, the head of the PC research library who had worked with Joe over the years, what he thought of him. His answer was clear. "Take the job. He's a great guy and a real gentleman." I later learned that Joe and I were both checking each other's references that week!

I was actually surprised when he called back and offered me the job and asked me to breakfast before his flight the next morning to "clarify a few things that needed to be done while he was away on the weekend." He left six tapes of dictation. He seemed to have forgotten that I could not type.

In the weeks that followed, I learned a great deal about my new boss. He was a thirty-three-year-old bachelor from High River, a small town in the foothills of Alberta. His father ran the family business, the *High River Times*, a weekly newspaper started decades before by Joe's paternal grandfather. He had a master's degree in political science from the University of Alberta. His mother had a university education and taught French, and his one brother, Peter, was a lawyer in Calgary. In his early teens Joe had earned a trip to Ottawa as part of the Rotary Club's Adventures in Citizenship program. He had travelled to the capital by train, arriving in time to witness the famous Pipeline Debate in the House of Commons, in the course of which the Liberal government had used closure to force an end to the parliamentary debate. John Diefenbaker, then the leader of the PC Party and leader of the Opposition, was in his prime as an orator, and Joe was caught in the passion of the debate and hooked on the excitement of Parliament. He returned to Alberta fired by the great issues of the day. Like me, he had then worked on campaigns and become involved in youth politics, ending with a term as national PC Youth President.

In a rare twist of fate, he had to deliver the difficult message to John Diefenbaker that he had lost the support of the youth wing of the party and should step down. In the leadership convention that followed in 1967, Joe supported B.C. member of Parliament and former federal justice minister Davie Fulton. When he dropped off the ballot, Joe moved to support the ultimate winner, Robert Stanfield, who had just resigned as Premier of Nova Scotia to run for the federal leadership. The next year, as a Stanfield staffer, he travelled with the new leader through the tough 1968 election when Trudeaumania swept the country and propelled Pierre Trudeau into office as Liberal Prime Minister.

Three years later, in 1971, Joe decided to leave Robert Stanfield's office in Ottawa and moved to back to Alberta to run for the nomination in one of the largest constituencies in Canada. Among other things, he wanted to bring a modern and progressive Albertan voice to Parliament. He understood his province's historic grievances against the concentration of political and economic power and control in the "eastern" part of the country, and wanted to present a picture of his home province in Parliament as a dynamic and exciting place of future prosperity and leadership. Ironically, he would rarely receive the support of Alberta elites in making this case to the country, nor the backing of its political leadership when he needed it most.

In October 1972, though, just before I met him in Ottawa, Joe had defeated the strong incumbent Liberal member, Alan Sulatycky, in the Alberta riding of Rocky Mountain and headed to Ottawa to claim his seat in Parliament.

From the beginning, Joe and I worked well together. As he became more comfortable in his job, he let his sharp wit and keen sense of humour show. I was not always in the office when he was. He left for Alberta Friday after question period, and returned either late Sunday night or early Monday morning. He knew that Pierre Trudeau would call an election as soon as the polls showed he could win a majority, and he didn't want to leave his constituency untended. Even when Joe was in Ottawa, we rarely saw each other. I had classes to attend and my work schedule was erratic. To make sure I was always on top of things in the office, I often worked late into the night and used the two-hour time change between Ottawa and Alberta to my advantage each day. I enjoyed the challenge and felt accepted by Joe's riding association.

One night in late January 1973, I left my office in the Confederation Building, just west of Parliament Hill, very late. I passed the Centre Block just as the clock in the Peace Tower struck midnight. I stopped in front of the Centennial Flame to listen to the toll of the bells, muffled by the soft snow that fell all around me. I suddenly remembered with nostalgia the same sort of night on New Year's Eve in 1967, when Prime Minister Lester B. Pearson had lit the Centennial Flame to mark the beginning of Canada's hundredth anniversary. As a teenager caught up in the excitement of Centennial Year, I thought of Lester Pearson as my country's special grandfather, kindly and safe. A month before, on December 27, 1972, he had died. I stood for a few more minutes alone at the flame, surrounded by the provincial coats of arms. Without warning it came to me that this was my place, and that it would play an increasingly important part of my life. I turned to continue my walk home; and as I did, felt a special and permanent link to this place of power.

During the winter of 1973, I was president of the English Debating Society and responsible for the annual high school debating tournament. Joe had agreed to be one of the judges at the tournament and had even asked some other members of Parliament to volunteer with him. The tournament was a huge success, with more teams than ever before and excellent judging. Traditionally, every debating-society president at the University of Ottawa was offered a place at its law school. Even though I planned to travel for a year before starting classes in law, I wanted to be sure I had the guarantee of a spot when I returned in the fall of 1974. I was the first woman president of the university's debating society, and I assumed that based on my marks and position with the debating society, I would be offered a place at law school. But when the day of the tournament arrived in early February, I had still not received any formal offer. At the lunch that day, I got up my courage and asked the head of admissions at the law school,

Professor Bruce Arlidge, who was the tournament's senior judge, when I would be offered a place. Professor Arlidge seemed startled by the question and admitted sheepishly that he had not even thought about it. He told me that the dean had a big say in all this, especially in how many women were accepted each year, but said he would look into the matter for me. I insisted that I be treated as all my former male colleagues had been and, as a member of the dean's honour list that semester, I expected an offer to attend law school. I came away from that exchange under the impression that Arlidge had not thought a woman would be interested in law. Later events proved this false, as Bruce Arlidge was one of the fairest and most supportive professors I would meet.

But on that day in 1973, his response summed up the attitude women of my generation faced as we sought access to professional schools in Canadian universities. I had been told by male classmates to expect that professional schools, including law and medicine, would resist admitting women. The argument was that we would "waste" our education by becoming pregnant and abandoning professional practice. Some schools even required higher marks for women seeking admission than they did for men. I had scoffed at the time, even though the memory of my lost hockey career still loomed large.

In May, true to his word, Bruce Arlidge advised that I had been offered a place at the University of Ottawa law school that fall.

———

Joe and I continued to work well together. I appreciated his commitment, honesty and intelligence, and he often thanked me for the excellent work I was doing on behalf of his constituents. We seemed to work hand in glove, and many a time we would catch one of us completing the other's sentences. We would laugh when this happened and I felt that, at last, I had overcome his initial reluctance to hire me because of my youth. While we enjoyed an effective and excellent working relationship, we did not socialize after work hours. In the three months I had been working for him, I had joined him only once for lunch, and that was with people from his riding. I kept my personal and professional life separate and had not shared with him the fact that my personal life was in a shambles as I had ended my long-term relationship with my high school sweetheart. It had been a turbulent year for me, made more so by all my commitments at work and university.

The first time I suspected that Joe's interest in me was more than platonic was on Valentine's Day in 1973, when a bouquet of roses arrived at my modest studio apartment with the note "From a secret admirer." I had no idea who they were from and decided to wait until someone owned up to the extravagant gesture. Later that day, Joe popped his head into my office on his way to question period and asked me if I liked the flowers. I was stunned, but alert enough to thank him and say that I did. Two weeks later, on February 27, I celebrated my twenty-first birthday. I had to work that day, but didn't mind. My thoughts turned to graduation from university and my plans for a trip to Europe that fall. But when I arrived in my office that morning, a huge bouquet of twenty-one yellow roses awaited me with a card announcing they were from Joe. I was surprised and pleased, and thanked him for his thoughtfulness. "You're only twenty-one once," he quipped.

Not long afterwards he left to spend the parliamentary break campaigning in his riding and I went home to my parents' place to rest. Upon his return, Joe asked me to dinner at the Café Louis IX, a popular French restaurant near Hull, "to discuss a few things." There was no flirtation in his voice as he issued the invitation and I was baffled. I even thought that given the volume of work in the office, he might want to replace me with another full-time secretary.

At dinner he asked me about my trip to Europe in September. He wanted to know if I would consider abandoning my plans for any reason. Surprised, I asked what possible reason could be compelling enough to keep me from such a trip. "You can marry me," he replied. I was speechless. I was about to ask if he was joking, but his face showed that he was dead serious. All of a sudden, we were talking about our lives and our dreams and what we wanted for the future. We stayed and talked until the restaurant closed and then drove back to Ottawa. I told him how unexpected his proposal had been and asked for more time to think about it. Marriage had not been something I was contemplating; I was nervous and even frightened at the prospect.

That night I decided to visit Colleen, who had finished university by then and was completing her education degree in Kingston. She had married while at university and now had a baby boy. I thought she could give me some mature, sisterly, married-woman advice. "Well, what do *you* want to do?" she asked me when I told her about Joe. "That's the starting point. Don't think about the rest of it, just what you want to do in your heart." I envy friends who talk about bolts of lightning and stars in their eyes when they met the men they married. My decision was more drawn out and difficult. I am a Pisces. The impulsive and romantic side of me was all for falling in love while the cautious side wanted to take it one step at a time. I was still not completely over the breakup of my first long-term relationship, and wanted no more painful personal commitments. Colleen made me think more about what was involved, including the price of marrying a politician whose life would be disrupted each election and whose days were dedicated to serving others. I knew from having seen him in action the previous five months that Joe would give his all to his political career and wondered where that would leave me. My romantic side, on the other hand, defined it all as the ultimate dream. Joe and I shared so many ideals and ideas. He was kind and funny and free of the ego and arrogance I had seen so much of on Parliament Hill. Even his proposal was out of the ordinary, but very much in his own style. Joe is not comfortable expressing his emotions but when he decided that he wanted to marry me, he set his normal reserve aside. I asked him once what he would have done had I refused his proposal. He replied, "I would have just kept asking."

To the extent that I had even thought about marriage as a life choice, I had not expected anything so sudden. And there was our age difference. While he was thirteen years older than I was, that did not seem to matter. My head was in a panic. My heart believed we were meant for each other and could manage all the rest. In the end, I chose to follow my heart.

One matter remained critical for me—my year in Europe. I had grown up in a crowded and noisy household and had worked hard to finish university. I wanted to be free of all constraints and be independent, even if only for a year. I had hoped that I would find that freedom at university, but my three years had been filled with politics, work and university causes. When I returned to Ottawa from my visit with Colleen, I spoke with Joe of my concerns and, while he understood, he did not want me to leave. He insisted that he would take me to Europe at Christmas that year if I wanted and urged me not to risk my place in law school by going away. Conscious that he had not finished his own law studies, he did not want me to make the same mistake. A two-week trip with a husband did not strike me as the same as a year away by myself, but in the end I agreed. I told him that I wanted to run for Parliament one day, and he promised to help me in every way he could. After another sleepless night, I decided that marrying Joe was the right decision and I told him yes.

That weekend, we went to meet my father. My mother was away and Dad's response surprised me. He disapproved, insisting that I was too young to make such an important decision. He felt my decision was rash and wanted me to think about it. It would take a long time to change his mind. He told me later that his worry had been that I would abandon all my own dreams and plans when I married and be forced to tailor them to Joe's life and career. He had seen what happened to many marriages that were subjected to politics, and he did not want that for me. When I told my mother, though, she was more optimistic. She thought it was wonderful that I had found a husband who liked politics and was as intense and serious about life as I was. She liked Joe's keen sense of humour and was delighted that I was going on to law school that fall rather than wandering alone all over Europe.

We then went to High River, Alberta, Joe's hometown, on the long weekend in May to meet his parents. His father, Charles, a newspaperman and photographer, became a fast friend, but I was never to enjoy much friendship with his mother, Grace. It was as if she never forgave me for marrying her oldest son. They agreed to come to the wedding, and upon our return to Ottawa we set the date for a small wedding. On the last day of June, about thirty-five of our immediate family and close friends would see us married in the chapel of my old school, Notre Dame, and attend a dinner afterwards at the National Arts Centre. My sister Pamela, an accomplished seamstress and a nursing student at Hôtel Dieu Hospital in Kingston, Ontario, agreed to make my wedding dress from a Vogue pattern I had chosen, and she and her twin, Patricia, were to be my attendants.

My life seemed a little unreal all that spring, and I felt sometimes that I was two people. One was a student writing essays and final exams; the other was a young woman preparing her wedding. We told no one but our families and somehow the secret held until after we were married. During the weeks leading up to the wedding, I saw first-hand what lay ahead for me as a political spouse and it made me nervous. Normally the House of Commons would have adjourned by the end of June, and we had planned to take two weeks right after the wedding for a honeymoon in Quebec City. But there was still a minority government in 1973, and no sooner had I made the wedding arrangements than Joe advised me not to lock them in. "You should know," he said in a most matter-of-fact way, "that if an election is called between now and the end of June, we will just have to put the wedding off until the fall." Since I had cancelled a year of travelling in Europe in order to marry that June, I wasn't sure what to make of this.

Looking back, I see that this was to be the pattern and norm of my married life. All major events, from birthdays and anniversaries to plain old time off for a vacation, risked being altered, marred or cancelled, depending on the exigencies of Joe's political life. I have always surveyed the parliamentary and political event calendar the way most people follow the stock market or their horoscope. All the signs were there, but in my romantic excitement, I was blind to them.

Parliament was still in session on our wedding day, June 30, and late that night after all the festivities we escaped to Quebec City, one of our favourite spots, for a short honeymoon. Midweek, we returned to Ottawa so Joe could finish up the parliamentary session, and we then spent July travelling around Joe's riding, visiting Banff, Jasper, Lake Louise and Waterton Lakes. We were feted by friends and supporters everywhere we went. In August, we travelled with a parliamentary committee to two of Canada's great national parks—Nahanni in the Northwest Territories and Kluane in Yukon. After a meeting in Yellowknife, we stopped at Norman Wells, Old Crow and Tuktoyaktuk to hear the concerns of the residents. It is a trip every Canadian should take at least once in her life.

As we left the last hamlet, our plane flew low over a herd of thousands of caribou racing across the bleak, black tundra below. We were above the treeline, and the only defining feature we could see were pingos, funnel-like structures that jut out above the horizon and serve as cold-storage points for trappers and travellers. I still have a picture of me walking along the shores of the Arctic Ocean, my long hair in pigtails and my arms crossed against the wind. It was a fabulous trip, and I was blissfully happy as I returned to Ottawa to start law school.

3

IN THE MONTHS AFTER MY MARRIAGE in 1973, my anonymity
ensured I could continue to live my life unnoticed. I was the
youngest political wife in Ottawa, and the only one starting law
school. No one knew or cared. Margaret Trudeau, on the other
hand, did not have that luxury. She had married Pierre two
years before, at twenty-two, and was the youngest "first lady"
in the world. She was expecting her second son that December
and media interest in her life continued unabated. Though she
had been born to privilege and into a political family, she railed
against the restraints that are intrinsic to life as a Prime
Minister's wife. She wanted her carefree life back, and made it
clear to everyone that she was unhappy and felt confined. I
could not have known in those months after my marriage, when
Joe was still a backbench MP, how much her public actions and
reactions to her life as a political wife would affect my own. For
years to come, whenever I would tell other political wives, parliamentarians or the media that I was a law student (or lawyer)
and living my own life as an equal alongside Joe, they invariably
rolled their eyes and said: "Just like Margaret."

From singing at a state dinner in Cuba to escaping to
Toronto to be with the Rolling Stones, nothing Margaret did
went unnoticed. It was not just that she was young and beautiful

and married to the most powerful man in the country. She had also come on the scene at a time when the media was more willing to pry into and publicize the comings and goings of senior politicians. There had always been tremendous interest in, and coverage of, Pierre Trudeau. Margaret's personality and her growing rebelliousness made news even as her activities and growing depression left her vulnerable. Being married to the Prime Minister ensured media interest and coverage. And it was not only a one-way relationship. Her husband's advisers saw the potential of her presence as a beautiful wife and new mother, and she would play a public part in Pierre's successful election campaign the following year. The truth was that Margaret was Canada's biggest media star, overshadowing Pierre on most occasions when they appeared together—not unlike Diana and Prince Charles years later. Margaret could do what she wanted. She had no responsibilities, unlike her powerful husband, whose popularity waxed and waned depending on his government's policies. I am sure, though, as the person who would replace her as the chatelaine of 24 Sussex Drive six years later, that her life was not easy. Her husband was thirty years older than she was, and I could only imagine the emotional and physical tolls that came with having three children in five years. As the Prime Minister's wife, she had established social protocols and political travel demands placed on her. Added to this were two national election campaigns, which are exhausting even without a toddler and newborn at home.

As I watched from the political sidelines in the following months, I couldn't help feeling sorry for her. I saw her as a young woman who needed protection, not publicity, and no one gave it to her. Instead, she seemed to be dangled before the public one moment as the ultimate "political" wife—pregnant and pretty—only to be reined in or criticized the next when she spoke about issues that mattered to her. Even though much of her behaviour seemed indefensible at the time, I have always thought that she was the victim in the sad saga of her marriage, seemingly abandoned by her husband and his entourage at the very moment in her life when she needed them the most.

As a young political wife, I learned a great deal from her treatment by both the media and the public. I saw that the stereotype of a political wife as a quiet, supportive, well-dressed and smiling helpmate was still the norm and what most Canadians wanted. Margaret's behaviour would have a negative impact on my own relations later with the public and the media, affecting as it did the perception of the sense and seriousness of other young wives, and making it even harder to be taken seriously. Her youthful and reckless acts left a legacy that branded young political wives as impetuous and self-centred. Three years later, when I faced the media and larger public for the first time as wife of the leader of the Opposition, my age and independence would be viewed with consternation. Canadians feared a repeat of Margaret's behaviour.

If I had felt like a fish out of water studying and preparing for a wedding earlier that spring, I felt positively marooned in the autumn of 1973. I wanted to do everything right and registered as a member of the PC Wives Association. Generally, the women I met in this association (and the ones I met later in the Parliamentary Wives group) were older than I was and some had been in Ottawa for many years. Even the name denoted an exclusive female club, and it would only change from "wives" to "spouses" a decade later when journalist Charles Lynch asked to join after his new wife's election to Parliament in 1984. Even though, as a brash twenty-one-year-old, I felt that the wives' association was outdated, I found the first meeting fascinating. For instance, I remember that it took place at Stornoway, then the home of Robert Stanfield. His wife, Mary, had invited us all for lunch and had invited her predecessor, Olive Diefenbaker, to lecture us on what to wear to Parliament when the Queen read the Speech from the Throne later that month. Those of us

in attendance knew that there had been some suggestion that
the Queen had been slighted by Pierre Trudeau, who wanted
to give some of her powers to the Governor General. Olive
Diefenbaker urged us, as political wives, to make her feel doubly
welcome. I assumed that in the regular pecking order, I would be
unlikely to get the chance to welcome her personally, but understood the message clearly. I was to be on my best behaviour.

I had skipped a class at law school to attend the lunch that
day, and as soon as I came in the door at Stornoway I realized
what an outsider I was. A mere child compared with the others
and dressed in an informal pantsuit, I stuck out like someone's
daughter who had arrived home early from classes. Seeing me
standing in a corner all by myself, Elizabeth McKinnon, whose
husband, Alan, was the member of Parliament from Victoria,
made her way across the room and invited me to sit beside her
during the lunch and speech. She had been a military wife and
was used to making others feel welcome. Her husband would
become Joe's minister of Defence in 1979, and her sensitivity and
kindness towards me made a painful experience into an enjoy-
able one.

During Olive Diefenbaker's speech, I saw how much I
would need to learn if I hoped to fit in as a new parliamentary
wife. I was intrigued that there were written rules for dress and
behaviour for parliamentary wives attending these ceremonies,
and realized that I would need a more extensive and formal
wardrobe. Student garb was definitely inadequate. As I sat there
listening to Olive Diefenbaker tell us we were never to wear
black in the Queen's presence and that a hat and gloves were
required, I resolved to find a wonderful long gown for the traditional Governor General's Ball to be held at Rideau Hall the
night Parliament opened. I was quite excited about it all and
even went off to shop as soon as I was able to escape. I looked
back towards the lovely lawns, cared for by Robert Stanfield
personally as there was no budget from the government for

their upkeep, and thought how magnificent it all looked. Little did I know that within three years Stornoway would be my home.

Throughout the first year of my marriage I vacillated between being an independent person and being a parliamentary wife. Among the wives I was known as Mrs. Joe Clark. Insisting otherwise seemed to make no difference. After all, I was there exclusively because I was married to a member of Parliament. I learned that you needed to emphasize that and tell people who your husband was, because the more important he was, the greater your status and position. I can remember years later, when Joe was Prime Minister, being asked by another political wife if I would now use his last name. "What on earth for?" I replied. "Because he is powerful and famous and people will then make the link and know who you are," she replied. I was startled at her logic but she was very serious. It made some sense, I suppose. Political wives pay a big personal price for being married to politicians and deserve some reward or recognition for all their efforts. What bothered me was that she saw a political wife's life as such a narrow enterprise and thought it acceptable—even expected—that the more powerful Joe became, the more I should abandon any independence and ambition for myself.

By contrast, my life at law school was a liberating and exciting adventure; there, everyone knew me by my own name. While I wore a wedding band, I rarely spoke of being married and only a couple of my close friends even knew my husband was a member of Parliament. I preferred it that way, as it ensured that as a student, I was anonymous and treated just like everyone else. I had worried that a political bias by a professor might affect my marks.

During my first weeks at law school, I was conscious of being one of only 22 women in a class of 120. One day I asked a friend in a senior class why there were so few women in second and third year and she told me the story, often repeated by

any other ranch wife would have done. When a senior law student explained the decision to my class, and urged us to lobby provincial members to change the law, I launched into action. I knew politicians in Toronto and Ottawa and wrote or called those I thought might be sympathetic. The decision, I told them, struck at the heart of our principles of equality and fairness. Surely, its outcome required legislators who believed in women's equality and justice to address the question, Why is the work of women who spend all their lives raising their families and keeping their homes not afforded any financial value? "And why is it," I added, "that only financial and economic considerations are seen as valuable contributions to a marriage?" The majority of women in law that year rallied around the cause of equality raised by the decision in the Murdoch case. I am not sure who raised this point, but each of us was aware that we saw our own mothers in Irene Murdoch. Few of us had children, and most of us who were married had been for only a few months or years, so we did not see how easily her plight could one day become ours. We were young and idealistic, believing in romantic love and the possibility of it lasting forever. As a group, we all planned to work, earn good salaries and have perfect children whom we would raise as we worked full-time. We insisted that all this would be done with the help of our spouses and partners who, of course, would divide domestic and child-rearing tasks equally.

So in those early days of law school, as we challenged legislation that discriminated against women, it was our own mothers we worried about. Mine had a clerical job with an insurance company in Ottawa, having worked outside the home out of financial necessity since my brother was four years old. But so many had always been "housewives." Indeed, before 1948 women had to quit work in the federal public service when they married. A man was judged by his ability to keep his family. But women who worked in the home were "nonpersons." As society grew more tolerant of divorce and many divorced men began to marry younger women, replacing my mother's generation with new wives their daughters' ages, divorce and property laws had to be changed to recognize women's work in the home. The Murdoch case was the catalyst for that massive legal and societal advance. From then on feminism took on a human face for me: the face of my mother. Legal change became personal. In those days, I took the goal of fairness and equality (and often myself) very seriously. It became my cause, and I gave speeches and lobbied politicians to reform outdated laws. Nor did I stop there. When the provincial laws were finally changed, I joined many of my former classmates to fight for further legal reforms—from human rights laws to the Charter. At least one friend, Peggy Mason, the brilliant gold medallist in the class before mine, worked for women's equality at the international level when, in the 1980s, my husband named her Canada's ambassador to the United Nations for disarmament, with a special responsibility for women's issues. As she said to my daughter's class one day when asked what she did as an ambassador to the UN, "I look after war and women—or bombs and broads, depending on the group I'm speaking to!"

While I became more committed to feminism and the cause of equality at law school, Joe was building a reputation as a tireless worker for his constituents and a seasoned parliamentarian. He loved the sharp give-and-take of question period and parliamentary debate. Each evening after class when he was in Ottawa, I would meet him in his office and we would have dinner in the parliamentary restaurant in the Centre Block. Then, if I had completed my assignments, I would sit in the Members' Gallery and watch the debate on Bills before Parliament. Other nights, I would work in the Library of Parliament, one of Canada's treasures and best-kept secrets. We discussed his work and my classes each day and provided each other with continuous support and ideas.

In 1973, the country was suffering the effects of worldwide recession, with high unemployment and inflation becoming serious national issues. Energy prices, always a concern for an Alberta MP, were exacerbated by the decision by the Organization of Petroleum Exporting Countries (OPEC) in the Middle East to raise oil prices unilaterally by 70 percent that year and to ban exports to all Western countries that had supported Israel in the Yom Kippur War. The provincial government in Alberta benefited from the increase, but the rest of the country felt the squeeze. That fall, among other drastic measures, the Trudeau government imposed a freeze on oil prices, precipitating a showdown with Alberta. In all this controversy, Joe expected an election at any time, and spent an increasing amount of time in his riding. When not in Alberta, he travelled across Canada to speak at nomination meetings for his colleagues and other Progressive Conservative candidates. He was articulate and respected for his loyal support of the leader and his team spirit and clear understanding of the larger issues in Parliament and in the country. As he toured, he saw the impact of the economic and social upheaval that faced Canadians, and joined Stanfield and the PC caucus in proposing a system of temporary wage and price controls to address the problems of inflation, high unemployment, rising costs and interest rates. Wage and price controls would become the main plank in the party's unsuccessful bid to form the government in the election in October of 1974.

I accompanied Joe to his Alberta riding whenever I could. While I was no longer on his staff, I often answered phone calls from constituents in the evenings and contacted his local organizers to be sure they were ready for an election. This kind of direct political and policy involvement would continue in different ways throughout our life in politics, although campaign experts and staff would do the lion's share after 1976. But in those early days before the 1974 general election, I offered strategic advice and prepared briefings for him on local and national issues of interest to his riding, including energy, forestry, agriculture, the environment, national parks and tourism. My earlier experience in the PC research office stood me in good stead and I continued to learn how to run political campaigns.

In early May, the Prime Minister called a general election. In many ways, the 1974 campaign was one of the most rewarding of my early life, where I proved I could contribute sound strategic and political advice as well as wifely support. Throughout the two-month campaign, we were equals and were unhindered by the presence of others competing for his attention and approval that would overshadow our working relationship later.

Election night on July 8, 1974, was both a victory and a defeat. A victory for Joe, who handily won his own constituency of Rocky Mountain in Alberta, but a defeat for Robert Stanfield and the PC Party, whose caucus was reduced to 95 seats to the Liberals' 141. Even though the PCs held almost all of the seats in Western Canada and did well in Nova Scotia, they had been nearly shut out of Quebec and were severely limited in Ontario. In the last week of the campaign, Joe and I could see there would be serious problems. We were travelling all over the riding and other parts of Canada trying to explain the complex scheme of wage and price controls. Each night on the news, Robert Stanfield would be shown soldiering on, while Pierre Trudeau was shot merely waving his arm like a wand at every crowd and shouting in ridicule, "Zap, you're frozen." I learned at least two lessons that election night. First, those who advocate the KISS system of political campaigning (Keep it simple, stupid) are right, and second, honesty in politics rarely wins votes or elections—a lesson I would relearn in 1980.

I remember crying that night in Drayton Valley, Alberta, and vowing that if that was what the people wanted, we would lie just as Pierre Trudeau did. I was inconsolable and beside myself with hurt and anger. Joe just let me rage on, drowning our pillow with my tears of youthful innocence, until he finally said, "Stop, Maureen; you don't mean that. If we do that, we are no different from him. There would be no purpose to our being in politics; we would have failed everyone, including ourselves. We fought a good campaign and we lost. It is a bad decision for Canada, but the people have decided. Now try to sleep." I have always hated it when I am on a tear and Joe quietly works to calm me down. But he was right, and reluctant though I was to agree with him, I knew what he said was true. So the next day, after we had cleaned up our headquarters in the riding and thanked our supporters, we returned to our apartment in Ottawa. Joe went to his office to pick up where he had left off before the election.

We needed a holiday. I had never travelled any distance on a train before, so we reserved a sleeper and went to the Gaspé Peninsula in Quebec, where we stayed at a little hotel that was also a culinary training school run by the Quebec government. For two weeks we played tourist in the Gaspé region. While we were there, former Prime Minister Louis St. Laurent died in Quebec City. He had been leader of the Liberal Party and Prime Minister before Lester Pearson took over in 1957, when I was five. I had known very little about him. Yet after his death, the whole province flew its flags at half mast and showed their respect to an important man.

The rest of the summer was spent with friends in Ottawa and Alberta rehashing the defeat and preparing for the fall session of Parliament. I looked forward to returning to law school. Like it or not, the Liberals had a majority government and Pierre Trudeau could govern for at least the coming four years. After all the chaos of the previous two years, I welcomed a break before the next election. Four years would give me plenty of time to finish my last two years of law school and decide where I went from there. When my second year of classes started in September 1974, I was glad to escape from politics back to my other love, the law.

4

DURING THE FALL, MY CYNICISM DEEPENED as the government introduced wage and price controls. I felt betrayed and terribly sorry for Robert Stanfield. I wondered if Canadians felt duped by Pierre Trudeau or if they thought him a clever rogue for playing his political cards so effectively. Even though Stanfield had been vindicated in policy terms, the sad truth remained that when a party loses an election, the leader has to pay. All through the year, there was speculation about whether he would step down as party leader and if so, who might run for the position. Many of Joe's colleagues' names were floated, and there seemed to be agreement that whoever ran had to be in Stanfield's mould—a social progressive and an economic conservative. The next leader also had to be bilingual and a bit more dynamic, as television was now the biggest communications tool for political campaigns. While I followed all the speculation of leadership candidates with interest, I firmly believed it had nothing to do with me. I was preoccupied with law school and working hard to finish my second year.

When my last exam was finished that spring, I told Joe that I was ready for a summer off, somewhere away from Ottawa. To my delight he suggested we go to France. When Joe was first elected in 1972, he could not speak a word of French. One of the first things he did upon arriving in Ottawa was enrol in French classes with Claudette Chemla, a teacher of talent and wit who over the years would make him bilingual. Many other members and cabinet ministers owe her a similar debt, and they speak of her with as much praise as I do. Claudette was a taskmaster who chain-smoked Gitanes and refused ever to speak anything but French to Joe or any of her other students. While I learned early that correcting a spouse trying to learn a new language is a guarantee of a household row, Claudette could correct Joe without a murmur of complaint from him. That July, on Claudette's advice, Joe enrolled in a French-language course at a school in Royan, a small city on the southern end of France's Atlantic coast in the Charente-Maritime. I was delighted to spend six weeks in France, where Joe would go to class each day to study French, and I to the beach to enjoy the sun. Each weekend we rented a car and travelled in a different direction, exploring the cities and towns all around Royan. Although I could not have known it at the time, it would be my last free summer for the next twenty years.

It was during that summer in France that Joe decided to run for the leadership to replace Stanfield. He had been thinking about it for a while, although he had only raised it directly with me once to see what my response would be. I was not opposed to the idea, and could see a real possibility for him. As his French improved daily, a significant impediment to his candidacy was eliminated. When we arrived back in Canada, I started my last year of law school and Joe began a new parliamentary session, amid all the excitement and intrigue that comes with a pending leadership race. All during the fall, I was naïve enough to think that a leadership campaign would not affect my life's plans or impose on my studies. I was still operating on the assumption that I had four years to finish law school, article and start to practice, and had even gone so far as to secure an articling position with the Calgary law firm Fenerty Robertson during the coming year. All during September 1975, I spent my weekends with my mother and sisters decorating the new house we had bought that summer in Ottawa. I suppose I could be forgiven for not seeing possible problems for myself in the coming months. In the press from this period, Joe's name was rarely even mentioned, usually near the end of the list of hopefuls. Yet he was already putting together an energetic, if young, group of supporters and spending every spare minute travelling across the country. He had decided to visit every delegate before the convention, which was set for late February 1976 in Ottawa.

It would become the classic grassroots campaign. We had to get along without the endorsement, the experience or the money of the traditional power brokers in the party. We enjoyed their goodwill and good wishes but, with a few exceptions, Conservative Premiers, MPs, senators, provincial leaders and party officials were either neutral or aligned elsewhere. There were a few exceptions, of course. Those included three members of Parliament—Harvie Andre of Calgary, Allan McKinnon of Victoria and Steve Paproski of Edmonton. The Attorney General of Alberta, Jim Foster, joined the team, as did Ralph Hedlin, who had played a key role in helping Duff Roblin win his first victory as Premier of Manitoba. Ralph was the only person who had actually run a campaign beyond the constituency level and with a little persuasion he accepted the title of national campaign chairman. MLA David King and Fred Bradley (both of whom were later in provincial cabinet positions in Alberta) came on board. Fred had co-chaired Joe's first run for federal office in 1972 and sometimes travelled with us.

But there had to be an organizational heart to every campaign and that task fell to Harvie Andre, Jim Hawkes and my father.

Harvie chaired the actual convention organization and was the strong, steady (and sometimes sceptical) voice at our Ottawa headquarters. His spouse, Joan, ran Joe's tour and loved to remind Harvie that she had committed to the campaign before he did. In fact, she had been one of Joe's supporters since 1967 when, pregnant with her first daughter, Coryn, she had campaigned with him in his unsuccessful bid for a seat in the Social Credit–controlled Alberta legislature.

Jim Hawkes, who later became the MP for Calgary West, was teaching at the University of Calgary. He stole time from his classes to commute to Ottawa before and during the convention to bring order to our excited chaos. Jim is a gifted manager who had grown up in the YMCA system and was a master at organizing volunteers and solving problems quietly. His spouse, Joanne, had similar skills and threw herself into the campaign in Alberta.

The third member of this triumvirate, my father, had run successful election campaigns and brought tangible experience to the campaign. He was in his element surrounded by enthusiastic young people. He was also on home turf. The convention site was three blocks from his childhood home, and he found a headquarters through a friend who owned the local IGA. Most days he walked two blocks over to his old house on Third Avenue to have lunch with his ninety-year-old mother. She no doubt offered him advice, like everyone else! Dad had a vast network of friends in Ottawa and everyone, from the grocer to the dry cleaner and the electrician, was invaluable to Joe's underfunded volunteer effort.

That campaign was an extraordinary experience. Old friends came forward: Jeff Lyons, who had been on the PC student executive with Joe; Toronto lawyer Jules Kronis and Ottawa businessman Ralph Tannis, who had been on the Ontario youth executive with me; Gerry Murphy and Bruck Easton, law classmates of mine from Ontario; David and Cecilia Humphreys, who had been on the *Manitoban* student newspaper when Joe edited *The Gateway* student paper at the University of Alberta;

lawyers George Cooper and Art Donahoe in Halifax, Peter Hayden in Toronto and Ed Poole from Corner Brook, who were all Joe's former law classmates from Dalhousie.

We met new people who disrupted their lives for Joe. Educator Barbara Drucker from Toronto quit her job and ran our Metro organization out of her basement; Toronto publicist and businesswoman Carol Jamieson volunteered to help with media and communications and attended all the strategy meetings; lawyer Pierre Bouchard, chiropractor Gaston Rivard and administrator Claude Boisselle took over Quebec organization; Lee Clark (later an MP) from Brandon and Bob Andrew (later provincial finance minister) from Saskatchewan helped on the Prairies; and Marjorie Carroll, Brian Turnbull and Peter Woolstencroft from Kitchener-Waterloo took over most of the Ontario organization. Allan Laakonen, a delegate from Thunder Bay, put Joe's name in nomination and symbolized the grassroots nature of our campaign, for the other candidates sought out Premiers and other "big names" to nominate them.

And of course, there was the team from Rocky Mountain, that magnificent stretch of national parks, ranch land and resource communities that first sent Joe to Parliament in 1972. Roy and Mary Ann Everest and Bob and Olga Dowling from Jasper helped Joe win his first nomination when he was "Joe Who?" to most of his constituents, and Roy was his official agent through six federal election campaigns. We trusted them with our lives. Marilyn Maclean of Drayton Valley, a no-nonsense nurse and one of the most generous and best-organized women I have ever met, was Joe's constituency president and ran his 1972 campaign out of her home. She was there again for us in 1976. Bill and Carol Herron each took their turn as members of Joe's riding executive over the years, when they were not running Mount Norquay in Banff. They were at our sides as "advance people" on the convention floor in 1976.

What the campaign might have lacked in experience, we certainly made up for in enthusiasm. Joe's recruitment strategy was simple. He made a list of all his friends and everyone he had ever gone to university or worked with in politics and called them, asking for their support. If they said yes, one of the senior campaign team in Ottawa would call them back with a list of how they could help. This included everything from being a delegate to the convention from their riding through to giving money or having a party for Joe in their home. We went into the convention with more than four hundred volunteers, many people who had just signed up to "work for Joe Clark."

We had real political and organizational talent in our youth volunteers, and many would later run for public office. David Hancock, for instance, is now the minister of justice in Alberta. Other young people signed on, including Ken Hughes who was elected in 1988 and served in Kim Campbell's cabinet, and Murray Dorrin, elected to Parliament from Edmonton in 1988. Brian Pell, Wendy Orr, Michael Ede, Karen Lynch, Tim Woolstencroft, Peter Bennett, Robert Baxter, Hamilton Greenwood and dozens of others were to form part of the youth brigade for Joe in 1976. Most of them took a semester off from their studies to do so, and I shudder at what their parents thought when their kids dropped out of university that Christmas to help this long-shot candidate. To balance all that youthful enthusiasm, we had a team of friends and family with the skills to guide them.

I tried to maintain my attendance at law school. I had also been asked by a Ph.D. student who taught us at law school to join a weekly discussion group. One week in late October I told the group that I had to drop out for a few months, as I no longer had the time to meet with them each week. "What's the matter?" Sandy Borins, one of the Ph.D. students, asked solicitously. "My husband is running for the leadership of the PC Party of Canada," I replied and asked if they would like to help. Surprised, they asked how four graduate students could assist a political campaign. "You can do research for policy and speeches," I replied, and we were off. Ian McKinnon, whose mother, Elizabeth, had befriended me two years earlier and whose MP father, Allan, was supporting Joe, took charge of our little academic team, working with Peter Woolstencroft from the University of Waterloo and Beth Bryant, who was later Alberta's deputy minister for multiculturalism, and her husband, Vic, from Calgary.

Leadership campaigns can cost hundreds of thousands of dollars and we knew that the leading candidates would spend a great deal. To save us from the poorhouse, Joe called on three friends, Edmonton lawyers Hal Veale and David Jenkins and Toronto lawyer Jeff Lyons, to take charge of fundraising. David and Hal agreed to take "temporary" responsibility for the whole effort, expecting to be replaced by some "big names" later. By the end of the campaign they were still in charge.

Raising money for that campaign was not easy. There were twelve candidates running and many were either going after the traditional party inside sources or relied on big-business contacts. Flora MacDonald had adopted a clever campaign of asking for five-dollar donations, raising considerable funds for her campaign. Generally, the big money was not donating to our campaign. In the end, the campaign received about $150,000 from over eleven hundred small contributions from across Canada. As a final demonstration of faith in Joe, just two weeks before the convention, Hal, David, Jim Foster, Robert Lloyd and Donald Mackenzie from Edmonton signed a promissory note to the Toronto Dominion Bank for forty thousand dollars, which let us pay for the rooms and operations we needed at the convention. Of course, we would have to pay it back, and I worried that we might have to mortgage our new home. To give the reader an idea of how limited our budget was, one day in January, Joe and I had to wait in Regina airport while Barbara

Drucker phoned ten friends and asked them to each put one hundred dollars on our VISA card so we could buy two plane tickets back to Ottawa!

By December, as the campaign took shape, I began to travel full-time with Joe. At Christmas, I thought seriously of taking the winter semester off, as most of the other young volunteers my age were doing. Convinced I could do both the campaign and classes, I decided to proceed with my last semester of law school and cram for my exams after the convention. This would prove to be a fatal mistake.

On days when I would become discouraged, my father, a political optimist and seasoned organizer, would always tell me that we were in the best possible position. Being labelled as eleventh in a field of twelve by the "experts" gave us breathing room, he insisted. (He was right there.) We had a strategy and were following it, and like a good general, Dad knew the value of surprise. Meanwhile, he worked his contacts to be sure that he understood the layout of the Civic Centre. He trained a group of "the kids" (as he called them) to know where every door, stairwell and closet was in that building and made sure they did the same for every hotel in Ottawa. When the sections for each candidate were assigned in the Civic Centre, he took his little team in to see how we would get candidates to Joe's box when they dropped off the ballot. Like Joe, he was counting on building support over the convention period, and he, Harvie and Jim spent a great deal of time figuring how that could be done.

After a Christmas rest, Joe and I came back ready to work flat out for the next two months. We needed media coverage. It was tough slogging. The press ignored Joe's campaign and kept reporting the race as a marathon between the two Quebec candidates, Claude Wagner and Brian Mulroney. Whenever Joe was mentioned by the media, he was always placed near the bottom of the list of candidates. The press refused to even cover him, let alone accept that he might win. Our volunteer communications expert, Carol Jamieson, was a new mother and could not work full-time in Ottawa. She worked her media contacts and always had her ear to the ground about developments in other campaigns. One day she was told that she should watch *Hockey Night in Canada* that Saturday, as one of the leading candidates, Brian Mulroney, would be there. In that ten-second clip, Brian would be seen by hundreds of thousands of Canadians from coast to coast. You could not buy that kind of coverage, and I could see that our lack of big corporate sponsors was having an impact beyond fundraising. We needed to find a way to get Joe covered by the media if he was to even be on the last ballot in February. After that, Jim hired a freelance media person to help address media concerns.

In the run-up to the convention, the tide began to turn in Joe's favour. At a series of policy sessions in which candidates were questioned by party delegates about the issues, Joe convinced delegates that he was a contender who knew the issues and could deliver his message forcefully and effectively. While Brian exaggerated and Claude Wagner looked aloof, Joe spoke directly to the audience, both in the room and on television. And he did it in both of Canada's official languages. Most delegates assumed Joe, like other anglophone candidates, could not speak French. But he had continued to practise his French with Claudette Chemla every day he was in Ottawa and it showed. The summer school in Royan was paying off for him, too. He was still nervous and hesitated when we were campaigning in Quebec, so I started a little routine to take pressure off him and give him time to understand the questions and prepare an answer. Whenever someone asked Joe a question at a delegate meeting there, I would repeat the question slowly so that it looked as if I was the one needing to be sure I understood them.

I am sure it was tiresome, but it paid off, and as Joe became more confident in speaking French, I could safely stop looking like a ninny with the Quebec delegates. Joe's strong showing at the policy sessions did two things. First, it brought delegates, alternates and volunteers to our campaign, promising their support either on the first ballot or later—if their first choice were to drop off. In a race with many candidates, no one can win fifty percent on the first or even the second ballot. It was clear that the voting would go on for three or four ballots, so our strategy was to line up support for the second and subsequent ballots. Achieving this momentum was key to Joe's ultimate win. Second, for the first time since his announcement, Joe was covered in the national press.

The next major break for Joe occurred in early February when journalist Jim Ferrabee joined us on the road in Ontario for a week. On his first day with us, Jim was surprised by the positive response of party members and delegates to Joe. By the second day, he was a convert. His stories became a running commentary on how Joe was the man to watch.

Joe's strategy was to make a decent first-ballot showing and to increase his support on each subsequent ballot. It was becoming clear that the polarization and campaign tactics of the Mulroney and Wagner camps would make it hard for one man's supporters to back the other. If one of them made it to the last ballot, the other's votes might just be available to anyone other than either Wagner or Mulroney. The media was beginning to show their scrapping as an issue, and their high-visibility campaigns made it hard for either of them to hide the disagreements. It is important to remember that in 1976, there was a strong and vibrant federal PC Party membership in most ridings across Canada and a family spirit among its supporters. Many of the delegates to this convention had been witness to John Diefenbaker's humiliation years before and knew the burden that had put on Robert Stanfield's leadership. The PC Party is known for eating its own, and this time, the party wanted the convention to heal those many internal wounds. But Joe and I saw something else happening among delegates as we travelled across Canada: most of the delegates wanted a new leader who was like Stanfield. The party trusted him and knew he had always done the right and honest thing. They wanted his successor to share those qualities. Of course, they preferred someone a little more dynamic and younger, but they wanted a gentleman. In the small groups in every town and in every province we visited during those four months leading up to the February 1976 leadership convention, more and more people saw Joe as that kind of man. They warmed to him, checked us both out, and thought Joe looked as if he had promise.

As Jim Ferrabee saw for himself and reported that week, Joe Clark had a lot of support. He had the potential to grow. That media coverage was the only truly national coverage we had the whole campaign, but coming as it did three weeks before the convention, it made a real difference. Carol and the communications team played it for everything it was worth. "Keep your eyes on Clark," she told her media contacts. On the crucial first day of the convention, a colour picture of Joe and me being welcomed by a crowd of enthusiastic supporters as we entered the lobby of our hotel in Ottawa ran on the front page of the local paper. Among the delegates, at least, and among the media that took the trouble to investigate, Joe had become the dark horse. And as anyone who has ever been in politics knows, the only thing people love more than an underdog is a dark horse.

This was my first national PC leadership campaign and I enjoyed the excitement of it all. I overcame my fear of flying and boarded one small plane after another to visit delegates in communities scattered all over the country. In Quebec, organizers found a small plane to fly us from Dorval to Thetford Mines in late January, where a group of delegates was willing to gather at the local airport to meet Joe. It was freezing and blowing snow as we boarded the plane. Our pilot was dressed in snow boots, a long raccoon coat and a ski tuque with the word "Quebec" across the front. It was too noisy to talk and too dark to see anything, and suddenly the plane began to descend into the darkness. "Where are we going?" I asked, as I saw no lights at all below. "To let my friends know we are here," he replied. I began to ask God's forgiveness for my sins. Down we went, flying perilously close to the top of a forest, and then suddenly the plane began to climb. We circled and started down again. I thought I would faint. Then, out of nowhere, about eight lights came on and there was a dimly lit snow-covered runway below. As we landed I saw that the lights were those of pickup trucks stationed along the short runway. As we coasted near the tiny building where pilots would normally file a flight plan, the trucks followed, sounding their horns in welcome. Lights went on inside the little building and at least thirty people were already in the midst of a party. Our organizer met us and made us wait while he hoisted a keg of beer on his shoulder and delivered it to the local delegates and party-goers, who were welcoming our pilot like a long-lost brother. He should be the candidate, I thought. "Best pilot around," our organizer said as he came out the door. "Still, I kept the beer out here just in case you didn't make it."

Two weeks before the convention, Joe and I were nearly killed in just such a small plane. As Joe's campaign's momentum built, so did interest in seeing him face to face. Canada is a very big country, and the only way we could keep his commitment to see the delegates before the convention was to fly to their towns and cities. Others in more financially flush campaigns bragged to our workers that "their man" flew in private planes. Some of our people decided that we needed a plane, too. It would help us cover more ground, and would send a signal that we had enough money to run a serious campaign. The problem was, though, that we had no budget for planes. We needed to rely on volunteers. No one has ever explained to me how we found the young pilot who flew us around parts of Ontario the second-last weekend of the campaign. Under the circumstances, I would have avoided the credit too. This pilot was still earning hours towards his licence, and flying us would also help him. I thought he did not look very confident when we shook his hand that Saturday morning in Chatham, Ontario. In fact, he looked a bit embarrassed, no doubt because he had just skidded to a stop by running into the snowbank at the end of the short municipal runway. I was all for calling the whole thing off, but Joe insisted that it was too late to change plans. It was to be a trip from hell, and I still don't know how we made it alive. We were heading for Goderich on our way to Owen Sound and a big meeting of delegates from several ridings. There was a family connection on both sides, so we were confident that at least some of the delegates were committed to Joe. We had to be there. Shortly after takeoff the weather turned nasty and the turbulence made my stomach sick. A voice came over the radio telling us that the airport was closed, but that we could make it to Collingwood— "if you hurry." At that point we hit a wind shear and flipped over. I was crying and screaming, and the pilot was struggling in the front beside Joe. Then I went cold and fell silent and thought, We are going to die. To this day, I have no idea how the plane righted itself. Neither did the pilot. But it did, and after another agonizing half-hour, we landed in a snowstorm in Wiarton. We were the last plane let in and again we stopped by hitting the snowbank at the end of the runway. I was shaking so hard by this point that I could hardly walk. I barely made it out of the plane before I was sick. We still had to drive to the meeting and were already an hour late. When we arrived, I begged for five minutes to brush my teeth and comb my hair, and then we went into the meeting as if nothing had happened. The next day, we thanked the pilot, rented a car and drove ourselves back to Toronto.

dance and don a yellow Joe Clark scarf. As we left the room to loud cheers and calls of "Good luck tomorrow," a drunken man fell towards me. Our organizers moved to protect me, but before they could, he grabbed and squeezed my right hand with such force that he sprained it. I cried out in pain and was swept along in a sea of supporters towards the lobby door and our awaiting car. That night, the hotel doctor arrived and offered me a cocktail of painkillers. I took one and slept for ten hours. The next morning, Sunday, I was still groggy and in pain, so my mother came to help me dress for mass. All that day I struggled along, refusing either to wear a sling or offer my hand to people to shake. When I could not avoid a handshake, though, it was torture.

That day nonetheless remains one of the most fascinating political days of my life. From the beginning there was a buzz around Joe. During the last three weeks, while the main camps warred or sniped among themselves, Joe was gaining. Yet on voting day, the bulk of the media remained huddled in front of the Mulroney and Wagner sections. They had predicted one of the two would win, and no amount of evidence to the contrary would persuade them to change their views or their plans. As the balloting started, our section was all excitement. Friends who watched it on TV told me that I looked calm and serene. The truth was, I was still under the influence of the painkiller, but for someone like me, whose emotions are usually written all over her face, that was a godsend. The first ballot was tough and we did not gain as many votes as we had hoped. Wagner was in the lead with 531 votes. Mulroney had 357 and Joe 277. We were third, a minor miracle considering where we had started five months before. Heward Grafftey from Quebec and Jim Gillies from Toronto were eliminated and came to us. Sinclair Stevens from Ontario moved at the same time and John Fraser signalled he would come to Joe, but for some reason did not remove his name from the ballot. Paul Hellyer, a former Liberal, stayed in but said he would go to Wagner.

On the next ballot, Joe moved into second place with 532 votes, behind Wagner (667) and ahead of Mulroney (357). His strategy was working. It was becoming clear that we had a real chance of making it to the final ballot. We did not have the numbers yet, but we had the momentum. While all these crossovers were important to the final result, two candidates in particular made the difference for Joe. The first was Sinclair Stevens, the independent-minded lawyer from Ontario whose campaign theme was "Back to Basics." A fiscal conservative, he had earned a reputation as a right-winger. As a so-called Red Tory, Joe was seen as more open and socially progressive. We had not counted on Sinc, thinking he would likely go to one of the Quebec candidates who had the support of big business. But Sinc had spent a good part of his legal and business career fighting the banks, and with his lawyer wife, Noreen, he was much more in tune with social and cultural issues than people knew. The second candidate who ensured Joe's election that day was Flora MacDonald. Hers was the biggest heartbreak of the campaign. So many people had pledged their allegiance to her and then either left her after the first ballot or did not keep their word. It became known as "the Flora Factor," a term that is used even today to describe the phenomenon of apparent support for a candidate that does not translate into votes. Joe and Flora were seen as political soulmates and social progressives, and there was a feeling of excitement and relief when, after the second ballot, she walked over and donned one of Joe's scarves. I watched her make her way through the crowd and the media, and I was delighted but sad at the same time. If Joe had not been in the race, I would have been on her team. Flora had confirmed for me that there was a place for strong and able women in our party. She knew her stuff and stood up to all the men in caucus. As she joined us in Joe's box, I touched her arm with my swollen hand and whispered, "Thank you."

There was no doubt now that we had a chance. As well as Flora, John Fraser came over then. Jack Horner went to Wagner and I don't know where Pat Nowlan went. Our people tried hard to get Brian to come over, but he refused, although one of his senior campaign advisers, Michel Cogger, called over to our box to say that while Brian would remain neutral, most of his supporters would come to Joe. A tense third ballot followed. Claude Wagner had 1,003 votes to Joe's 969. Brian was reduced to 369 votes and had to drop off. The final vote was Wagner against Clark. By this time, our supporters were in a frenzy. This was the moment we had worked and planned for, and our team knew what it had to do. Some had gone immediately to solicit workers from the boxes of other candidates as they dropped off, and there were clusters of yellow Clark scarves strategically placed all over the convention centre. Anyone who knew uncommitted delegates pressed them to support Joe. Brian and his close workers were obviously crushed. His campaign team had been confident of victory, yet the Baie Comeau boy, transplanted to Montreal, had been bettered by the boy from High River. Still, as Cogger had said, most of Brian's people came to Joe on the last ballot. We sat there numb with fatigue as we waited for the final results.

We won by a whisker—Clark 1,187 to Wagner's 1,122. The numbers were barely out of the Convention chairman's mouth before our supporters went wild. Joe and I were swamped and literally carried from our box to the stage. I turned around and saw that my father and mother and most of my family were cheering and crying with relief. I gave my father a smile, blew him a kiss and formed the word "thanks." He nodded and waved his yellow scarf. I remember standing on the stage with Joe as he made his acceptance speech. It was vintage Joe Clark— straight, concise, passionate. He had won, he said, but that was just the first step. He looked at the thousands in the stands in front of him and ended with a sentence that I remember still.

"We will not take this nation by storm, by stealth or by surprise. We will win it by work." It was both an invitation for them to join him and a warning to the party members of the task that confronted them. But for me, those words were an omen of what lay ahead for the two of us.

—

One of the benefits of hindsight is its clarity. Had we known in 1976 what we learned later, our first task would have been to establish a strong relationship with the key media opinion leaders immediately after the campaign. During the months leading up to the convention, Carol Jamieson, our volunteer press adviser, did everything but sell herself to get any coverage at all for Joe. The minute he was elected leader, the press liaison job demanded a very different strategy. But we had no seasoned political press person on staff or in the wings. Within hours Joe had hundreds of media requests from across Canada and around the world.

We were not prepared.

That night, after the convention was over, Carol went home to Toronto and her six-month-old son whom she had brought with her to countless meetings since the previous September. With her went an important link to the Ontario media. During those crucial first days, we were without a definite media plan and a professional press person to carry it out. I have never underestimated the damage that void created for Joe in those first days of his leadership. The *Toronto Star*'s "Joe Who?" headline was the sign of a media group that had not done its homework. But rather than be apologetic, the media went on the offensive. Who was this upstart that beat the frontrunners? Who said he could win when we did not agree to his coronation? There were a lot of red faces that day and there should have been. But that did not change the fact that the media has more power than any other group in Canadian society and they number of women keeping their surnames had increased from less than 10 percent in 1980 to about 20 percent between 1984 and 1998 to nearly 35 percent today. In 1973, when I married, very few women in English Canada kept their own family name. In my experience, with the exception of my law classmates, I did not know another woman among my family and friends who made this choice. Legally, women can use whatever name they want when they marry, provided it is not for an illegal purpose. Taking a husband's name is a cultural, not a legal, requirement in every province but Quebec, where women keep their surnames. So why was there such a fuss? I see now that the issue was control—about a woman's independence and about equality within a marriage. These were neither accepted nor popular concepts among the party or the press when Joe was elected party leader in 1976. Rebellious behaviour among young women like me needed to be quashed in order to maintain the social status quo.

Three years earlier, when I married, people just ignored the fact that I used my name and called me Mrs. Clark. Others added the words "Joe's wife" whenever they introduced me. For some, like my father, it was an embarrassment. Every card or letter he ever sent me was addressed to Mrs. Joe Clark. For others, it was a sign of an eccentric and self-centred personality. But in 1976, in a desperate attempt by the media to know *anything* about me, the "name issue," as it was always referred to by Joe's staff, party members and press alike, took on a life and significance of its own. I did my best to explain my decision, but no reasoned explanation satisfied the media or the larger public. It was considered ridiculous for a young woman to make such arguments and heresy that a prominent man would let her. Joe was now the leader of the Opposition in Parliament. He had an image to maintain, his critics charged, yet he supported me in my "unacceptable" decision. He "allowed" his wife to use her own name and then encouraged her to pursue her own life and career. Unlike Pierre Trudeau, he was a traitor to the macho cause and had ostracized himself from his own gender group by breaking an unwritten male pact of dominance and, worse perhaps, by opening the door to demands from other wives for similar treatment. He was a heretic and anyone in the media or the public who attacked him as weak and henpecked could be forgiven for their belligerence, because, after all, he had asked for it by refusing to "put me in my place." Those were the standards by which a man was judged less than thirty years ago and my decision and actions required my husband, as well as me, to be censured. For years after 1976 we received letters from Canadians demanding to see a copy of our marriage certificate to convince them that we were not "living in sin." In 1978, my right hand was broken by a man who said he wanted me to know what he thought of women's libbers. I have even been attacked by other women, including political wives, who were concerned that my example would force them to try harder and to have a career, because "if you are doing it all, people will want to know why we can't."

As I look back now, the whole controversy about my name seems ridiculous. But in 1976, such was the stuff of criticism and gossip. Within the party, the issue was hotly debated, and I can remember the day that two Ottawa matrons took it upon themselves to call me to a meeting in my own home to tell me that my husband was doomed unless I changed my name. My husband just laughed at their presumptuousness and insisted I take no notice. "We are the future," he had said. "Remember the Panasonic jingle. We're just slightly ahead of our time. Look at your own classmates. How many use their husbands' names? How many plan to practise law after they have children? How many support you and are willing to fight for better laws to ensure women are treated fairly in the home and the workforce?" He was right, of course, but at the time the vocal public reaction was very upsetting to me and left me with a real sense of insecurity. I worried that maybe the critics were right and that I had misjudged the larger public's desire to see new and younger people involved in political activity and social and legal activism.

Joe has always supported me in my life choices. But his reassurances in 1976 could not stop public criticism, which extended to attacks on him, too. I can remember the last time before the general election that the party was actually asked to debate the "name issue" at a provincial annual meeting in Manitoba. I was in the room that day as a show of defiance, but also of solidarity with those who supported me and wanted the matter laid to rest once and for all. After some negative comments, a wonderful lady in her late seventies stood up in the crowded room and asked, "Who is Elizabeth Windsor? She is our Queen. I am tired of hearing our leader and his wife criticized. If it's good enough for my Queen to keep her name, then it's good enough for my leader's wife." When this tiny, elderly lady in her special hat sat down, there was silence and then applause. From then on, the "name issue" was either ignored or whispered about behind the scenes. Ironically, it would really only resurface as an issue again in the 1983 leadership campaign, when Joe was attacked as being a weak leader because he "let" his wife do what she wanted and couldn't even make her take his name. This was again presented as a negative for both of us and we were derisively compared to other candidates whose wives were, according to their logic, far superior to me because they did just as their husbands told them!

emotion. I drove to my parents' home and told my mother, asking her to keep it secret, as I had so much to do and needed time to absorb this incredible news. Mom was delighted. She hugged me and promised to tell my father as soon as he got home.

The second challenge I had to face in March was law school. I was hopelessly behind, but with about six weeks left until exams, I still believed that I could finish the term. I decided to visit Dean Hubbard at the law school to explain my dilemma. We both agreed that my situation was unprecedented, but differed on how to resolve it. I asked that given my serious morning sickness and all the publicity that surrounded me, I be granted permission to do either a paper for each course or be given a take-home exam. I knew a classmate who had been granted the latter because her mother was sick and she had to help care for her. I thought that my own situation was more extreme than hers was, and felt it was a reasonable request. He refused the take-home request out of hand, and I pushed for permission to at least write the exams in the afternoon. He refused that too, suggesting that I might cheat by getting the questions from friends coming out of the exam room. I was furious, and startled that a law school could have so little trust in the integrity of its students. He told me that my best bet was to quit, insisting that I was at a crossroads. I could have babies or I could be a lawyer, but I could not do both. My Irish temper exploded. "I will do both," I told him and left. There was no support for me there.

The third challenge facing me was the move into Stornoway. In 1976, there was little budget for decorating and no budget for staff. It was only in 1979, when Pierre Trudeau took up residence there, that staff positions would be set aside at his request for the leader of the Opposition. Previous party leaders had to pay for their own staff. And so, in 1976, I once again called on my family and friends for a helping hand. I turned specifically to my friend Cecilia Humphreys, an Ottawa architect whose eye for architectural detail would ensure we set new trends in colour and design. The result was brilliant if controversial. That year she had the living-room walls at Stornoway transformed from institutional pink to chocolate brown with high-gloss winter white for the window frames and beautiful mouldings. The walls in the dining room were covered with an expensive ochre-coloured shot silk from Mrs. Pearson's years in the residence, and rather than remove it, we had the dado below it painted coral. We then hung brown and cream curtains in a traditional English cotton and used the same material to cover the twelve chairs around the Regency mahogany dining table, which looked spectacular when set with the residence's formal gold-trimmed china.

It was in 1976 that I began my lessons in Canadian art, and filled Stornoway with paintings on loan from the Canada Council Art Bank. Joe and I had a few pieces that we had purchased after our marriage, but after we moved to Stornoway, I started to read all the books on Canadian art that I could find. My taste was eclectic at first, and soon I favoured experimental pieces, which did not always sit well with our visitors.

It was at Stornoway that we started the trend away from serving the regular variety of heavy, hot hors d'oeuvres at our receptions and parties to lighter and healthier alternatives. At our first press gallery lawn party in 1977 we chose strawberries and champagne, using local fruit and an excellent sparkling Ontario wine. That marked our "coming out" as the first public figures to highlight exclusively Canadian wines at an official reception. The following year, we went further and served crudités (raw vegetables) and sliced fruit as part of a "healthy" buffet. Canadian cheeses and smoked salmon from the East Coast were on offer. We also chose only Canadian wine and beer—no small feat given the choices in 1976. The press response, while laughable today, surprised and hurt me. We were accused of being cheap and not knowing how to entertain. I learned a valuable lesson from this—don't surprise people with food changes they are not used to, and when you do introduce new foods and wines, make the act of introducing them into an event so people think they are among the chosen few who have been invited to share in a new trend.

The months after our move into Stornoway were a blur of activity and angst. I crammed for my final law exams in late April and wrote them in spite of persistent morning sickness that lasted my entire pregnancy. Despite my best efforts, I could not salvage my year, and had to decide if I would go back and try again in September. I hoped that I would only have to repeat the courses I had missed, but that was denied too, and I would have to repeat the entire year. As part of his decision to meet other leaders internationally, Joe undertook a visit to some of the world capitals and I joined him in Washington, D.C., the first week of June. It was from there that we announced my pregnancy, which at almost five months was becoming increasingly hard to hide. We spent two weeks in Prince Edward Island in a cottage in July and then at Shaw's Resort with George and Tia Cooper of Halifax. George had been a key supporter and would briefly represent one of the Halifax seats in 1979.

In early September, Joe went to Europe with caucus foreign affairs critic Claude Wagner, trade critic Jim Balfour and labour critic John Fraser to meet government and opposition leaders. Even that trip was not without controversy, as messages went back and forth between his office and the Holy See. Joe and his delegation had been granted a papal audience during their visit to Rome, and there was a disagreement about what I would be called. I preferred to be called by my own name and wasn't sure what the problem could be, but I very much wanted to be blessed by the Pope as my husband and I were about to begin our lives as parents. I told the staff to just give them my name and not to worry, as I knew the Vatican officials would do whatever their protocol required. In the end, I did not go to Rome, opting to remain in Ottawa for the first important week of law classes—a decision that resulted in many months of answering criticisms that I had slighted the Pope because I was too proud to let him call me by my husband's name.

Near the end of Joe's European tour, I joined him in London, where I waddled through the National Gallery and toured Westminster Abbey with Diane Berlet, whose husband, Ron, was a senior trade person at our High Commission there. Diane was both a professional London guide and a midwife, which was an additional safety precaution for me.

I did not have a particularly pleasant pregnancy and suffered throughout with migraines. By the end, I was painfully swollen and spent the last days before Catherine's birth in bed. She was due on Halloween, but as I told my mother, the press would kill us. I could just see the headlines: "Two Trudeau angels born on Christmas Day and Catherine Clark, the little Halloween witch!" Thankfully, she was born November 6— a week late.

In the months after Catherine's birth in 1976, I found reconciling my private and public roles particularly difficult. I did my best to balance my new life as a young mother and wife of a prominent politician. I found time to attend class full-time to finish law school. On the motherhood front, breast-feeding was the order of the day. I failed at it dismally. Catherine was always hungry, but my schedule would not allow for the trendy "on demand" feeding regimen. I still see it as a form of infant indulgence bordering on tyranny. Catherine also suffered from colic and it seemed that she cried all night for six months straight. Like most new mothers, I rarely had more than two or three hours' sleep each night. When I see new parents who look exhausted, I always feel I should offer to babysit so that they can sleep a whole night. It took me years to sleep through the entire night after Catherine's birth. Until I finished my studies the following April, I found I was struggling. I had always been able to take care of everything on my own or to rely on Joe on the rare occasions I needed help. That was no longer the case. He had other professional responsibilities and was surrounded by his own political staff, who took over the many roles I had played during the leadership process a year before. They set his travel schedule and determined a lot of our home life—from early-morning briefings through to parties at the house.

After the initial euphoria following Catherine's birth, I felt alone and depressed. I cried a great deal and seemed unable to pull out of my funk. I saw everything in a negative light and was listless. While I was very tired, I still awoke at all hours of the night in fits of anxiety. One day, unable to cope at all, I skipped my classes and called Joe's office to have him come home. He was in a meeting and I was put through to his press secretary, Donald Doyle. Fortunately for me, his wife had suffered post-partum symptoms when their child was born, and he knew what to do. Within fifteen minutes he was at the door, followed closely by my mother, whom he had called at her office and asked to come over. Both my parents showed up that day, and came regularly each evening after work to offer support. My doctor began to treat the symptoms I was suffering. It took longer than I would have liked to return to "normal" but after a few months, I began to feel that I could manage. I was less traumatized by the sheer responsibility of caring for a baby and worked to screen out the criticisms against Joe from within the party and in the media that marked this time. I saw that my sadness was not unusual and learned how to deal with it.

Because of Catherine's late arrival, I missed two weeks of classes, including important Christmas exam preparation lectures. My parents came as often as they could, but my brother was only fifteen and they had other responsibilities and could not always be in Ottawa with me. In early December, encouraged by my mother, I decided that I needed full-time help with Catherine during the day so that I could study. I hired a Mothercraft nurse who had been recommended by a family friend, and she came to Stornoway each morning for the day until I finished my exams. Mom spelled her off by coming on the weekends and I handled the nights. Joe was away most of the time, making up for the period during the fall when, near the end of my pregnancy, he had remained in Ottawa to be with me.

Our new nurse was worth her weight in gold, and Catherine became calm and contented. "You're starving her," was her diagnosis after one day on the job, and after a few meek protestations to the contrary, Catherine was introduced to a bottle. Although relieved that she was satisfied, I worried that I had failed an important test as a mother. I had been told at the hospital and by most of my friends that breast-feeding was the only way for a healthy, happy baby, and I had taken them all seriously. My mother scoffed at their claims, pointing out that she had raised all six of us on a bottle and we had never missed a day of school. In spite of her reassurance, I still felt a failure, and Catherine's enthusiastic acceptance of a bottle confirmed my view that as a mother, I was rather a pathetic case. There was one real benefit to bottle-feeding that I later discovered— Joe was able to spend time holding Catherine and helping me feed her. Each night he was in Ottawa he would come home before eight to give her the last bottle before bed. From there, the two of them graduated to reading together each night he was home, a ritual that over the years of her childhood created a strong and enduring bond between father and daughter.

By the time my last exam was over in mid-December, Joe had finished his travelling for the month. He offered to help where he could and would take Catherine for long walks around Rockcliffe Park, where Stornoway is situated, carrying her against his chest in a baby pack. But even when he was in Ottawa, I could see that he was terribly busy and I did not want to burden him with my own worries. He could not help seeing, though, that I was sad and we discussed what could be done. Part of my concern was that our life had changed so dramatically since the leadership convention and we could no longer easily share experiences and ideas as we had done before. While he agreed, he also insisted that this was to be expected and I began to see that this was a permanent change and, just like motherhood, would alter our relationship. It all seemed like too much at once, and I was unsure how to handle it. It took me a long time to put all the emotional pieces together to make a whole picture, and they never really fitted as perfectly as I would have liked.

I have often thought back to those days and wondered what I could have done differently. All women have to adapt to the monumental changes a new baby brings. Some cannot cope at all, while others breeze through without a complaint. But usually they get to live these adjustments privately, turning quietly to family and doctor for personal and medical support if needed. That was never an option for me, and I see now that being constantly in the public eye was a huge part of the problem I faced at this crucial point. The press maintained an interest in our life, and Catherine's birth added to that. At the same time, it was stressful trying to finish law school. At twenty-four, I was out of my depth and feeling very vulnerable. Several women came to my aid. Grete Hale and her sister Gay Cook helped with catering and advice about food and entertaining, and Dale Johnston, whose husband, Howard, was a member of Parliament from B.C., came over frequently to lend a hand with actual preparation. I relied heavily on Wendy Orr, a staffer in Joe's office, and Joan Andre was always there to help with Catherine when Mom was too busy and I had to be away. Joan's two daughters, Coryn and Lauren, were like big sisters to Catherine from the time she was two. They all had asthma and Joan knew exactly how to manage it.

Once Catherine passed the colicky stage and started to be her own little person, I felt much more comfortable with her and found her a true delight. She has always had an independent spirit and is loving, kind and sensitive. As she grew up, Joe and I found every stage of her life a treat. Friends often ask me what was the best stage of my child's life, and I had to honestly tell them that I had loved them all. Children are a marvel and teach you as much as you teach them. As Catherine moved from the infant to the toddler stage, we decided to make her as much a part of our life as possible. As she grew up, I tried hard to have her understand her responsibilities within our family. I always saw my job as a parent to care for and love her and to prepare her to grow and mature into a sensitive and creative member of the community. I never thought of her as mine alone, and I owe so much to Joe, to my mother and to her godmother, my sister Jane, for their roles in helping raise Catherine to be a beautiful and loving young woman. I know that I was strict with Catherine as a child. Society has all kinds of limits and rules that we must follow, even when we don't want to. Respecting these and the rights of others in our community is part of the price we pay for living in a free society. Catherine was a child who always preferred to know where she stood. She delighted in having responsibilities and roles in our family, which increased as she got older. From her earliest days, I wanted Catherine to know the demands of her father's position and to have a part in his life. I worried that she would feel isolated from him if we did not find a way to include her in his public and private life each day. Although we shielded her as much as possible from the press and public as she grew up, we found other ways to include her at many events, some at the official residences.

With this in mind, I decided that Catherine would attend her first reception at Stornoway in the fall of 1978 when she was not quite two years old. As she sat in her highchair the morning of a caucus reception, I told her we were having a party that evening and she could attend—this party was for Daddy's colleagues at work and all of us had to help. I insisted that I really needed her to hand out the cocktail napkins—one to each guest—and then showed her where they were. "Will you do this for me?" I asked her. Of course, she wasn't talking yet, but she smiled and kicked her feet to show her excitement, and I said, "Good, then let's get them ready." She spent the day piling and re-piling these little white paper napkins in a corner of the pantry. After her nap that afternoon, she had a snack and then chose one of the two party dresses I had set out for her. When she was young, I would always choose two or three complete outfits for her to select from when she was going to appear in public. Generally, this avoided wasting time and energy fighting over what to wear, and ensured she was colour-coordinated. I had suffered enough criticism to know that if Catherine arrived dressed inappropriately at a public event that it would be my fault as a "women's libber" and not her father's because he didn't pay attention to ensuring that she wore what had been set out or packed for her. The rest of the time, though, we were fairly casual about clothes and she could choose what she wanted to wear.

When the waiters arrived and the standard rush to prepare the food and the bar began, Catherine was pretty much on her own. She knew that the kitchen was off limits during a reception and went to the pantry. I confess she did cry at one point and wanted me to go with her, although I thought she wanted me to read her a book. As the guests arrived, they were offered a drink and were sent into the living room. Soon I noticed little puddles of water on the floors and asked the waiters what was happening. They had no idea. Then one of the MPs asked Joe, "Can I put this ice cube in my drink?" It turns out that the waiters had taken Catherine's little piles of napkins off the floor and placed them on the counter out of her reach. She could, though, bend over into the big tub on the pantry floor and retrieve ice cubes. Like a whirling dervish, she would run into the pantry, get an ice cube and then run back to the living room and hand it to a guest. The women had taken the proffered cube, thanked

her and promptly put them in their drinks. The men, on the
other hand, held the melting cubes gingerly. It was, after all, a
token from the boss's daughter! We all laughed at the two very
different responses from the female and male guests and celebrated Catherine's first official party.

As we entered 1978, there were rumours of a federal election call, and I began to prepare myself for a campaign. In this
endeavour, I relied heavily on my father. He knew what was
involved and wanted to be sure I understood how big a task lay
ahead for me. It was his view that I should campaign on my
own as well as with Joe so that we could address different constituencies, including women and young people. He also felt
that I could relieve the need for Joe to travel to every constituency himself, especially those where we might not have any
chance at all of winning. That would allow Joe and the campaign organizers to focus on those ridings where polling showed
we were in a tight race with the Liberals. In early March, Joe
and I were to go on a campaign-style trip to northern Ontario,
and Joe asked Dad to come with us. We were to visit North Bay,
where Dad had played junior hockey and attended high school.
He had many friends and contacts there, and was pleased to be
included.

That year, my father had often felt unwell and had lost
weight, although he had refused to see a doctor, insisting it was
just stomach upset. After Joe's speech in North Bay, the three of
us joined the local organizers for dinner, but Dad had to leave
early, as he was feeling ill. I asked a doctor friend who was travelling with us to go up and see if she could offer him some
advice. I was startled when she came back downstairs and said
she thought that he might have a growth on a major organ. It
was a measure of how sick he was that he promised to see a
doctor as soon as we returned to Ottawa the next day. He
underwent a battery of tests and the results were due within ten
days. Meanwhile, Parliament rose for the Easter break, and Joe

and I left to spend a week in Florida. A few days later I learned that my father had inoperable lung cancer that had spread to his liver. His treatment options were bleak and brutal. After one session of chemotherapy that made him violently ill, he decided to let the disease take its course and refused any further treatment. He insisted on palliative care and pain management only, and prepared to die.

I was devastated and overcome with grief. What would I ever do without his daily guidance and advice? In those six weeks before he died, I thought a great deal about my father. We had often disagreed about things, including my outspokenness, independence and refusal to conform to a narrow view of women's roles. My father embraced a traditional view of male-female relationships. But he also made tentative attempts to understand the way life was changing, and women's roles with it. He did try to imagine what my life and that of my sisters would be like. What he saw, though, didn't please him much because he felt the changes ignored his view that women should be protected by men. My father was racked by financial insecurity and by the nonconformity of his daughters. It made him a complex and contradictory man. Now I see that with the exception of family life, he was really a man who felt most comfortable fighting, not defending, the status quo. He had his pride and was a "man's man" and I know that it hurt him when, after my marriage, his friends made fun of the fact that I kept my name. Yet he also wanted my sisters and me to succeed in a "man's world" and was willing to put up with the "silly things," as he called them, in order for us to do that.

I remember when he was in the hospital, a friend who had ridiculed him when I kept my name after my marriage sheepishly told him that his own daughter planned to do the same. "Well, Maureen has always been a kind of trailblazer," my father said. "I am sure lots of others will follow her example." In repeating the story to me later that day, I could see he was quite proud of himself. It seemed to him a real personal victory. He was ahead of the curve on an important issue, and his friends were forced to watch as their daughters followed the example of his own. It almost seemed as if all the snide remarks he had endured about "the name issue" were worth it for him. But it was more than that. I think it also made him realize that my choices and independence had been partly his doing and that his girls would set the trend in this new era that he found so confusing. Maybe, he hoped, we were not going to have lives of bad luck, as he believed he had had, but rather fight for changes to systems and attitudes that would otherwise hold us back.

Caught in a time warp, my father personified the generation that had been shaped by the Depression and World War II. His ultimate act of teenage independence had been to flee the constraints of home and enlist in the war in Europe. Some of his friends never returned. For almost all of his adult life, he lived in a house full of women. He was often a lonely, solitary man. Backroom politics and sports were his only real releases. He loved political strategy and the thrill of winning but preferred working on behalf of others who had the social skills he knew he did not. He also pushed us continually to be educated; his own lack of education had prevented him from attaining the financial independence so many of his educated friends enjoyed. Financial security was not just desirable for a married man with a large family back then. It was everything. I sometimes think that as he aged, my father grew more cynical about life and lost faith in his own advice about education. He was burdened by his financial responsibilities, and after browbeating Colleen and me to strive and achieve, he seemed to skip over my three younger sisters, instead pouring all his energy into his only son, the last of his six children. In the end, when he was ravaged by the cancer that killed him at fifty-nine, his view of life swayed back and forth between his firm belief that you make your own luck and a growing awareness that systems bar some people from achieving their potential while allowing others an easy time of it. It was this view that encouraged me to become a lifelong advocate for equality. I like to think that he would be proud of my stances, even though he rarely agreed with my stating them as candidly as I did.

The demands of politics, my father's pride and my own sense of duty would prevent me from being with him at the end of his life. The day before his death, he refused to let me cancel a speech I was to give on Joe's behalf in Alberta. "I'll see you Monday when you return," he insisted. "There will be an election soon, and you must do all you can to help your husband." Just before I left for Alberta that last day, I went to visit him. He was swollen and yellow, his liver failing. When I was about to leave, tears suddenly started to flow down his cheeks. He had only once before cried in my presence, in the bleakest of days when as a child I saw him face the possibility that our family would break up if he continued to drink. He had stopped drinking then, but I remember the feeling of fear and insecurity that had overwhelmed me as a six-year-old during those months before my youngest sister's birth when he was struggling so hard. The feeling then was the same as I felt that day. That no matter what happened, things would never be the same again. And so I told him quietly that he must not cry. His life had been too short but he should think what he had achieved. I told him that our mother would want for nothing and that we would all take care of each other. I told him I loved him and I wished that he would not die—all the things that a child tells a parent on the eve of their death. All the things so often left unsaid as we live and pretend that our lives will never change and that death will never come. I like to think that my words made a difference to him that day, that they set his mind at rest. We spoke of Catherine and how she would have the pony he had promised her. I kissed his emaciated cheek for what I did not know then would be the last time, and I left.

And so I was away when he died, doing my duty to one man I loved at the expense of the other. My sister Pamela, a registered nurse, was alone with him when he died that night, his lungs rotted by the cigarettes to which he had been addicted since they had been offered as treats to soldiers. She had seen death before and could follow his last moments with both a clinical eye and a daughter's heart. I could not have, nor could my mother or my other sisters or brother have. I saw a sign in this that God was looking out for us, saving us from the sight of his painful death, although not the pain of our loss.

In writing this I have faced again and finally resolved my fear of having failed him in some way by my absence that night. He was right to make me leave, to maintain his own pride and to save me from the anguish of being there with him at the end. I could not help him and so I had again done what he had wanted. I had gone to help my husband.

6

AFTER MY FATHER'S DEATH, Joe urged me to consider articling with an Ottawa law firm so I could do the bar admission course and be licensed to practise law. I had taken a year off after graduation the previous summer, but I had not ignored law completely during this time. During January 1978, before my father had become ill, I had joined a group of academics to write a chapter for a book called *Violence in Canada,* edited by Mary Alice Beyer Gammon. Concerned about the proposed changes to the federal rape laws, I agreed to write a chapter entitled "Rape and the Canadian Legal Process," which was my first attempt at publication. In it I severely criticized the bill for maintaining the admissibility of evidence of a woman's prior sexual conduct with a person other than the accused in a rape trial. If the law was not changed, women would continue to be victimized twice in rape cases, first as the victim of the violation and later at the trial. During that fall I was to participate on panels, radio and television shows and in university classes, which eventually attracted considerable press attention, something that worried Joe's staff, who felt I was upstaging him in the crucial months leading up to an election. Joe, however, urged me to speak out, as he knew that this was an issue of public importance to Canadian women and one of great concern to me. As the weeks went by the writing would distract me from my sadness following my father's death.

In May 1978, it looked as if Pierre Trudeau would not call a summer election, and I decided to look for an articling position. About a week into my search, a former classmate, Jacqueline Viau Fitzgibbons, called unexpectedly and offered me an articling position with a small but prestigious francophone law firm in Ottawa called Paris, Mercier, Sirois, Paris and Bélanger. Catherine was eighteen months and Joe urged me to accept, insisting that it would do us all good if I was back in law. I agreed and began the required year of articling before writing the licensing exams. I warned the senior partners about the upcoming election, and all of them (who were Liberals!) understood what was involved. They would free me for the two months of the campaign on condition I make up the time.

It was during these years between 1976 and 1980 that I came to understand the meaning of being a political spouse. I thought when I married that I knew what was involved in politics. But I did not. And in 1976, after Catherine's birth, I saw that politics could be a cruel mistress that threatened all other relationships. Joe's life as party leader demanded total loyalty and the full commitment of his time and energy. His political success required that he make it the centre of his life. Other plans and people unrelated to political life just had to adapt. I guess I should have been more astute about Joe's total commitment to politics and been ready for what lay ahead. Although he supported my decisions to study law, to do graduate studies when Catherine was still young, to practise law in Toronto and even to run for Parliament, I learned early in our relationship that if I planned to stay married, at least four things would have to happen.

First, I would usually have to give in to the demands of his life and their imposition on my own. That has always been easier said than done, especially if I wanted to be taken seriously as a professional. Second, to withstand the loneliness and pressures that politics imposed on our family life, I would have to develop my own world where I could live and work and find solace and strength. Third, I would have to accept the primary responsibility for raising Catherine. Finally, I would have to insist that family time was built into Joe's schedule as much as possible, especially for special events like vacations, birthdays and other family milestones.

I tackled each of these with different degrees of success. In some ways I was fortunate because I knew and liked politics and had personal experience in election campaigns before getting married. Politics was nothing new to me, and during the first couple of years of our marriage, we were mentor and adviser to each other as Joe pursued his early parliamentary career and I studied law. This is the pattern lived by many couples, who start off their married lives together sharing an emotional and intellectual bond and closeness. But after the 1976 leadership convention, when Joe was elected party leader and became the leader of the Official Opposition, that easy rapport changed due in part to my pregnancy and my own developing maturity. By the summer of 1979, though, the pattern of our political life together had been set. Cabinet secrecy and caucus confidentiality would require that we clearly separate our private life together from Joe's new political responsibilities.

Throughout Catherine's childhood, I was faced with the usual problems of a working mother combined with the added obligation of political life. Not only was I absent during the day, but I often had to travel with Joe on the weekends. There were times when Catherine was young that we were away half of each month, and I worried that our many absences would affect her. In early 1978, when my father was dying, I hired a housekeeper named Pauline Cook, a middle-aged widow and mother of four grown children. Catherine called her "Polly" and, to my great relief, took to her immediately. Pauline lived in the apartment over the garage at Stornoway and was available whenever we needed her. I was, of course, one of the fortunate women who could count on both my family and full-time support at home. I know how lucky I was and I am grateful. I started articling in June 1978, and each morning as I left, Catherine made a fuss. "Don't worry," Pauline insisted, "these tears are to make you feel bad. She's fine the minute you leave." I was unconvinced. Then one morning I forgot my sunglasses and returned home to get them. I had done no more than go around the block, but when I entered the kitchen, there was Catherine, all smiles, banging a wooden spoon on a kitchen pot, while Pauline cleaned the breakfast dishes. My housekeeper looked at me and said, "You see what I mean? Kids like to do this to their mothers. It's a built-in guilt inducer. Don't you feel better? Now go to work!" Nevertheless I faced criticism from party supporters for leaving Catherine in the care of a "stranger" at home. I began to see that this harping was not going to stop and decided that the only way to respond was to move ahead with my own career in law.

I found articling liberating, as it allowed me to accomplish something on my own merit. I was assigned to Jean-Charles Sirois, one of the senior lawyers, who later was named a federal judge. He was a superb mentor and taught me a great deal about litigation. He told me once that there was still a little resistance to women in law, but that this was changing. The following week we ran into an example of how some judges responded to the novelty of women in the courtroom. Jean-Charles had asked me to accompany him to court on a divorce matter, where he was representing the wife as his client. I wore my new navy blue suit and thought I looked like a smart young lawyer. A former male classmate of mine was the junior with the lawyer representing the husband, and before we joined our senior counsel on opposite sides of the courtroom, we laughed at how lawyerly we looked. No sooner had the case started than the presiding judge said to Jean-Charles, "Please ask your client to sit behind you, Mr. Sirois." He thought I was the woman seeking a divorce! Jean-Charles burst out laughing and said, "Your Honour, this is not my client but my articling student." I was mortified. To give my law-school friend credit, he sought me out after the court adjourned for lunch and told me that the judge was getting on in age and his eyesight was obviously failing. "You look like a lawyer to me," he added kindly. Jean-Charles just laughed and said, "What did I tell you?" During the afternoon session the court clerk passed me a note from the judge who asked to see me in his chambers at the end of the day. When Jean-Charles and I went in, the elderly judge rose to his feet, shook our hands and apologized for his earlier mistake. "I am not yet used to young women in my court," he said.

This incident reminded me of the time I attended a law association meeting two years before. I asked the woman in charge if there were any tickets left for the lunch. "Wives are not allowed," she replied haughtily. "Are you a wife?" I told her I was married, but that I was there as a law student. "Well, the wives are all trying to sneak in," she retorted. I was startled by this statement. Certainly the wives of affluent and influential lawyers whom I knew never needed to *sneak in* anywhere!

In January of 1979, as part of Joe's international trip to Asia and the Middle East to meet their political leaders, we visited Israel and Jordan. Several friends joined us for that trip, including Jeff and Sandy Lyons and Irving and Gail Gerstein from Toronto. Ron Atkey, Sinclair Stevens and Rob Parker, all Progressive Conservative MPs, were part of the delegation, as were Bill Neville, Joe's chief of staff, and Ian Green, his executive assistant. I missed the first part of the trip because of work and joined Joe in Athens, where we spent two days before going to Israel. Even though I had read a great deal on the Middle East and on Israel and Jordan before leaving Canada, I remained a neophyte in international affairs. The complexity of Middle

East politics eluded me, and for once, I just gave myself over to the sights of the places we visited. No one can leave Israel untouched by its diversity and history. As a Roman Catholic, I found that travelling to the birthplace of Christ and seeing Jerusalem and the holy places of his Passion and death were deep religious moments for me. I was touched to the core by Yad Vashem, a monument to the six million Jews killed in the Holocaust, and will never forget the sheer horror of each room, each picture and each artifact that told of this time of hate. My Jewish friends shared their perspectives with me as we visited these holy places and memorials, and we supported each other during a highly emotional week there.

After our trip to Israel, we went to Jordan, where I visited with Queen Noor, the young American wife of King Hussein of Jordan. We were almost the same age and shared a commitment to public service. I liked her immediately. We drank coffee in her magnificent home and she told me about some of the challenges she saw ahead for her adoptive country and the role she planned to play in helping her husband fulfill his work in this explosive part of the world. Her role would turn out to be much more difficult than mine. When we met again in Banff twenty years later at a dinner Joe held to welcome King Hussein and Queen Noor during their official visit to Canada, we reminded each other how innocent we had been then and how much life had offered us in the intervening years.

When we returned to Canada, our time was devoted entirely to election readiness. Pierre Trudeau had no choice constitutionally but to call a general election within months, and Joe set to work immediately. During February and early March, Joe was on the road, travelling to nomination meetings, giving speeches to business and social clubs and raising the hundreds of thousands of dollars it would take to run an effective national campaign. He tried to be in question period as much as possible during the week and had weekly meetings with the organizers

7

FROM THE MOMENT THE ELECTION WAS CALLED we were on the road. It was our first national campaign with Joe as leader, and it was brutal. Joe had staffed for Robert Stanfield when he ran in the 1968 election and had some idea of the stress and strain that faced us. I had no idea at all what awaited me.

For six months, Lowell Murray had assembled and chaired a talented campaign team. We knew the issues we had to champion and had prepared a media campaign that focused on the changes a new government would bring. We could call upon the organizational skill of the "Big Blue Machine," a group of Ontario PC provincial party supporters who had brought modern election campaigning to Canada. Bill McAleer of Toronto was in charge of the "hands on" logistics, and travelled with Joe throughout the campaign. Art Lyon, a former law classmate of mine, was the wagon master, which involved making all the trains (and the plane and buses) run on time.

Before his death, my father had urged me to undertake a parallel campaign to Joe's, and I had decided I would. Joe had agreed and told the campaign organizers to see how this might be done. He suggested we start and end the campaign together and then have a specific strategy for my travel to meet several key objectives, including promoting women candidates; campaigning in

Quebec, where my fluency in French was a real asset; and appearing at high schools and universities to urge young people to vote. This strategy was not uniformly popular, as some of the election team had never seen me campaign and worried that I would fail. But Joe was the leader and if he wanted it done, then they would do it. Wendy Orr, Joe's scheduling assistant, was assigned to travel with me. Campaigning on my own would demand a great deal of energy and stamina, and Joe warned me about how hard it would be to be out there alone. He suggested we start slowly at first, adding to my schedule as we went along. As delicately as he could, he reminded me that my openness and candour were not always helpful. I agreed with him and managed with difficulty to discipline myself to the rigours of following the briefing notes.

Perhaps ignorance really is bliss, for had I known how demanding the travel commitments were to be during the next two months, I am not sure I could have made it. Most days I would attend between two and five coffee parties in homes and town halls, meet with the mayor and other dignitaries, speak at a high school or community college, have a half-hour standup sandwich lunch with women workers in a party supporter's restaurant downtown, visit businesses or a factory, do some media and speak at a service or women's club dinner. My message was clear—Joe and his team were young and dynamic and would provide the leadership needed for the new decade. At the end of each day, I would dictate "action required" notes for Wendy to transcribe and send back to headquarters. These notes usually related to travel needs, policy requirements, speech notes and details as mundane, but essential, as our candidate's name and those of the local organizers. There was neither e-mail nor laptop computers. Wendy used a word processor that looked like an old electric typewriter and weighed a ton. We were just impressed that she could correct mistakes automatically and save up to five hundred words at a time!

There were days in that campaign when I did not even have a chance to speak to my husband. If I needed research help quickly, I would call Bob Laing at our research office, with whom I had worked during previous summers. If there was a political question, I would talk to Bill McAleer or Lowell Murray. Jock Osler and Donald Doyle, the English and French press secretaries respectively, would give me media advice. It was terribly lonely for me during those early days of the campaign, but Wendy and I fell into a routine and enjoyed each other's company. As the leader's tour proceeded, Lowell was able to find the time necessary to focus more closely on my parallel tour. He saw its positive impact as local organizers fed their comments back to headquarters, and he did everything possible to make my tour a success. A staffer in each of the leader's office and PC headquarters was assigned to me, and after the second week of the campaign I appreciated the backup. By the end of the campaign, I even had my own campaign structure, with advance people in each province and women in each riding in charge of my tour.

As an assistant, Wendy had the one asset that makes a gruelling campaign tour possible—a keen sense of humour. At the time, Bobby Orr was a popular NHL hockey player, and at each hotel we would be shown our rooms and take bets on who would be assigned a suite. She usually won, and each night she would accept yet one more request from the bellman for an autographed copy of her "brother's" picture! She was his best promotions agent. Wendy knew about my fear of flying and always did her best to distract me. When all else failed she would tell jokes. I remember one day in Winnipeg when we were met by a very young man who carried our bags to the plane. "Looks like they're robbing the cradle for our advance team," Wendy quipped. It turned out he was the pilot. We crawled onto the little plane for our flight to northern Manitoba and about two hours into the flight noticed that our young friend seemed to be totally absorbed in his map. Wendy was crammed into the back of our four-seater plane and asked if she could help. He handed her the map. "What am I looking for?" she asked. "Lynne Lake," he said. "What's it near?" she asked as she turned the map around. "A lake," he replied, sending Wendy into gales of laughter. She said, "Didn't the Manitoba licence plate used to say 100,000 LAKES? Which lake, exactly, am I looking for?" "I don't know" was his only reply. In a panic, I began to search the horizon for a landing strip. "You've got to be kidding!" Wendy shouted. "Are you with some co-op pilots' program? Don't you have a licence to fly this thing? What do you mean, you don't know?!" Of course, the last thing to do to a young and insecure pilot is to challenge him while he is at the controls, so Wendy promptly switched to her mother-hen mode and talked him into action using her own version of "Twenty Questions." Finally, we managed to get a response on the radio and landed without incident. The main campaign heard an earful that night and sent an experienced pilot for the return trip to Winnipeg.

I have always needed a lot of sleep, and after a while, I became run down from the long days of campaigning, travel and tension. During the middle part of that campaign I broke down and cried in public one morning when I was speaking at a high school. I realize now that I had underestimated the impact of my father's death the year before. When he died in April 1978, the frenzy of pre-election campaign activity, combined with my busy life at the law firm, allowed me to pretend that I was fine. Sometimes when I rode our horses or walked with my sisters Pat or Jane near our family home, we would share our sense of loss. But generally, I kept my grief to myself and firmly under control. It worked—until that morning when I was asked by a teenage boy, yet again, why I "refused" to use my husband's name. I started by repeating the answer I had given hundreds of times before but, without warning, when I mentioned my father, I started to cry and could not stop. It was as if something inside me had snapped and I could not fix it. The story and TV footage of me in tears, confronted by this kid in a local high school, sent the campaign team into spasms. Was she having a breakdown? Was she strong enough to continue? What damage control was needed? Those who thought the parallel campaign idea too risky waded in, wanting me to return to the campaign plane immediately. Others merely shrugged. Joe called to ensure I was okay and my mother told me to get some sleep. It was a one-day media wonder but it was pivotal for me. It forced me to realize that it was normal to miss my father. I decided that I had to find others who could help me as he had done. I turned to my youngest sister, Jane, who had been living with us during the campaign, and she joined me for the following two weeks, beginning a practice of sisterly support that has seen her campaign with me in every election since 1979. Like me, Jane had been a bit of a family rebel, although she expressed her rebelliousness in a different way. She left home after high school and spent a year on the road in Mexico before working as a gas station attendant and a bus tour guide in B.C. and in Banff so she could spend her spare time skiing. When Dad was dying she came home, and later went to Algonquin College in Ottawa to study child care and social work. She graduated at the top of her class and worked with teens in trouble with the law and in vulnerable family situations. Over the years she would become my closest sister, even though she is six years younger than I am.

My outburst of tears during the 1979 campaign also forced me to finally address the "name issue" and what it meant to me personally. At twenty-seven, I was a young mother and articling student whose life could very easily become submerged in that of my famous husband. I could see how easy it would be to let that happen. Several party members had already demanded that I conform and keep my opinions on everything, from women's equality to child care, to myself. Backing down would have been so easy. It was such a seductive and simple option.

But in facing this question about my name, I realized how important it was to live the reality of the answer. I had to stand up for what I believed, weathering blistering criticism because I refused to drown my own ambitions and dreams in those of my husband's. I had to fight for women's equality because I believed it was essential in a modern Canada. I went to law school and continued my legal career because I wanted to have the tools to make a difference for all women. I kept my own name because it allowed me to affirm who I was. I could not accept that I was to start a marriage—a relationship of equals—by giving up my name and becoming someone else. Where was the fairness in that? As a prominent public figure I had to take a stand. On a personal level, I had to keep myself whole. I had to be equal and fight for my space and my place—both in my marriage and in my professional life. My name defined who I was, not just who I'd been. It didn't matter to my sisters, each of whom took her husband's name upon marriage. But for me, keeping my name was my way of ensuring that everyone, including me, knew who I was.

For the campaign, something also happened that day to my image. The people I met after that event were concerned about me. In the public's mind, I had shown human feelings and it put the lie to the critics' argument that I was a hard-nosed "women's libber" without a heart. My campaign was focused on women, and in the coming days they all seemed to be offering me extra support. It is a practice to give a speaker a gift, and women's groups started to give me personal things, like bubble bath for a hot relaxing bath after a long day of campaigning or a gift certificate to a spa on a day off. Such shows of support encouraged me to move ahead with the parallel campaign, to start to create my own public persona and to understand my own inner strength.

Throughout these two long months, I tried to speak to Catherine every day. Unfortunately, I found that this upset both of us, as she only wanted to know when I was coming home. It was during this campaign that I started the practice of leaving a little present for her to open each day I was away. It was never anything big—just something new and fun, with a note about how much I loved her and hoped she was being a good girl for her grandma. On the morning when the last present was opened, she knew that I would be home that night. This simple routine seemed to comfort her and gave shape to the promise that I would be home in "ten more sleeps." After all, what is "ten sleeps" to a two-year-old? Years later, I would continue a version of this, writing her notes and short poems on the paper napkins I stuffed into her lunch bag so she would know that I loved her. In this campaign, Catherine would meet us at the plane in Ottawa whenever we got a chance to return for a break, and near election day Mom and Jane flew west with her to spend the last weekend in Jasper and Edmonton with us. It was a huge boost to us to have her there, as her presence always reminded us of what is really important in life. Joe was in his first major national election race, and Catherine would buzz around the place, oblivious to everything but the attention she was getting on the campaign plane from staffers and journalists, whom she seemed to think were there just for her. Even at two, she just made herself at home and joined the group. There's a picture of us all standing beside the plane on the last day, and Catherine is there, front and centre, hugging the big stuffed green frog the French media crew had given her.

In that election Joe and I showed that by campaigning both together and apart we represented a new kind of political relationship. In 1979, Canadians were being asked to choose a new generation over the old. As a couple, we embodied that new generation in both our youth and outlook. The Liberals had been in power most of the post–WWII period. History had shown

---

8

AFTER TWO MONTHS OF NON-STOP CAMPAIGNING back and forth across Canada, election night, May 22, 1979, was chaotic. While the mood of the campaign had been positive, especially during its last frantic days, we knew that the vote would be tight. A minority government would be the worst of all scenarios for Joe. His platform was a reforming and activist one that really required a majority government to carry it out. On the last weekend, we left Nova Scotia for Edmonton, leaving the campaign plane there and boarding two smaller ones bound for Hinton, fifty miles from Jasper. Mom was waiting for us in Edmonton with Catherine, as were my sister Jane and my brother, John. We spent the night at the Jasper Park Lodge, where Roy Everest and Bob Dowling had organized a big Western barbecue for the press and all the campaign staff. It was an idyllic setting and seemed far away from the pressure of those last days of the campaign. On the morning of election day, we made our way by bus to Edmonton, stopping en route in the town of Edson to vote. We whistle-stopped at polls in several small towns and villages in the riding as we travelled along the Yellowhead Highway towards Edmonton and arrived at our hotel around the time the first polls were closing in Newfoundland.

There the Liberals took four seats to our two. The Maritime results were next, and the PCs shut out the Liberals in P.E.I., won four to the Liberals' six in New Brunswick, and eight to their two in Nova Scotia. Quebec was a wash, with only two seats for the party, and after all our work there we were truly disappointed. Ontario, though, was strong for Joe and he won fifty-seven seats to the Liberals thirty-two; six went to the NDP. We knew that Ontario was key to Joe's victory, but with Quebec a wasteland for us, we needed more riding victories in the West. Several ridings in Ontario were lost by a handful of votes, which made the evening even more frustrating. As we crossed our fingers and moved west, it did not seem possible that Joe would form a majority government. Still, he won big across the Prairies, in B.C., the Northwest Territories and Yukon, while the Liberals won only three seats. The NDP, though, showed more strength than we had predicted and won eighteen seats in the region.

I was not as discouraged as others were that night about the minority government status. I believed that Joe's platform commitment to ensure a greater role and more equal treatment for the Western provinces in Canada's future would mean the New Democratic MPs from there would support him. Furthermore, the NDP had supported Pierre Trudeau's minority government for the two years from 1972 to 1974 and had insisted at the time that a minority government was good for Canada. I assumed they would work with the new government, as key promises, like mortgage interest deductibility, a balanced budget and freedom of information legislation, would appeal to them.

At about nine o'clock on election night, after a buffet dinner with family, a few close friends and key staffers, we went to Spruce Grove, a town west of Edmonton in Joe's riding, where all our campaign workers were gathered in the local arena. It was one of the rare times in Canadian history that people in Ontario and Quebec had to wait up to hear their Prime

Minister–designate deliver his victory speech. I can remember arriving in the car of one of our local organizers and being ushered into the arena, hugging friends and supporters all along the way. It was their victory as much as ours and we were all ecstatic at the results. Joe spoke and thanked his workers across Canada and those Canadians who had entrusted him with the honour of being Prime Minister. We stayed an hour or so after Joe's speech and then prepared to return to our hotel.

There was a scuffle at the door and I saw one of our workers in an argument with two strangers. He was supposed to drive us back, so we made our way towards him. "Follow me, sir," one of the strangers said. "This way. We're with the RCMP." Within a minute we were whisked into a limousine and the doors were locked. We couldn't even lower the windows to speak to our friends outside, and all of us looked confused as we waved to each other through the thick glass. The RCMP had arrived and assumed security for the country's new political leader. Our friends and family were left behind to fend for themselves, and we were driven back into the city. A new and very public chapter of our life had begun.

The next morning we all returned to Jasper. Joe had decided to have a real base in Western Canada, and he had chosen this Rocky Mountain town. Jasper was in Joe's Yellowhead riding and was a natural choice for the Western equivalent of 24 Sussex Drive. He called together his transition team, headed by former MP Jim Balfour from Regina and lawyer David Jenkins from Edmonton, and spent the next three days listening to their proposals and being briefed by the clerk of the Privy Council and other senior government officials. He decided that he wanted to be sworn in as Prime Minister on June 4, the day before his fortieth birthday. The transition to power was in motion and so much needed to be done in the ten days ahead.

Of course, it was not all work. Joe's staffers took on the press contingent at baseball and won. It was then that I discovered, as

the team's worst ball player, that there were real benefits to
being followed by the RCMP! We had barbecues and picnics
and Joe took Catherine to play on the swings every afternoon
after her nap. An old back injury was bothering me, and so
I rested when I could, while Mom and Jane took care of
Catherine in their cabin. It was a wonderful few days, when
everything seemed possible and the future looked promising and
bright. Joe had achieved his dream and now could turn his
attention to leading the country along a new path. He was
bursting with ideas and had the cabinet team to back him up.
I was proud of him and convinced he would succeed. We spoke
briefly about what lay ahead, but the truth was, neither of us
had any idea.

At the end of the week we flew back to Ottawa and
returned to Stornoway. I took an extra week off from articling
and began to prepare for our move to 24 Sussex Drive. Pierre
Trudeau had asked if he could stay at Harrington Lake until his
children finished school at the end of June, and Joe had agreed.
I asked Cecilia Humphreys to assess the changes needed at 24
Sussex and to report back as soon as she could. In the meantime, we would stay at Stornoway and move up to Harrington
Lake for the summer at the end of June. Wendy Orr was assigned
as my special assistant and liaison to Joe's staff, and the two of
us worked with the protocol staff to put together lists of people
who were to be invited to the swearing-in ceremonies at Rideau
Hall the following week. I decided to organize a fortieth birthday party for Joe on June 5 so that friends and family could
come over to Stornoway for champagne and birthday cake.

June 4, 1979, was a superb day filled with sun and friends
and family. Joe took his oath of allegiance holding the Clark
family Bible, and his parents and I sat proudly in the front row.
I knew my father would have relished this moment and I missed
him, but my mother and siblings were there, brimming with
pride. It was a historic moment for our family. But it was for the

West, too, because Joe was the first born Westerner to serve as Prime Minister.

There was so much for Joe to do that June. Within two weeks of being sworn in, he left for the G7 economic summit in Tokyo. When he returned we celebrated six years of marriage by going to dinner at La Ferme Columbia on June 30, one of our favourite restaurants. At the end of the month, we moved up to Harrington Lake, located in the Gatineau Hills about a half-hour drive north of Ottawa.

During the potato famine in Ireland in the 1850s, land in what is now the Gatineau Hills had been given to Irish immigrants fleeing starvation. Unable to do anything but eke the barest of livings from the rocky soil, most left as soon as they could to seek their fortunes elsewhere in Canada or the United States. After the farmers left, Harrington Lake became first a summer home for wealthy industrialists and later the official country residence of the Prime Minister. Isolated from the general public by a gate and the RCMP, and surrounded by hills on all sides, it became my refuge. Built in the early twentieth century in the cottage style of many of the large summer homes of the day, it had a boathouse and a little beach where Catherine and I would sit when by ourselves. Our Great Dane, Taffy, would stretch out on the sand beside Catherine and never let her out of her sight—a habit that nearly resulted in my drowning when she tried to "rescue" Catherine one day while I was swimming with her.

Over that summer, Harrington Lake offered me the sanctuary I needed to put recent events into perspective. I was raised in the country, and I revelled in the natural beauty that surrounded me at the lake. Each morning I would watch a mother loon lead her little ones in a single file along the beach and into the water. She would make them follow a rigid drill, and I would watch with amusement as one of them refused to cooperate. The little bird was either terribly uncoordinated or a loon's version of a free spirit. Every day the mother would bat it with her wing, ensuring it conformed for a few minutes before it strayed off on its own once again. I would lie in bed at night and listen to the sounds of the forest and of the lake and feel safe and isolated from the chaos and craziness that marked my life back in the city.

—

It was during the summer of 1979 that I met the Queen Mother for the first time. Joe was away, and it was arranged that I would represent him in Halifax. This included attending a lunch hosted by the Lieutenant-Governor of Nova Scotia and a dinner in the evening, hosted by the federal government. A few Tory supporters and MPs were hastily added to the guest list, as the invitations had been sent weeks before the Liberal defeat, and there was really no way to un-invite their party faithful without a fuss. The wind was howling as we stood out-doors at a military ceremony at the Citadel that morning with the Queen Mother. While all the other women held or chased their hats around the site, she stood serenely, making it clear that this was but a small wind of no consequence to her. Standing there with my beret crammed down around my ears, I loved her instantly.

At lunch, I was not just the only Tory, I was also the youngest person at the table by about a quarter of a century. All the Liberal women at my table called me Mrs. Clark and seemed a little disappointed that I did not contradict them. One asked the Queen Mother how she managed to keep her hat on in the gale-force winds. She replied by retrieving from her hat the longest and deadliest hatpin I had ever seen. For a moment I hoped she planned to use it on the questioner who had been particularly snooty towards me. Instead, she regaled us with the story of her hatpin: how it had been her constant companion ever since it was given to her as a gift as a teenager, how it was a perfect weapon if ever needed (an impish smile from her at this comment) and how, anchored in both her hat and her hair underneath, it was a hatpin that had never once let her down.

After lunch, as I walked her to her waiting limousine, she stopped on the steps, touched my arm and thanked me for accompanying her. As if sensing my hurt at the way I had been treated by the other women, she said, "I always tell my grand-children that they must be themselves and do what they believe best in life. Don't be bothered by criticism." As the limousine door was opened for her, she turned and looked at me and said quietly, "Good luck . . . Ms. McTeer." She then offered every-one her trademark royal wave and smile, head tilted slightly. She would never know what strength her few words gave me that day.

—

It would be wrong to suggest that I came to the position of Prime Minister's wife with a personal agenda. That would have required more understanding of the potential of the role than I had at the time. I did know, though, that I wanted to make the home of the Prime Minister an elegant and accessible place for all Canadians, and set about doing just that. Joe had given our architect, Cecilia Humphreys, a ridiculously low budget of thir-teen thousand dollars to carry out whatever changes we made. When I protested, he insisted that since he had been elected on a platform of economic restraint, both of us had to set an example. In the end, 24 Sussex and Harrington Lake were redone at minimal cost to the public purse, and I remain proud of the inspired scrounging Cecilia and I did to showcase Canadian art and artifacts while creating a livable family home. Part of my goal of accessibility was to open 24 Sussex Drive to public tours the following summer during July and August, something that had never been done before, but that I felt would make Canadians feel a part of their Prime Minister's life.

As I had done at Stornoway, I insisted that we serve Canadian foods at official functions. I felt it essential that we stop serving modified versions of French cuisine and begin to highlight Canadian products and methods of preparation. I also wanted to use only Canadian wines and decided that the best way to do this was to have a special cuvée made for 24 Sussex Drive. In 1979, the Canadian wine industry was in its adolescence and thus we had two difficult tasks. We had to find a quality red and white wine to use for this special cuvée, and then we had to convince people to drink Canadian wine. For the first task, I turned to Peter Ward, a respected wine critic in Ottawa. Peter introduced me to Donald Ziraldo, then president of Inniskillin Wines in the Niagara peninsula, who came to Ottawa to offer me his advice. We ignored the chef's disdain and moved ahead to order the special cuvée for the next year. I planned to have an artist design a label and to launch the cuvée with a special party the following fall. History, though, had other plans.

The summer of 1979 was a busy one for me. I moved homes, finished my articling commitment and travelled with Joe to Cameroon, Tanzania, Kenya and the Commonwealth Conference in Zambia. In Cameroon, I visited the children's polio clinic with its founder, the Canadian Cardinal Paul-Émile Léger. He had given up his position of comfort and influence in the Roman Catholic Church's hierarchy to serve the poor and sick in this African country, and after a day with him, I was deeply moved by his example of humility and moral leadership. He showed me a true vocation of sacrifice for others' well-being. It was Cardinal Léger who encouraged me to see the world beyond the confines of my previously insular life. In August I decided to tackle the Ontario bar admission course that fall and winter so I could start practising law the following summer. At that time the bar ads, as they are affectionately called, consisted of a gruelling six-month marathon of fourteen courses and exams. The course is strenuous at the best of times, but with all the additional responsibilities I had that year, I knew that it would be particularly demanding.

I also discovered over the summer that the household staff were spoiling Catherine terribly. Whatever she wanted, she could have—from cookies to candy. If she did not get her way, she would scream. I raised this problem with Laura Lefebvre, who had been on staff for some time and had grown children of her own, and she agreed that it had to stop. Still, Catherine managed to get her way; some staff just ignored my request, including Pearl Gordon, who had come from Jamaica to live with us when Catherine was a baby, and for whom Catherine could do no wrong. One day after my bar admission class I came upon the two of them in the den. Pearl was rubbing Catherine's back as Catherine teethed on her hand. I was shocked to see teeth marks on Pearl's hand and told her never to let Catherine do that again. "Her gums are sore and her little teeth hurt her," was Pearl's reply. I enlisted Joe and he took Pearl aside and told her she had to stop. "Lincoln Alexander is in my cabinet," he told her. "How would we all feel if he extended his hand to Catherine and she bit it? That is the lesson you are giving her. It is all right to bite people. Help us teach her respect for all people. Do not ever let her bite you again." Pearl agreed but after this and other incidents of indulgence, I decided that Catherine needed to attend daycare. As expected, everyone had an opinion on the upbringing of the Prime Minister's child, and I was roundly criticized again for falling down on my maternal obligations by "abandoning her to strangers" in a daycare centre.

That September, I arrived at the centre with Catherine in tow, just one of the many mothers there with their children. The supervisor assured me that Catherine would be fine, but I lingered out of sight for a few minutes. Catherine sat down with the other three-year-olds, started to play with a toy and seemed content. But could she really manage without me? This is the classic maternal question. We raise our children to interact with the world and then part of us is profoundly upset when they do so beautifully without us. But this was the first time Catherine had been cared for by strangers outside our home, and I was worried. Just then, one of the little boys in the circle bent over and took the toy she was playing with from her hand. The look on her face was one of stunned surprise. "Give me my toy!" she said. He ignored her. She added the magic word "please." No response. Then, pow! She banged him on the arm and took her toy back. "I said, give me my toy!" she told him in her best little don't-mess-with-me voice. He was an only child too, and the look of surprise on his face was as funny as the one Catherine had displayed a moment before. Yes, I thought as I went out the door. She'll cope.

I could see after the first week at the bar admission course that once again I had been unrealistic about my ability to find the time I needed to study, just as I had in law school a few years earlier. As has so often been the case over the years, my professional life had to take second place to public responsibilities and domestic realities. From first ministers' conferences through to official travel, the fall of 1979 required more hours than existed in a day. It became a massive organizational task. Pierre Trudeau had had a public servant, Heidi Bennett, as a household manager who performed the various household and protocol tasks traditionally expected of a Prime Minister's wife, and I left the arrangement in place for the summer while I assessed my household needs. In September, I foolishly opted to take charge of everything myself, and Heidi was promoted to the protocol office. Household staff are the people closest to you each day, and I hired three women whom I knew and trusted to take care of our personal household matters. Laura Lefebvre, who had owned her own restaurant, was appointed cook, Cory Henry oversaw the other staff and Pearl Gordon looked after Catherine and spelled everyone on the weekends. Cleaning staff came in each day, and the chef, who had been there when we arrived, cooked when we entertained.

This set-up was not perfect, and I knew that changes were required, but in the meantime, it would have to do. As backup when I was at class during the day, I began to rely on Marilyn Neville. She was a friend and an experienced hostess whose husband, Bill, was Joe's chief of staff. Her help was invaluable. One day that fall, the Premiers were in town for a meeting with Joe, who was trying to bring them all onside for major economic and energy reforms. It was a tense meeting and they were scheduled to join him for lunch at 24 Sussex. Marilyn was overseeing the event, and as I returned from classes that day I found her speaking excitedly to one of Joe's staffers. "They want to continue their meetings here this afternoon," she told me, "and each Premier needs a separate room for his staff to work from, and a phone line." We set to work resolving that crisis, only to have another of Joe's staffers tell us nonchalantly that the Premiers and their staff would be staying for drinks later—and maybe even for dinner. Marilyn knew I had an exam the next day, so while I found a corner that was free and went there to study, she cancelled her own plans for the evening to create a menu. I am sure not a single Premier realized the amount of work that had gone into their afternoon at the official residence.

Each day I was reminded how complicated my life had become. That fall my professional and private life seemed always at loggerheads, and I felt as though we were on a merry-go-round that sped up every time it should have been slowing down. I am an organized person, yet each time I thought I had my day ordered something unexpected happened, requiring me to change my plans. I never saw Joe alone except late at night when he came home exhausted. I followed the press analysis of his government closely and understood that as an activist government with many legislative proposals in the works, it was a huge task to effectively communicate the government's message to the public. My concerns that fall were trivial compared with the immense pressure Joe endured as he directed the affairs of state. Still, I missed his guidance and his company and longed for the days when there had been time to be together and to share our professional as well as personal lives away from staff and state duties.

The fall of 1979 was one of unending, crushing pressure for Joe. At their best, Prime Ministers are both a reflection of who we are and a guide of what we might become. As our highest elected official, the Prime Minister presents our common face, embodying our values, our aspirations and dreams. A prime minster should be dynamic and bold, as well as solid and sound. She or he should be generous of spirit, experienced and wise, with a national vision and an understanding of how to bring a country together, and should know when to refuse the complaints of one and repair damage done to others. In 1979, Canadians had been asked to choose not just a new national leader, but a different vision of Canada. In doing so, they elected the youngest Prime Minister in their history, the first native-born Albertan, a respected parliamentarian and a man committed to building on Canada's economic, cultural and energy strengths for the future. His very presence—young, determined, a modern Westerner—reinforced his image as a man who would challenge the status quo. He was committed to a greater voice for the provinces in federalism, legal equality for Canadian women and greater autonomy and control for First Nations people. He looked for consensus—on issues as diverse as Quebec and energy policy—so governments could move ahead and beyond old constitutional wrangles and gridlock.

Joe had been elected on this platform of change and spent most of the summer working with his cabinet and senior government officials preparing the Speech from the Throne and the budget; he knew these would set his stamp on government policy. It was an ambitious agenda, even for a majority government.

Since Joe led a minority government, he had to worry about finding support among the six Créditiste members from Quebec and among the NDP caucus to ensure his agenda was accepted. His government held 136 seats to the combined opposition parties' 146. Each vote was potentially one of confidence in his young government.

Chief among his immediate tasks was keeping the promises he had made in the recent election. Over the summer he decided that he would govern as if he had a majority. His policies were needed and sound. He trusted that the opposition would not dare defeat such strong and important initiatives. Mortgage interest deductibility was one such measure. It meant something to Canadians. It was money in their pockets at tax time, but it was also symbolic and showed that Joe supported Canadians in their daily lives. A major theme of his government was embodied by this one policy. But there were so many others that he would have to introduce immediately to counter the economic crisis Canada was in and to build for the future. At the time, Canada's oil supply was insecure and expensive, as the federal government subsidized the cost of imported oil. Joe proposed a national energy policy that would build the Canadian industry, mainly in Western Canada, and provide a reliable and bountiful source of fossil fuels for the whole country. He also proposed funding research into alternative and less polluting energy sources, like solar and wind power, to ensure sustainability of power sources in the long term. As an MP, Joe had seen how outdated the institution and processes of Parliament had become and had proposed a comprehensive reform package. The final touches were being put on a Freedom of Information Bill so Canadians would be able to get answers from their government on issues of importance. He believed that the opposition parties would put the country first, and that the NDP in particular would continue the policy they had started in 1972, when they supported Pierre Trudeau to make minority governments work.

I had heard him make all these major commitments in speeches over the summer and fall, and knew he was under tremendous pressure to deliver on his promises. Expectations were high and the risks were monumental. As I prepared for my tax law exam in early December, Joe worked day and night on his first budget. Its purposes were clear—to tackle the huge public deficit (which cost over eight billion dollars a year in interest alone); to bring restraint to government spending; to encourage the private sector to create new jobs; and to create a national energy policy that would encourage production and develop alternative, environmentally friendly and sustainable energy sources. To do this, the cabinet had made the decision to increase taxes on gasoline by eighteen cents a gallon beginning July 1, 1980. He knew that this would be controversial, but believed that Canadians saw, as he did, the need for discipline and restraint. He argued in his speeches, both in the House and in the country, that all of our cherished social programs, from health care to public pensions, were being put at risk by the mounting public debt.

The week Joe was to bring down his first budget in early December 1979, did not start well. The U.S. President, Jimmy Carter, was expected in Ottawa for meetings with Joe but had to cancel at the last minute due to illness. This was at the height of the American hostage crisis in Iran and he was under intense pressure. Unbeknownst to most Canadians, Canada was playing a major role in helping six Americans escape from Iran. They had fled undetected to the Canadian embassy when their colleagues had been taken hostage, and Ambassador Ken Taylor in Iran had devised an escape plan that required the hostages to have Canadian passports. Their escape would put all of their lives at risk, and yet it was a gamble they were all willing to take. During these crucial days of budget preparation, Joe spent many hours holed up with Flora MacDonald, Canada's foreign minister, going over the details of the proposed escape from

Iran. As I studied for my exam that week, Flora would appear at any hour of the night and the two of them would go to his den to talk. I did not know what they were discussing, but I did know that it was important.

On the morning of December 13, Joe flew to Burlington, Ontario, where he outlined his national energy policy to the Burlington chamber of commerce. Ontario is Canada's industrial heartland, and it was important to convince sceptics in the provincial government and among Ontario members of his own caucus that the increased cost of energy was not going to burden Ontario taxpayers and businesses while giving Alberta windfall profits. It was a hard sell, but as he always did, Joe went to the centre of the controversy and defended his policies. While he was speaking I handed in my exam and went home to catch a nap with Catherine. It was my last exam until January, and I looked forward to a rest and a big family gathering at Harrington Lake over Christmas. Joe returned to Ottawa from southwestern Ontario and went straight to his office in the Centre Block. That night there would be a confidence vote on an NDP motion on the budget. The government's future was at stake.

Around suppertime, rumours began to spread to his office that the government was in for a surprise. The rumours were not taken seriously by the staff. It seemed impossible that without a leader (Pierre Trudeau had just stepped down and announced his retirement) the Liberals would vote with the NDP. Yet press rumours persisted that during their Christmas party the night before, Liberal MPs and senators had decided to try to defeat the government. Most people had thought that their enthusiasm would wane as the effect of the party wore off, but that had not happened. Worse, some of our MPs were away on public business, and it became clear that the government did not have the numbers to defeat the motion. Back at the residence, I fed and bathed Catherine and put her to bed. I toyed with the idea of going to Parliament to watch the vote, but

decided that it was better to stay with Catherine, whose aller-
gies that night were making it hard for her to breathe. I read for
a while and around nine o'clock went for a swim and a sauna.
When I returned my mother called. "What does it mean that the
government was defeated on an NDP motion?" she asked. "I'll
call you back," I said and slammed down the phone. I finally
got through to Joe's secretary, Adèle Desjardins, who confirmed
the news and hung up. She was typing Joe's statement to the
House and had no time to talk. I was sick and confused. I
watched him on the news and, when he came home later that
night, he sounded both defeated and defiant. He would see the
Governor General the next morning and there would be another
election. He had already asked the party's national director to
prepare for a campaign. We would start immediately and plead
our case directly to the Canadian people. They would see what
scoundrels the opposition parties were in defeating this activist
government rather than continuing to make it work. He stayed
up most of the night preparing his first speech of the 1980
campaign.

—

Pundits have offered their views on the defeat of Joe's government on a budget vote. I have often thought about what went
wrong and understand that there was a combination of factors.
One of the dilemmas facing parties that are out of office more
than they are in is that they must come to office ready to imple-
ment their platform immediately. The first few weeks are crucial,
and for Joe and his minority government there had been no
honeymoon. He had come to power on the promise of fiscal,
energy and social reform and a specific campaign commitment
to introduce mortgage tax deductibility for all Canadians who
owned a home. To do that, he had to ensure he could count on
the smaller opposition parties. In a minority situation, every
vote is critical, and a budget vote is a matter of political life and

death. Someone should have been on top of the numbers and they were not. Also, proceeding as if his government had a majority gave a signal that he was a confident leader, but it required a level of political depth and parliamentary control that had yet to develop among most of Joe's caucus and political advisers. It wasn't just a matter of counting votes, but of cajoling support. The rump group of six Créditistes wanted something in return for their votes in support of the government, even if it was only access to government funding for their constituencies' needs. They were ignored, yet their votes could have kept the young minority government in power. More careful attention to the dynamic of parliamentary politics could have made all the difference.

But from my point of view, the biggest disappointment was the NDP, who had kept Pierre Trudeau in power from 1972 to 1974. I could not believe that they would defeat a budget that contained mortgage interest deductibility, because it would have helped so many Canadians, and I thought that at least their Western members would support the new government's energy policy. But they did not. In the end, Joe's government was defeated by an NDP motion of non-confidence.

The government's defeat on December 13, 1979, changed my life once again, and I faced another huge challenge—this one caused by rules in my own profession. That fall, I had successfully completed eight of the fourteen courses required for the bar admission course and had six left to go in January and February. I knew from my experience the year before that the election, set for February 18, would demand all of my time, so I called the head of the Ontario bar in Toronto to ask permission to complete the last six courses the following year. To my astonishment he refused and advised that if I stopped at that point I would forfeit the entire course, including the eight exams I had already passed. I was angry and hurt by his inflexibility, reminiscent as it was of the trials I had endured in law school. What kind of a profession did I belong to, I wondered. Did campaigning for a husband who was Prime Minister not seem serious enough for the legal profession? Or did they just assume the party he led would not be there for long?

Joe was as angry as I was and suggested I call lawyers I knew to explore the options. They inquired and it appeared that there was no appeal process open to me. They worried that a fight with the Law Society would reflect badly on Joe. When I raised it with him, he scoffed and told me to fight. But my friends' concerns were well taken. We were vulnerable and had just been defeated. We needed to focus on the election. I decided that I would not challenge the decision but try to write the exams without going to the classes. There was no other option, unless I wanted to start again from scratch the next year. In 1979, the bar admission course was offered in Ottawa, London and Toronto. One day in January, when I was campaigning in Toronto, I took two hours and attended a class there and met Bob Rae who, while a sitting member of Parliament, was also doing his bar ads that year. He complained about how hard it was to campaign for re-election in his Toronto riding each day and study for exams at the same time. "Well, whose fault is it that we are in an election campaign anyway?" I retorted. "Try travelling back and forth across Canada each week," I went on. "At least you get to sleep at home in your own bed each night!"

I had no idea how I would pass the exams without class notes. Then one day in early January, a group of my classmates organized a study group for me. Their goal was to ensure that I knew enough from each required course to pass the remaining six exams. I was delighted by their generosity, and during the next two months I spent every available moment using their notes to cram for my remaining exams. When I stopped in Ottawa, they would come over and brief me about the courses; but as election day neared, I was in Ottawa less and less and relied exclusively on their notes. I owe these women my licence to practise law; and their support became symbolic of all the female friendships I have had over the years—friendships that have helped me survive and thrive.

As the election drew to a close, the polling news was bad. We were having real trouble in Ontario, where the gas tax was being rejected, and Quebec remained an impenetrable Liberal fortress. In the days after bringing down the government in Parliament, Pierre Trudeau had reversed his decision and was Liberal leader again. In this campaign, he used the same tactics against Joe that he had used in 1974 against Robert Stanfield. Instead of "Zap, you're frozen," as he said about Stanfield's wage and price controls proposal, he would wave his hands and say "Remember eighteen cents a gallon." The Liberals attacked Joe's government, saying his energy policy gave millions to Alberta at the expense of Ontario. They ridiculed his gas tax and insisted he had broken his promise on mortgage interest deductibility. The fact that the Liberals had defeated this measure by bringing down the government seemed to go unnoticed.

I clearly remember the last week of the 1980 election. We had campaigned in the Prairies and B.C. and then flown back to Toronto on the last Wednesday night for a blitz in Metro Toronto. I was beside myself with fatigue and worry about the election and about the remaining two exams I had to write that Friday in Ottawa. In the frenzy of the last three weeks of the campaign I had not touched any of the notes my classmates sent me faithfully by fax each night. When we arrived at our room at the Royal York around eleven that night, I started to cry. I could not imagine failing now, at the very end of the course. Joe told me to take a bath and rest for a while and he left the suite. When he came back he confessed that he had called Helen Pierre, my Ottawa classmate in charge of sending me notes each day, and that she had offered to arrive the next morning at eight to help. Once again, despite all his own worries, he had come to my rescue. As I went to sleep, he closed the door to the dining area and started to work on his speech to the Empire Club the next day at noon. Helen flew to Toronto on the six o'clock flight the next morning and tutored me all day. She was a natural teacher, and it is no exaggeration to say that I would not have passed without her help. That morning, as we started, I broke down again in tears of exhaustion and despair. "I can't do this," I told her, "I really can't." She looked at me sternly and in her Scottish brogue said, "Maureen, there are two kinds of people in the world—those who cope and those who do not. You can cope." And so I did. We spent the morning on one course, estate planning and the afternoon on the other, administration of estates. Helen gave an entirely new meaning to the verb "to cram"! At six o'clock, one of the staff drove her to the airport and I started to prepare for the huge rally in Etobicoke that would mark our last big event of the campaign in Ontario. Thousands of supporters were expected. For the first time in days, I felt that I knew enough to pass, and I was almost happy as I left the hotel with Joe that evening. Yet an incident after the rally later that night almost prevented me from writing the exams at all.

Political campaigning is not only exhausting, but it can also be dangerous. Over the years, my right hand has been sprained and broken on two separate occasions—once by a drunk and once by a bully. I also suffered a sprained ankle and a mild concussion when I was caught in a crush of reporters and cameramen. That night in Etobicoke, thousands of people were at the rally, and the Premier, Bill Davis, thanked Joe and wished us luck as we left the hall. As we headed for the campaign bus, I was blinded by television lights. A male voice in the crowd called my name and I extended my hand. All at once, I was pulled forward and felt a searing pain in my upper right arm as the man pulled and twisted the flesh above my elbow. I screamed in pain and an RCMP officer broke the stranger's hold on me while another tackled him to the ground. But by then the damage was done. The ligaments under my arm had been torn and the pain was unbearable. Within minutes my arm was black and blue. I cried in pain a good part of that night but my hurt and anger were not just because of the injury. I cried because another Canadian, whom I did not even know, would hate me enough to hurt me in this way. What kind of a man would be so cruel? Of course, having researched issues of violence against women, I know that such violent and sick men exist. But that night, as I refused painkillers for fear that I would not be sharp enough to write my exams the next day, I was depressed and frightened. This is the purpose of such violence—to make women afraid and to ensure we know our place. Brutality against women by men is about control and hate. Bashing women with bare hands is a special tool of terror. The message this man was sending me was clear and terrifying—There's more where that came from, and not even the police around you can protect you. He was arrested and charged, but I remained afraid. That night, it took a supreme act of will and Joe's continuous reassurance to allow me to focus my mind on two immediate goals—passing my exams the next day and finishing the election campaign that weekend.

The next day, I wrote for five hours with a throbbing and painful right arm. I remember only feeling a kind of numbness the whole day, as if my mind were in one place and my body in another. At the end of the exams, I went back to the residence to shower and change for three campaign events in Ottawa later that night. Catherine was in the care of a very pregnant friend, Katie Chapman, whose husband was on the campaign plane with Joe while she stayed at 24 Sussex. She was due to give birth any time, but both she and Catherine were in good cheer. I ate something and went to the campaign events trying not to wince every time a well-meaning supporter grabbed my right arm. At the end of the evening, I invited my campaign team—Russ Wunker, Peter Holland, Wendy Orr and my sister Jane—for a nightcap at the residence. Around midnight I went to bed, and set my alarm for seven so I could prepare for the drive to meet Joe in Montreal early that morning. At dawn, Katie woke me from a deep sleep to tell me her water had broken. There was no one else to drive her to the hospital, so I took her there myself. Meanwhile, she had called her husband at his hotel in Montreal. The poor guy had not yet gone to bed, so he just grabbed his bag and drove to Ottawa. I left her at the hospital and went home, where I called my mother to ask her to come and care for Catherine, and then I left for Montreal.

When I arrived in Joe's hotel room in downtown Montreal, he looked glum. The latest polls showed us losing Ontario and making few inroads in Quebec. He put his arm around me and said quietly, "We're going to lose this one." He knew what a shock this was for me and did his best to look as though there was still something we could do about it. Nothing seemed to make sense to me at that moment. I was running on empty emotionally and physically, and the news was devastating. Joe had two options for the last two days of the campaign: he could slow down or go into overdrive. He told his campaign manager that he wanted to campaign full-out to shore up his candidates and prevent further erosion in popular support. We left Quebec that night, made another stop in Toronto for the Metro and area ridings and, before the polls opened on Monday morning, had stopped in a dozen ridings across the country. We slept in Edmonton that Sunday night, and many of our friends who had celebrated with us less than a year before flew out to be with us again. Unlike the mood in 1979, there was little celebration as we awaited the results. It reminded me of a death watch—not an entirely inappropriate analogy.

The election results, when they came in that Monday night, confirmed the polls. We lost seats in most provinces. Only Alberta, Newfoundland, the Northwest Territories and Yukon remained unchanged. But the real damage was in Ontario, where we fell from 57 to 38 seats and the Liberals picked up 20 new seats. We were reduced to one seat in Quebec and the Créditistes were eliminated. The Liberals now held all but one Quebec riding and ended the night with 147 seats to our 103. The NDP were up 6 seats to 32 from their total of 26 a few months before. Their game had paid off.

This was Joe's first major political defeat. It is hard to explain to people without political experience just how high or low one can feel after an election. Winning erases all fatigue, while losing unleashes a wave of exhaustion and depression that is hard to master. That is how Joe and I felt on election night. That is how our entire team felt too, and Joe and I tried our best to console them as our campaign plane flew us all back to Ottawa one last time. During that week in Ottawa we had a reception at the residence to thank the campaign team, and I celebrated my twenty-eighth birthday. Joe took me to a movie that night, and as we returned to the house a group of friends greeted us. Somehow, in spite of all that was going on around him, Joe had thought of a surprise birthday party for me.

9

AFTER THE DEFEAT IN 1980, we went to Maui for a month to recoup and regroup. No one cares about you much when you lose an election, and with a majority government, Pierre Trudeau would have the luxury of four more years as Prime Minister. Once again, we had to move homes—from 24 Sussex Drive back to Stornoway. We left the bulk of the work to my family and the movers. During our time away, Cecilia would assess the changes in Stornoway, and, when we returned, would bring us a proposal for action. I trusted her judgment completely on such matters.

As we prepared to leave, we lived in a surreal world. On the one hand, we had lost the election. On the other, Joe was basking in recognition from the U.S., which was grateful that his government had helped free Americans from Iran. As was their due, Ken Taylor and his wife, Pat, earned the lion's share of the publicity and praise for this daring plan of escape, but Joe, as the Prime Minister who made the decision, was also recognized in the United States. As his harried staff tried to empty the office of all official papers, thousands of letters of thanks and hundreds of civic commendations poured in. Throughout the summer of 1980, he would be honoured at several American events. But when we left for Hawaii, we just wanted to be away, to

her and sit in the sun, reading and talking, as sisters can do with little effort. While I love the ocean, I am rather afraid of it and so I have always kept close watch on Catherine when we are near water. One morning, in the blink of an eye, Catherine disappeared. Even now I cannot think of this moment without feeling ill. She had somehow wandered out into the waves, and the incoming tide was rolling over her and pulling her out to sea. I screamed and we rushed out into the water. After a few more waves had knocked Catherine down, Jane reached her and managed to grab her and hold on. With her body between us, we made our shocked way back to shore. Catherine was sick and water poured out of her little mouth. I was shaking and crying, and passing my fear and panic to her. Jane simply ordered me to go back to the condo, telling me I was scaring Catherine even more. She then picked my daughter up and carried her along the beach, walking slowly, talking to her and reassuring her she was fine. Catherine was wheezing, whimpering and clinging to Jane with all the strength of a terrified toddler. She wanted to go back to the condo but Jane just kept walking. Then calmly and slowly, she turned towards the sea and started to wade into the shallow water, where the waves lapped against her knees and then her waist. At a distance, I could see Catherine screaming her protest while Jane turned deliberately, still talking soothingly to her, and carried her back to the beach and into the condo. She did the same thing each day for a week before Catherine would let herself be dipped in the waves again.

Some may think that this was an unusual way to handle such a situation. But Jane comes from my father's school of tackling fears. When we were young and would fall off our ponies, he would ensure there were no broken bones or concussions and then make us climb back into the saddle. He did not want us to fear things. Jane was doing the same with Catherine. She wanted her to have a healthy respect for the sea, but she did not want her to grow up to fear it. By the time the two of them returned to the condo that day, I had composed myself somewhat and went into the bedroom with Catherine to lie down. Joe had been away when this all happened and now came into the room with us and rubbed her back. The rest of the trip, she did not make a single move without me beside her. I could not leave her as she fell asleep that day, and I lay there beside her, silently praying and unable to stop the images that raced through my mind. In one dream that recurred for months after this incident, I chased her through the water and screamed as a wave rose behind her. She just laughed and waved her arm as the wave crashed over her. In another dream I was calling for her to come back as the tide kept rising around her. Neither of us could move.

For a long time I could neither sleep nor eat. I had to fight the urge to set up a bed in her room so that I could protect her and never again let her out of my sight. Recently, I read a book about Anne Morrow Lindbergh and wondered how she could ever sleep again after her precious son was kidnapped from his crib and murdered. What does a parent do when the unspeakable happens? How do you ever again believe in your own power and ability to protect those you love? Does anything ever matter after such a tragedy?

That incident changed forever how I thought and acted towards my only child. After worrying about her safety and relying on the RCMP to protect her from the "crazies" and from the cruelties that mark the families of prominent public figures, I had almost lost her to the sea, in a spot that had always given me comfort. For the longest time, I tortured myself in the middle of the night. What kind of a mother was I that my child nearly drowned on a public beach? This image of her drowning remained with me as the vision of my worst nightmare. It would be there just like the hint of a migraine, waiting to burst into full pain if I allowed it the space it wanted in my mind.

It lurked there until, one night, when Joe was foreign minister, it was replaced by another threat—a phone call on our unlisted home number in the middle of the night from a man who told me confidently that he could take my daughter whenever he wanted, a man who was never caught. But that brutal voice would enter my life years later, and by then I would understand the purpose of security and the possibilities of its failure.

After the Hawaii incident, what had once mattered to me in terms of politics and life seemed quite irrelevant. In my exhaustion after the defeat in 1980 and the marathon of the bar ads, everything seemed out of focus. The near-loss of Catherine compounded my own dark thoughts and deepened my sense of despair. I felt I needed to profoundly alter my priorities and start living more in the present, to be aware of the frailty of our lives and to recognize what matters and what does not.

That night in Hawaii, I went to bed and clung to my husband as if he could force these horrible thoughts out of my mind. The next morning, Catherine's little cotton sun hat lay in the sand. It had been torn from her head by the waves and then returned on the morning tide.

10

DURING THE SPRING OF 1980, we limped along as a family, bruised, hurt and exhausted. When we returned from Hawaii, the party recriminations had already begun. Joe's critics labelled him "naïve" and condemned him for being "too honest"—an astounding accusation to make of a Prime Minister. The party faithful who had not seen a government of their own since 1963 had expected a share in the perks of power. That is, after all, the way governments work and how the game is played. After more than a decade in the political wilderness, they assumed that Joe would reward the party faithful immediately for their loyalty. But so much needed to be done during the summer and fall of 1979 that Joe had just begun his appointments when the government was defeated in December. On principle, Joe had refused to appoint anyone after the 1980 election had been called, arguing it was both unethical and illegitimate for him to do so. The Liberals, on the other hand, had continued all through the 1979 election campaign to appoint as many of their own supporters as they could to public boards. Joe would pay a high price for his integrity on the matter of appointments, and after the defeat in 1980, his critics in caucus and in the party used it as a rallying cry against him, insisting that he did not reward his friends and supporters after all the work they did to elect him in 1979.

In April 1980, I was called to the Ontario Bar. Joe and my mother came with me to the ceremony in Ottawa. Gowned and feeling rather proud of myself, I received my licence to practise law and knew that I had managed this milestone in my life with much personal effort and with the support of many friends. I was relieved to have the whole process behind me and started to think about next steps.

The tension of constitutional politics continued unabated that spring in Canada. The governing Parti Québécois in Quebec scheduled a referendum on sovereignty. Pierre Trudeau promised that if Quebeckers voted against the proposal of "sovereignty-association"—an independent Quebec with an economic union with Canada—he would renew federalism to meet Quebec's concerns. In May, the *Non* side won the referendum by a margin of sixty to forty. English Canadians breathed a sigh of relief and believed the "Quebec issue" was finally solved. I could not have known that it was just the beginning of a long and painful constitutional battle that would dominate our political life for the next fifteen years.

In the midst of the 1980 referendum campaign, I had dinner with a friend, Ginette Asselin, whose husband, Martial, was the Quebec senator whom Joe had named minister responsible for the Canadian International Development Agency (CIDA) in 1979. This allowed Joe to have Quebec representation in his cabinet even though the party had only won two Commons seats in that province. Ginette and Martial had travelled with us to Africa, including the Commonwealth conference in Zambia that summer, and she and I had become friends. We talked about going to Europe together, which I thought it was a wonderful idea. Joe encouraged me, saying it would do me good just to be away where no one knew me. He had some travel to do, especially to Alberta, and assured me that he would take Catherine along with him. And so at the beginning of June, Ginette and I flew to London for the first week of a month-long trip of adventure and rest that included England, Ireland and France.

I returned to Ottawa on the eve of my seventh wedding anniversary feeling rested and more optimistic than I had in a long time. But being back in Canada was a shock after the anonymity and privacy that had marked my time in Europe. I travelled west with Joe in early July for the Calgary Stampede and then spent most of the summer in Ottawa. We had returned to Stornoway in April, which had been a bittersweet experience. Before leaving for Europe, I had agreed to the proposal for repair and redecoration that Cecilia Humphreys recommended, and when I returned in late June, all the work was finished. Catherine knew Stornoway well and settled in quickly. Her childhood routine of waking, eating, playing and sleeping provided an anchor for me. She and Joe had had a great time together during my absence in June, and I saw at dinner my first night home why they had got along so well. "Eat your dinner," I told her as she dawdled and pushed the food around her Bunnykins dish. She ignored me and turned to Joe. "How many more bites, Daddy?" "Four should do it," he replied. Later on I tried to put her to bed and she insisted that she had to have a walk, a treat and reading in bed before she would go to sleep. The treat was candy. She had trained her father well in just a month!

The trip to Europe had helped settle my nerves and allowed me to overcome the sense of powerlessness that had marked the previous months. It would take me the better part of a year, though, to work through the impact of the election loss and the uprooting that moving twice in a year caused us. This was a very lonely time for me. Again, Joe was working hard to prepare for the new session of Parliament that fall and was very focused. He was trying to keep the caucus together, but there was no doubt that many were angry that they were out of government and held him personally responsible. It was as if a cloud of polluted air hung over the caucus and the party, and we both knew that there were political storms ahead.

I thought about starting to practise law, but did not feel I had the stamina yet. During these months, I had come to rely on a small group of friends, especially Barbara Drucker in Toronto, for support, and these friendships were pivotal in helping me get back on my feet.

It was Barbara who proposed a birthday party for me at her place the following year with Toronto friends Sandy Lyons, Gail Gerstein, Andrea Alexander, Sarah Band, Lee Hayden, Nancy Eagleson, Marie Rounding and my sister Pam. Over the twenty years that we've repeated this ritual, others occasionally joined us, but this group remains, even today, the core participants at "Barb's annual birthday bash," which has little to do now with my birthday and everything to do with friendship. We have survived the crises of childhood, adolescence, weddings and deaths, and are now into the next generation of issues, including grandchildren, aging parents and retirement. It remains one of the events I really look forward to each year; but when it all began, it was the lifesaver I needed to be able to cope with the strains of public life.

The capacity to trust others is one of the most elusive, yet essential, elements of all human interactions. In politics, one tends to protect oneself by trusting only a very few people. It is the nature of politics that a friend today may not be a friend tomorrow. I learned that lesson in 1980, when the many "new best friends" I had acquired while Joe was Prime Minister disappeared. But trusting people is essential and sometimes one just has to take the risk. Slowly, during this period, with help from friends and family, I managed to find my way again.

By 1980, I had learned another lesson: in order to survive these traumatic political experiences, I had to keep myself at a safe distance from politics whenever possible and to forge my own identity based on my own accomplishments. I had started my married life as an equal partner in Joe's political career, but after 1976 I discovered that I could not be a political adviser or even a confidante in a formal sense. His staff was there for that and they all guarded their turf jealously. A fine but real line existed between us on this point, and at the beginning, I found it difficult to be excluded because my own life was so affected by the turmoil of Joe's political life. But after a time, I realized that I had effectively developed my own interests and built a comforting wall around Catherine and myself. We were a part of Joe's life, but at the same time, we had our own. Being together and yet separate sometimes strained our personal relationship, but it helped me survive the mental darkness that had overcome me during the turmoil of the defeat in 1980.

While I knew I was not ready to start practising law, the question remained of what I wanted to do. Two events pointed me towards writing. In 1980 I was named Chatelaine's Woman of the Year, and I was asked to write a monthly column entitled "Report from Ottawa." I accepted and started to teach myself how to write for magazines. Then, shortly after my return from Europe, I was walking into the laneway of Stornoway when yet another tour bus stopped to let its passengers take pictures. A passenger hopped off the bus and asked me about Stornoway's history, and I had to admit that I had no idea. Recounting this to Joe that evening at dinner, he said, "Maybe you should research and write a book on the official residences." I decided to give it some thought. Like most women faced with a new challenge, I meticulously went through all the reasons why I could *not* write such a book. The following week, a Toronto friend recommended Lucinda Vardey, a prominent literary agent, to represent me in my efforts to find a publisher. Lucinda asked me to put together a slide presentation on the three residences—24 Sussex Drive, Stornoway and Harrington Lake. Under her direction, I visited five publishers to pitch my book proposal, and in the end Prentice Hall published my first book, *Residences: Homes of Canada's Leaders.* The well-known Montreal publishing house Les Éditions Libre Expression published the text in French, and over the years I developed a close and lasting friendship with its founders, Carole Levert and André Bastien.

The writing and successful publication of my first book did three things. It showed the interest that existed, especially among women, for a book about our Canadian heritage. It put the story of the public homes of Canada's political leaders together in one place. And it gave me the courage to become an author. Writing *Residences* was a fascinating experience for me, but it also served a historical purpose. None of the people who had lived in the residences before me was under eighty, and while their short-term memories were not always strong, all of them remembered vividly what had happened fifty or more years before. I learned, for instance, that Stornoway had been the wartime home of the Dutch royal family, which meant that Catherine was the first child to be born and live there after the youngest of the Dutch princesses. I learned that 24 Sussex Drive had been expropriated from the Edwards family and that Mackenzie King's government had refused to accept the owner's extensive art collection of post-Impressionist paintings for the National Gallery in lieu of taxes. The collection was then sold at auction in New York and dispersed around the world. The son of the man who built 24 Sussex had celebrated his hundredth birthday by the time the book was completed and regaled everyone with his stories the night of the launch.

I decided to hold the launch at Stornoway in 1981, and as the guests left I gave them each six tulip bulbs called "Chantilly Lace," one of the late Mary Stanfield's favourites. Mary had introduced me to Stornoway, where she and Robert Stanfield had lived while he was party and Opposition leader. After Joe won the leadership in 1976, Mary welcomed me back to the house and gave me the cook's tour. Sadly, she died of lung cancer in 1977, and I decided to offer one of her favourite tulips to honour her.

The national tour I undertook that October and November to sell my first book was perfect therapy for my tattered sense of self. It was a busy time of travel, but quite pleasant and so much easier than an election campaign. The many media interviews gave me an opportunity to speak knowledgeably on historical and heritage matters of importance and interest to me personally. During previous interviews while campaigning, I had had to talk mainly of political issues. Now, I could recount fascinating stories of history and human interest, allowing me to present a new and different face to the public. It was one of the few periods since my marriage when partisan politics were far away and I felt strong and focused doing something that was my own.

It was at this time that I decided to found a small art company to promote the works of young and recently established artists in regions other than their own. I had become a collector of art in 1976 when we moved to Stornoway the first time and had learned a great deal through reading and visiting galleries across Canada. I saw that I could encourage artists to get recognition outside their own region and, in so doing, increase their understanding of the culture and artistic influences in other parts of the country. In 1981, I joined two friends, Joan Andre and Dreena Jenkins, to form a little company called Canadian Perspectives Canadiennes, and during the three years we were together, we mounted art exhibitions in Ottawa, Calgary and Quebec City, and hosted many art shows in people's homes. We collaborated on a *livre d'artiste* with Libre Expression and Art Global. With the help of Quebec City lawyer and art collector Michel Doyon, I travelled throughout Quebec, meeting artists, especially those working with Albert Rousseau, who had gathered together dozens of talented artists for his annual *expo champêtre* at his famed art studio, Le Moulin des arts, near Quebec City.

During these years, political turmoil engulfed Joe and often denied us time together as a couple and family. The chance to meet artists whose lives were so different from my own gave me a sense of purpose and allowed me to escape, however briefly, the tensions that politics imposed on my marriage and my public life. When I was working with artists, I felt distant from political affairs; I remember even pretending that perhaps this new focus would ensure that politics would not interfere too much with my own life ever again. Little did I know what trials lay ahead for me.

—

When Parliament resumed in the fall of 1980, Pierre Trudeau's one dominant goal was to address the constitutional concerns of Quebeckers. To do that, he proposed to patriate Canada's Constitution from Great Britain. The bill he tabled contained an amending formula and a Charter of Rights and Freedoms to replace the 1960 Diefenbaker Bill of Rights. Joe was concerned about the bill, whose amending formula would have made the Western provinces second-class citizens. It also failed to address key provincial concerns about the centralization of power in Ottawa. Both nationalists and federalists in Quebec criticized the bill. Joe travelled across Canada to galvanize those who opposed it, and three provincial governments—Quebec, Manitoba and Newfoundland—raised doubts about its legality, referring it to their courts. The federal government then referred the question of legality to the Supreme Court of Canada, and on September 28, 1981, the court held that it was legal. But while the majority of Canada's highest court agreed that the federal government had the legal authority to patriate the Constitution, it expressed reservations about its legitimacy, arguing that it ran counter to the conventions and spirit of the federal system. As leader of the Official Opposition in Parliament, Joe seized upon these reservations and asked the government to reconsider the bill's provisions. The government, on the other hand, interpreted the court's decision as giving it the green light to proceed and, after a year of delay while the matter was before the court, the government forged ahead. Opposition to the bill would not keep it from being passed.

While Joe was preoccupied with the court decision and the bill's provisions, especially concerning the amending formula, I and many other women were concerned about the bill's equality provisions. Like the 1960 Bill of Rights, the proposed bill guaranteed procedural but not substantive equality—a right that had been ineffective in promoting or ensuring women's equality in the past. The 1960 bill had offered a guarantee of equality for all Canadians, but had proved insufficient to achieve real equality (also called substantive equality) or correct discrimination against women. Fundamentally, that law failed to recognize that women's lives were different from those of most men. Take pregnancy as an example. The Supreme Court had held that because a federal law about unemployment insurance treated women and men equally, there was no discrimination under the Bill of Rights against pregnant women who could not collect it. That is *procedural* equality. Under the new law, the courts could hold that because women become pregnant and men don't, any law that adversely affects them on the basis of pregnancy denies equality. The 1960 Bill of Rights treated people as if they were all the same, and this resulted in discrimination and inequality—not what the legislators in 1960 had intended.

Unfortunately, two of the important bodies that should have been lobbying for changes to the 1960 bill were proving themselves totally ineffective. The National Action Committee on the Status of Women (NAC) was in the midst of an internal battle, and the Liberal appointees on the Canadian Advisory Council on the Status of Women supported the government throughout. Fortunately, one Liberal appointment, the council's president,

Doris Anderson, refused to give in to her political masters and resigned in protest. The advisory council meeting called to discuss the proposed bill in November was cancelled, and another meeting was to be held the following February. In all of this mess, the task of defending women's equality interests was taken up by a handful of women in the justice department, private practice and Parliament. Concerned women parliamentarians, especially Flora MacDonald and Pauline Jewett, demanded the Prime Minister amend the bill to guarantee women's equality. But women's equality was the furthest thing from the Prime Minister's mind. He was furious that Joe kept challenging his bill and dismissed concerns raised by some of the provinces and by women. To Pierre Trudeau, this bill was about a showdown with Quebec's PQ government and all the rest was window dressing.

Around this time, Ottawa lawyer Peggy Mason, a classmate from law school, resigned from the staff of the advisory council and joined Joe's office. She argued convincingly to Joe and the PC caucus that they should endorse amendments to the equality provision to guarantee women's equality "before and under the law." This wording would guarantee substantive as well as administrative, or procedural, equality, and other lawyers were endorsing the wording. There was already concern that a new section in the Charter of Rights and Freedoms would be needed to protect women's equality guarantees in case of the inclusion of a "notwithstanding" clause in the Constitution. This latter clause would allow the federal and provincial governments to deny certain rights to Canadians if a significant majority of members of Parliament or the provincial legislatures agreed to it. The War Measures Act a decade before had made me wary of such exceptions, and feminists wanted a guarantee that women's equality would be a fundamental constitutional right, free from the threat of the notwithstanding clause.

During the early winter, the official opposition demanded that the bill be withdrawn and redrafted to take account of the major changes proposed by the provinces, women and the parliamentary opposition. Joe argued that to do otherwise would put the whole process at risk because some provinces, including Quebec, would not sign the new Constitution. He argued that the Trudeau bill would divide Canada rather than serve as a unifying constitutional tool for the future. The government refused to budge, and tensions and tempers were high in Parliament and across the country.

To understand the concern many women had about the Trudeau bill, it is important to remember that this debate was taking place at a turbulent time for women's equality in North America. American feminists were failing in their own efforts to have the Equal Rights Amendment passed by a majority of state legislatures. In Canada, the federal government's unilateral decision to withdraw funding for the national women's conference, called by the advisory council to discuss the bill, reminded feminists that what was happening in the U.S. could just as easily happen in Canada. Like most women interested in this debate, I knew that this would be our only chance to ensure that a guarantee of women's equality was enshrined in our Constitution. As a lawyer, I preferred a law that was clear and unequivocal about the guarantee of women's equality, and was lobbying for the introduction of a new bill that would achieve that goal. The only thing worse than no law is a bad one, and I believed that mere tinkering with the current bill would only lead to confusion when Canadian courts were later called upon to interpret the law's equality guarantees for women. Even among feminists, though, opinions differed on the best way to achieve full equality for women under the new Constitution.

As 1981 began, another women's meeting, called for February 14 by the advisory council to address amendments to the bill's equality provisions, was cancelled by the council itself at minister Lloyd Axworthy's request. Many women across Canada objected, and a group led by Doris Anderson decided to go ahead with an ad hoc meeting in Ottawa on the same dates. Donations and offers of billets were made from supporters across the country, and in Ottawa, Joe and I volunteered to host a reception at Stornoway for the participants. I went to that women's meeting convinced that the bill should be withdrawn and a new, amended and acceptable bill introduced in its place. The organizers disagreed, and my position was attacked by them as being partisan and obstructionist. Most of those in attendance saw their role as limited to getting the best deal possible for women within the wording of the current bill. If they could improve the equality provision, that would be enough. Other groups and the provinces concerned with the bill's provisions could look after their own interests; these were not women's problems. That attitude was clear to me the moment I entered the room and saw that the discussion of a recommendation for a new bill was at the very bottom of the agenda.

I felt uncomfortable all day, as several women I did not even know came up to me and demanded I not "sabotage" the meeting by discussing the recommendation for a new bill. I reminded them that our reason for being there was to be sure we had the best possible Constitution and Charter of Rights, and that meant all options should be considered. I noted that Flora MacDonald and Pauline Jewett had almost single-handedly held the line against the government on this issue since October and that cabinet ministers Monique Begin and Judy Erola had risked their own political necks within the Liberal caucus to try to make the government change the bill. I was hurt that my presence was seen not as that of a committed feminist, but rather as a mouthpiece for my political husband. This gathering had been billed as an open meeting of women concerned about our equality rights within the Canadian Constitution, and the current bill did not protect them adequately. Certainly all those in attendance had a right to be heard. I began to worry that the organizers had already made a decision about the bill and that we were there essentially to endorse their plan. Trust was in short supply on both sides of the House of Commons, but there was also little of it at this women's meeting.

Near the end of the afternoon, needing to return to Stornoway to help prepare for the reception we had agreed to host later, I raised the matter of a new bill, asking the organizers if there would be time to address it. You would think I had asked if I could replace the Prime Minister, and I was told by those at the head table to sit down and to stop trying to politicize the meeting. I was stunned, furious and hurt. Some women there actually booed and told me to sit down. I was upset and unprepared for this response and left the meeting. I heard later that evening from Jean Piggott that my sudden departure had played into the hands of my critics, who were accusing me of being petulant and partisan. Obviously, at twenty-nine, I still had to learn how to play the political game.

After our reception, I talked to Joe about what had happened that day and asked him what lay ahead for the new law. He was disappointed by how I had been treated by other women, but not surprised, given the mood in Parliament, where he lived with this kind of behaviour daily. He reminded me that many women, and men, who had attended our reception had supported my right to raise the issue and had found the attacks on me personally insulting. As we cleared the dishes from the dining room, he kindly suggested that I needed to toughen myself up a bit if I wanted to survive political life. One more thing for me to learn, I thought, even though I wasn't sure I could ever manage that kind of toughness. Later he told me that the meeting had been an important threat to the government. It would force the Prime Minister and his cabinet to address women's equality rights directly. He believed that revised equality provisions would be included in the final bill and that the opposition parties would suggest a clause to put women's rights above the notwithstanding clause. He promised me that he would propose it himself if need be. Days later, a majority of parliamentarians from all parties supported a provision, Section 28, to guarantee women's equality. It was not a perfect solution and remained open to judicial interpretation, but at least it recognized women's fundamental equality rights. In spite of my personal disappointment, I felt that the ad hoc meeting had had an impact. It gave credibility and confidence to those in Parliament who had been fighting for changes to the equality provisions, and confirmed specific legal wording to make those changes work.

The Charter of Rights would include the principle of equity as part of its definition of equality for women, and allow for affirmative action by governments. This was essential because the charter is a special law. If we think of our laws as a pyramid, it is the law at the top. It sets the standard against which all other laws must be read and to which they must conform. Getting it right the first time around was essential. Our equality in the future depended on it.

The signing of the new law giving Canada a Charter of Rights and Freedoms and the power to amend our own Constitution took place on the lawn of Parliament Hill on April 17, 1982. The weather that day was unpredictable, and included rain, snow and sun. Joe and I sat in the audience on the lawn in front of the Peace Tower and watched Her Majesty Queen Elizabeth sign the act into law. It had been a tough and bitter fight to make this a sound and effective law for all Canadians and in the end it had failed. Quebec had not signed the Constitution, feeling betrayed by both the federal government and the Premiers who had decided to proceed over its objections. Joe had argued passionately for more time to allow Quebec's objections to be addressed, but had been refused. Canada remained sharply divided on the very law that had been introduced to make us whole.

Many of us watched the procedure with a heavy heart, including my seatmate, the late Senator Jean Marchand, who had come to federal politics with Pierre Trudeau. Jean and I huddled together under my umbrella in a sudden downpour and, visibly upset, he hissed the word, *traître* when Pierre Trudeau signed the official document. I was startled by his vehemence, but said nothing, aware that the anger he felt was shared by many others and would fan the fires of Quebec separatists in the months ahead.

After the ceremony, members of the Privy Council attended lunch with Her Majesty in the Centre Block. Given the downpour near the end of the ceremony, many of us were soaking wet, but traffic on the Hill prevented us from going home to change. I ran up to Joe's office in the Centre Block and begged my husband's secretary, Adèle Desjardins, to lend me her dry dress. She laughed and told me I looked like a *chat noyé*, a drowned cat. "Precisely my point," I told her. And so after a little more begging, I went to lunch with the Queen, dressed in Adèle's brown dress and my soaking grey shoes. As I stood in line to meet Her Majesty I noted in a panic that my gloves were too wet to wear. I apologized as I took her proffered hand and, without skipping a beat, she replied that I needed someone like her lady-in-waiting to carry an extra pair of gloves for me. "Excellent idea," I replied, smiling. "I must raise that with the finance minister the next time we meet!"

11

IT WAS NEAR THE END OF 1982 that the storm clouds around Joe's leadership began to gather in earnest. Even as I tried to pretend that our lives could be lived peacefully without the daggers and drama of politics, I knew that we were about to face a very difficult challenge at the party's annual meeting in Winnipeg the coming February. The party's constitution requires a vote of confidence in the leader after each election loss, and Joe's supporters in caucus and the party were already working to organize a strong vote in his favour. At the same time, his critics were planning to use that vote to undermine his leadership and force him to step down. The positive side to this campaign was that it gave renewed energy to Joe's many supporters as they organized for the vote, but fighting the phantoms of opposition sapped his energy and forced him to waste his time on petty internal party fights and power struggles when we needed solidarity. Joe and I were ready for a break after Christmas and accepted Ted and Loretta Rogers's invitation to stay with them in Lyford Cay in the Bahamas. Ted had always supported the leader and knew politics well enough to see the difficult days that lay ahead for us. Joe's mother, Grace, joined us and we all relaxed and enjoyed the Rogerses' hospitality for ten days.

When we returned to Ottawa, the grumbling about Joe's leadership continued. I just wanted Winnipeg to be over with and Joe's leadership reconfirmed. Without it, he could not lead a strong opposition in the House or prepare for the next election. Meanwhile, the Liberals were talking of changing leaders, and two of the likely candidates, John Turner and Jean Chrétien, were vying for media attention. As I travelled with Joe to meet delegates in January and February there seemed to be a good mood among long-time Tories, and a feeling that Joe should remain as party leader. Still, I worried that there could always be surprises. I had seen conventions before packed with instant party members. But we seemed to be well organized, and I was beginning to feel that Joe would obtain the necessary fifty percent plus one required in the confidence motion at the Winnipeg convention. Then, as the meeting neared, a senior Clark strategist from Ottawa told the press that Joe would get at least 70 percent of the vote. He thought that such a bold assertion would be helpful, a sign of pre-convention strength that would serve to sway some of the undecided votes.

We would pay heavily for his bravado. From that moment on, the figure of 70 percent became the benchmark against which the vote for Joe would be judged. Anything below that would be seen as a defeat. Still, when Joe and I arrived in Winnipeg, the mood seemed upbeat and the naysayers kept to themselves. There did seem to be an unusually strong showing of Quebec delegates who appeared just before the confidence vote, to the surprise of many of us at the convention. After the vote, while the delegates were dancing and having a great time, one of the convention organizers came and asked Joe to follow him. It is common practice that the leader is advised of the results prior to their announcement to the crowd, and Joe and I went to a room nearby. The official handed Joe the results, and to our dismay, only 66 percent of delegates endorsed his leadership. We had failed to reach the magic 70 percent that had become the minimum for his leadership. Terribly disappointed, we began to discuss our options. For Joe, the vote he had been given, while more than a clear majority, was just not enough. Terry Yates, the head of the PC Canada Fund, and MP Jake Epp, who were there with us, made it clear that our own supporters were very tired and that it would be difficult to find the money to mount an effective leadership race that year. They recommended caution in rejecting the vote out of hand. They thought that 66 percent was respectable and argued that the 70 percent figure could be talked away. I saw how let down and discouraged Joe felt, and told him that whatever he decided I would be there for him. He decided to step down.

———

Joe's decision to resign as party leader and to call a leadership convention after the vote in Winnipeg cannot be assessed without remembering the context of the time. A leader must have the support of his party in order to do his job. At the very least, he needs to know that he can wake up in the morning without a daily crisis created by his own members or parliamentary caucus and that he need not worry about being knifed from behind. Since his government's defeat in 1980, he could count on neither. We were not the only ones demoralized by the continual attacks on Joe's leadership from within: many of our supporters were suffering from "leadership fatigue." It reminded me of a game we had played as children, in which one person would turn his back and all the others would sneak up behind him, trying to stand dead still when he turned around, as if they had not been gaining on him when he was not looking. After the defeat in 1980, Joe could never be sure who was organizing against him.

Calling a leadership vote in 1983 was a huge risk, but its purpose was clear. It was not a decision Joe took in haste, but rather a calculated risk to force those who opposed him to meet him in public, face to face. The back-stabbing and endless undermining of his leadership and personal integrity had to stop. If he won, he would have the authority to move forward with confidence to lead the party in Parliament and into the next election, expected within the year. Even with all the under-handedness and the bad press this internal challenge to his leadership had generated, Joe still managed good ratings in the polls. If he lost, well . . . we did not think about losing. That is lesson number one about political campaigns. Run as if you are ten votes behind, but run to win.

I cannot overstate the impact all this intrigue and betrayal had on my own health. My migraines increased and I was often unable to eat. I lost weight, felt weak and had trouble sleeping. During the weeks between Winnipeg and the leadership con-vention in Ottawa in June 1983, I travelled with Joe as much as possible. I had hired a professional nanny, a young woman named Susan Baxter, who took care of Catherine—and often me—in those trying days. All of us were under strain, and these were some of the most difficult days of our political life. There was, of course, a positive side. I doubt if any leader in a crisis like this has ever enjoyed the kind of loyalty Joe had from his supporters. I used to tell people that person for person, in the 1983 leadership convention Joe had the A-team. So many of his parliamentary colleagues put their careers on the line to support Joe, knowing that if he lost to the main contender, Brian Mulroney, they would have burned their political bridges.

It was unseasonably hot on voting day that June and the Civic Centre in Ottawa was like a pressure cooker. The voting seemed to take hours and the atmosphere was charged with ten-sion. Yet spirits were high among our team and Edmonton MP Steve Paproski led us all in enthusiastic song. As the field nar-rowed, the three main contenders were Joe, Brian and John Crosbie. When the results of the next-to-last ballot were read, Joe maintained his lead, but it was clear that the final result would depend on the third-place finisher, John Crosbie. As we waited for the balloting to begin again, no one knew what would happen. Then, the most bizarre experience of my political life occurred. As we waited for reports from our workers on what the Crosbie people were planning, one of Crosbie's senior organizers, Brian Peckford, made his way, gesturing frenetically, to Joe's box in the Civic Centre. Hordes of press people with cameras and microphones closed in for the show. Such a dramatic act usually means that a losing candidate, who will be eliminated and forced to step aside before the next vote, is sending over his senior campaign adviser to "strike a deal." In this case, it could only have meant that Crosbie knew he had to drop off the final ballot and had decided to throw his support behind the front-runner. That would be the logical assumption—but that was not what Peckford was proposing. Instead of bringing delegate support, he was demanding ours!

We listened in stunned silence while this emissary begged Joe to move to Crosbie. "You can't win, Joe," he said. "Come to John. It's the only way to stop Mulroney." The number-three person on the ballot was asking the number-one candidate and the current leader to fold up his tent and join his camp against the number-two contender. It might have seemed logical to the Crosbie team, but it made no sense at all to us. Our campaign team was shocked, but within seconds, that changed to anger. I can clearly remember my response. I turned to Doug Bassett, who looked as surprised as I was, and said, "Get this stupid bastard out of here." Doug reminded me in a whisper that there was a boom mike over my head, but immediately ushered Peckford out of our way. At that moment Joe turned to Robert René de Cotret, who spoke to him in French, saying, "You have not come this far to throw away your reputation for honesty and integrity now. We will fight to the end and see what happens." A campaign worker came up to tell us that Crosbie had "released his people" which, in convention terms, meant that he was not taking a stand. In this case, it meant that he was not supporting Joe, for if he had come to us at that moment, the convention would have been won.

I believe that the charade we witnessed was about John Crosbie protecting his own interests. He wasn't sure Joe would be able to win and he was likely unsure if he could bring his delegates with him if he moved. By doing what he did, he could answer the charge that he had defeated Joe by saying that he had tried to forge a last-minute alliance to stop Brian, but Joe had refused. If Brian won, Crosbie was safe, as he had not come to Joe. By then, Brian and Mila Mulroney had already left to change their clothes, confident of a win. Our supporters fanned out and worked like mad to convince Crosbie's delegates to vote for Joe. In the end not enough of them did. Brian Mulroney had won the convention, and the party had a new leader.

12

I CAN REMEMBER STANDING ON THE STAGE in the Civic Centre in Ottawa after my husband's leadership defeat in 1983 and saying over and over to myself: This has nothing to do with me. I am a whole person and I am free. I was completely numb and just wanted to be away from the place. While the electoral defeat in 1980 had been traumatic, this was devastating. Unlike 1980, when Joe committed his energies to building the party for the next election, the events of 1983 effectively ended his dream of leading the country. When I went home to Stornoway that night, I was too tired to cry. I felt that years of painstaking and exhausting effort had been a monumental waste. There was no doubt that the party would be very different under Brian Mulroney, but I had no idea how different, or if there would be a place for Joe and those who had supported him.

Marked by the memory of John Diefenbaker's refusal to resign as party leader in 1967 when Robert Stanfield was elected, Joe took the high road and urged his stunned supporters to stay and work with Brian. I found Joe's generosity remarkable. As always, he put party and country first and moved quickly to ensure that the party was united and in a position to win the coming election. He knew that would only be achieved if he worked with Brian, who had no parliamentary experience but lots of political talent. And so Joe and I stood together later that night of defeat in the Adam Room of the Château Laurier, where the ghosts of PC conventions past still lingered, and Joe urged his supporters to pull together with those who had spent the past three years plotting his defeat. The whole scene seemed cruel and senseless to me. It marks me still and tempers my interest in active politics, although not its higher purpose.

That evening, I decided to turn off my mind and just live in the moment, leaving all other considerations until later. In my heart, I wanted to just run away and never come back. When we got home that Saturday night, I had a more immediate task at hand. Weeks before, I had invited forty people for brunch the following day. Two of the staff were ill, and although Laura Lefebvre would be coming in early the next morning to prepare food, I had to set the tables and prepare the house. The luncheon guests were all old friends, among them Lowell Murray and his wife, Colleen; Jodi White; Bill and Marilyn Neville; Roy and Mary Ann Everest and Bob and Olga Dowling from Jasper; and staff members Jock Osler, Donald Doyle and Peter Harder and their spouses. Joe's family was there too; and, as always, my mother, Jane and Colleen came in to help me. They all tried hard to cheer us up that day, and we discussed what lay ahead well into the evening. Nothing was left out as these campaign strategists talked about what had gone wrong, the tactics of our opponents, what we could expect in the coming months, the influence of money on this leadership campaign and the difficulty Joe had had leading a party still bitter from being left out of the spoils of office. One friend summed up the situation when he said, "Maureen, you have to remember the prize of winning this leadership is power. Joe has laid all the policy and parliamentary groundwork and the time is ripe for change. Brian will be Prime Minister. He will pay back all those who expect it and more. That is what the party wants." At that point I left the group and quietly went to my room and cried.

As the day drew to a close, it was as if no one wanted to leave, and I saw that several would be staying for supper. The Everests and Dowlings had to catch a plane back west, but others remained. At this point, my sisters and mother just took over and organized an impromptu barbecue in the backyard. As darkness fell, we continued the post-mortem of the convention and I listened to people who had seen it all. The experience of this campaign defeat was new to me and I sat on Stornoway's screened-in porch, absorbing the stories and the history being revealed to me by Joe's old political friends. I knew instinctively that it would be harder to work our way through this defeat than it had been in 1980. One of the problems with living these kinds of events for the first time is the lack of context, since context comes only with experience. Most of those with us that day were veterans of previous defeats and knew what to expect. They did not like it but they knew the game and the price they would pay for not supporting Brian for the leadership. As I heard them all dissect each element of the campaign and talk about what came next, I thought, How can these people be so calm? I was baffled by it, and in my hurt and anger thought their sang-froid and logical discussions were a sign that they did not care about what Joe and I were feeling. Of course, I was wrong. They all knew what had been lost and understood clearly what it meant for us and for them now that Mulroney was leader. To his credit, as Prime Minister later, he recognized the character and ability of many of them and eventually would seek their advice and participation in his government. Late that night our friends finally left, and once again Joe and I were alone.

When I awoke the next day, I decided to stop feeling sorry for myself and to focus on Catherine's needs. She was six now and aware of events taking place around her. In the days following the Winnipeg meeting earlier that year, she had refused to go to school and did so again. She stuck by my side, and I tried to prepare her for the inevitable move from Stornoway, where she had lived since her birth except for the brief interlude at 24 Sussex Drive. She had trouble understanding why we had to move. I decided that as it was only the beginning of June, we would just stay for that month, finish school and give ourselves some time to come to grips with what had happened in the shelter of the place we had called home for so long.

Within a few days those plans were changed. In a nutshell, we were being evicted. Brian was already campaigning in Elmer MacKay's seat in Nova Scotia and wanted to move in as soon as possible after the by-election. They were planning extensive renovations over the summer and we were not in much of a position to object. This was one of the few times in my life that I did not even bother to protest. I didn't even tell Joe, as he was involved in the terrible job of leaving his office and had enough to worry about. Instead, I called a real estate agent and started looking for another house. By the end of the week I had found one in the nearby community of New Edinburgh, which I chose in part because it was on a street that shared a name with my father—John. In my state, I saw that as a good sign. We closed the deal and started to pack our belongings for storage. I called public works to come and ready Stornoway for its new occupants, only to be told that they had no intention of sending anyone over to help clean the place. We were out of power, and in Ottawa, power is all that matters. In the end, I called in my family. My mother, two of my sisters, my auntie Vi and our housekeeper, Laura, came over to scrub Stornoway with me from top to bottom. We worked until late that night to make the place spotless and left for good the following day.

Often things happen for a purpose. In the spring of 1983, as we struggled with the nastiness of the leadership campaign, I signed a contract to write a book on Parliament to be used in Canadian schools. I decided then that win, lose or draw, I would use the advance money to take us all to England and France for six weeks' rest after the June leadership convention. And so, with everything in storage and our future home being painted and updated, we boarded a plane for London. During that summer, we were lucky to have Susan Baxter with us. She cared for Catherine and served as a real support for me. I could not have managed without her. She had a lasting impact on Catherine, and over the years we always did many things "Sue's way"— from making crafts to creating pizzas.

When we arrived in England in late June, we met several friends and celebrated our tenth wedding anniversary with Al and Nancy Eagleson. Like many of our supporters at the time, Al would pay a price for backing Joe and would have many of his own troubles later. But in England they soothed and consoled us in a way that only people who understand politics can. They are both exuberant people and were more so that trip, as they tried to make us see that there was so much more in life for us to experience. We felt so many emotions that evening. We drank champagne, ate, laughed, cried and remembered the excitement of our many victories and the pain of this particular defeat. Joe and I had been married for only ten years, but during that time, I had borne a child and watched my father die. I had helped my husband in his political career, and had taken part in three riding victories, two leadership races and two national election campaigns. I had attended law school and completed the bar admission course, run a small art company, written a best-selling book and was completing another. I had just turned thirty-one. Thus began what I think of as a forced sabbatical, a year that started with the most bitter pain and anger but ended in victory with Joe re-elected in his Alberta riding of Yellowhead and named Canada's secretary of state for external affairs.

But in early July 1983, we only wanted to leave Joe's political life at home, and after our anniversary celebration in London, we spent three weeks in a little place in Cornwall called New Polzeath. There, sweltering in the most unusual heat, we walked the cliff paths and quietly started to put body and soul back together. We went on to the south of France for two weeks, and in early August returned to Canada, where we lived like nomads until Labour Day, waiting for our house to be finished. I felt lost and sad, and we all faced yet another difficult change when Susan left us to start university that September. Catherine was upset for a long time after Susan left. In her absence, my daughter seemed to rely even more on me. Having her need us so much at that particular time was really a good thing for both of us, as it forced us to set aside our own concerns to meet her needs. Joe had always been a doting father, and he relaxed and played and read to her each day. He has a great sense of humour and they would often play jokes on me. At other times they went to movies or stores together. Their relationship grew stronger than ever as we lived through this tough period.

In the fall of 1983, we became more self-sufficient and independent as a couple. Joe was still active as a member of Parliament, but I knew that he was being excluded in the shaping of the party's policies and in caucus. A party person to the core, he still travelled extensively to help new candidates prepare for the coming federal election. Old friends and supporters naturally fought to be noticed by the new leader, which meant distancing themselves from us, and we steadily established our own life away from them. We avoided political gatherings where we would be seen as outsiders and spent more and more time alone. On one trip to Florida that year, Joe decided he was interested in knowing more about the drug trade and asked for a briefing from the responsible American agency in Miami. During the fall of 1983, Brian asked him to prepare the party's policy on disarmament, and during the coming months Joe travelled extensively around the world with his legal assistant, Peggy Mason, to interview experts and prepare his report.

When we finally moved into our place on John Street, which Cecilia Humphreys had redone for us over the summer, I thought we would be there for quite a while. New Edinburgh was built in the late nineteenth century as a community of small homes for those who worked at the door and sash factory on Green Island nearby. This factory was part of the estate of Thomas MacKay, who had built Rideau Hall, the residence of the Governor General. Our new place was one of the original houses in New Edinburgh—and had only a crawl space for a basement. We invited my family for Thanksgiving, and that evening turned on the furnace to guard against the night's chill. Within a few minutes it exploded, spewing thick black soot all over the new white furniture and freshly painted walls. It was to be downhill from there on in our little place on John Street.

I can laugh now, but after all we had been through, I was really in no mood to find humour in the events of the weeks that followed. Because the crawl space was so small, we decided to try a new furnace that fitted neatly into the narrow space. It had two parts that arrived in separate boxes. The company owner arrived and carried one part to the basement crawl space, leaving the other piece near the front steps. There was only one problem. It was garbage day, and when he came up for the second part, it had been picked up and taken to the dump. After much haggling he agreed to fund another second part and install it before we all froze. It seemed to work all right until Christmas Day, when we lit the fireplace again. It turned out that there was a design flaw: lighting the fireplace somehow blew out the furnace pilot light. That night the temperature plummeted in the house, and the three of us and one of my nieces huddled in the kitchen close to the hot oven. We took turns holding candles to warm the water pipes and gave the furnace supplier a day to figure out what was wrong. To his credit, he admitted that it was his responsibility and covered the cost of a conventional furnace.

Our house in New Edinburgh fronted directly onto the street, and during that winter I came to miss my privacy and longed for a place in the country where I could walk alone and cross-country ski. One day in late March 1984, an ad in the local paper advertising a place on the Chaudière golf course near Aylmer, Quebec, caught my eye. In bitter freezing rain, I went to see the place and bought it on the spot. Joe knew I wanted to live in the country, but he did not relish the busy commute to Ottawa each day over one the interprovincial bridges. The owners of the house in Aylmer would not leave until Labour Day and our Ottawa place sold immediately. Once again we would be nomads for a summer.

That year, I turned my attention back to writing and worked on my second book, *Parliament: Canada's Democracy and How It Works*—for students as well as the general public. It was the first book of its kind, and I relied heavily on editor Barbara Hehner to help make it readable for a grade eight reading level. I enjoyed writing this book but it also gave me an excuse to be away from the political scene. Whenever anyone wanted me to volunteer to endorse their cause or speak to their association, I could truthfully say I was too busy. It seems that when you are writing a book, people respect your need for time much more than if you are simply leading a busy life. This period of intense focus and isolation helped me recover from the chaos of the previous few months. Catherine had adjusted well, but I thought that after five years at a French-language Montessori school that she should begin to study in English. I had enjoyed my years at a girls' school and felt it would be a good experience for her to try, too. We talked about it, and as some of her friends were already students there, she agreed to start grade five at Elmwood, a girls' school in Ottawa, that fall.

Since June 1983, the political landscape of the country had undergone radical change. Both major political parties had a new leader. Pierre Trudeau had left politics, for good this time.

He had waited too long, however, and his successor, John Turner, had no time to establish himself or his government before going to an election. The intensity of the nomination contests in our own party reflected our high standing in the polls. Barring disaster, it looked as though the PC Party would win the next election. Joe's support of Brian and the latter's efforts at conciliation meant that there was peace for once within the PC Party and caucus. Ironically, it would be the bench strength from Joe's cabinet in 1979 that would form the basis of the Mulroney cabinet in 1984. Caucus members were on their best behaviour. I found it all hard to stomach in the circumstances, but I was pleased that there would be a new government at last.

I cannot imagine how hard all this was for Joe. I did know, though, that he wanted the country to be led by a new government that would squarely face the economic and constitutional issues that plagued Canada. He had done his own soul-searching about what role he could play in making that happen, but it remained a painful place for him to be. He could see the polls and he realized that the Liberal blunders were paving the way for a PC victory. A stoic, Joe held his head high and kept working to win his riding. Serving Canada in Parliament had been his life's work, and he would pursue that goal selflessly and with a commitment I deeply admired.

13

WHILE JOE WAS PRIME MINISTER, he had received several invitations to visit countries around the world. We had not had a chance to accept many of them at the time, but some invitations persisted even after Joe returned to his role as leader of the Official Opposition. One of these was from China and in May 1984, we made our first trip to that fascinating country. In all, we visited five major cities—Beijing, Chengdu, Xian, Guangzhou, Shanghai—and the new industrial zone of Shenzhen, before ending our trip in Hong Kong. Our first stop was Beijing, where Gordon Houlden from our embassy joined us. As we drove in from the airport, we were surrounded by a sea of bicycles. Millions of old and sturdy single-speed bikes flanked us, ridden by people dressed in grey or brown. The city smelled of dust, and for a Canadian used to lots of space, the atmosphere was claustrophobic. As soon as we arrived, we were taken on a tour of the city by a young Chinese man who knew every minute architectural detail of each massive building but absolutely nothing at all about what went on inside them. No doubt he knew more than he admitted, but in controlled societies, this continuous recital of numbers is often all a tourist or visitor can expect as historical commentary and analysis. As is my custom when travelling, I had read a great deal about each city we were to visit. It was a process that had always worked for our North American and European trips. Yet when we arrived in China for the first time, it was as if I was lost and wandering on another planet. My normal sense of direction and cultural balance was all askew. Part of it was the language, of course, for when you are limited to English, French and a smattering of Spanish and Italian, as I am, visiting most countries can be a superficial experience. But I wanted to know more about the people who lived there and what they thought about the massive changes underway. Many huge cities on the southeast seaboard, for example, were becoming mini economic states unto themselves. I wanted to see what their houses were like and what kind of goods the Chinese would need as economic prosperity, trickled down to the individual. I wondered what the words to their songs meant and if there were any plays or books that could help me better understand the new China. Our poor translator became as tired of my questions as I did of his answers.

After Beijing, we began our trip to the four other cities on our itinerary. We took a plane to the city of Chengdu in Sichuan province, and on our first morning there, I was wakened by the eerie sound of singing, muffled by the dense fog that enveloped the city. Still jet-lagged, I thought I was dreaming, but as it continued, I awoke fully and opened the window to a surprising sight. In a park near the hotel were row upon row of people dressed alike all moving in ghostlike rhythm in the bleak light of dawn. I watched in amazement as they all swayed in sync and sang a song that sounded melancholic and haunting. Then, as if on cue, the music stopped and the people dispersed, leaving nothing behind but heavy mist. As I closed the window and turned back into the room, I was startled by a man who had silently entered and was filling our tea thermos. He spoke not a word, pretended I was not there and left as silently as he had entered. I tried to lock the bedroom door, but there was no lock. These were two scenes—that of the early-morning mass exercises in the parks and the omnipresent tea servers in our room—that would remain with me as vivid images of my first days in China.

As fate would have it, we managed somehow to be following some of the travel itinerary of U.S. President Ronald Reagan, who had visited China a few weeks before us. As we moved around, we realized that we were the real beneficiaries of China–U.S. diplomacy. Knowing that the U.S. President would not be allowed to wander far from his motorcade, the Chinese merely set the route he would take and modernized everything in the vicinity—a sort of swath of modernity cut across centuries and thousands of miles of geography. In Xian, we visited the terra cotta soldiers standing armed and ready at a recently excavated burial site. It was an incredible spectacle. Before the Reagan visit it would have been impossible to go down to the site, but a presidential platform with newly constructed wooden stairs brought us as close as possible to this incredible ancient military honour guard of earthen men. On a more practical level, the platform saved our fancy Western shoes from the surrounding mud.

All the hotels we stayed in had had just enough floors renovated to house the American delegation. On those floors the rooms were filled with furniture covered with the most luxurious silk brocade. Wonderful Chinese rugs lay at our feet and works of art hung on the walls. The electrical outlets all worked and the bathrooms were fit for a President. The remaining floors were untouched. As special guests, Joe and I were given renovated rooms, but our friends who were travelling with us ended up in economy. I remember Joe's executive assistant, Bill Chambers, arriving at our hotel door in Xian one morning with a tattered piece of towel, while our bathroom was stacked with fluffy new ones. Another friend, Brenda Yates, nearly met her maker when her hair dryer blew the fuses in her bathroom, and finally, one night, they all showed up asking if they could just camp out on our beautiful silk rug rather than try to stay in the rooms below. We eventually managed to persuade our hosts to transfer our friends to the renovated floor, but it took a while.

During our visit, we attended many dinners in our honour. On one of those evenings we were hosted by a senior woman official. Like all her peers, she wore a grey suit. As the evening wore on and all the platitudes common at such events had been exhausted, we asked her how she came to be involved in politics. It was, she said, an attempt at returning to normal after the Cultural Revolution, during which she and her educated husband had been "rehabilitated" for their bourgeois ways. She had been shipped off to an isolated rural area to swill pigs. Her husband had been sent to a farm somewhere else and her children dispersed around the country. All but one of her children had found their way home at the end of this gruesome period. They had never heard from the lost child, but she still held out hope that some day they would. It was the price she and her husband had paid for being educated. Her life had been altered forever and her family shocked and shattered. Yet she seemed neither bitter nor angry. Instead, she was candid and optimistic about China's future and insisted that the new leadership would avoid the extremes of the past. She spoke of how difficult it would be to find the middle way between economic development and the demands of a controlled economy and reminded us of the entrepreneurial spirit of the Chinese. She saw many opportunities for Canada in China, including in the agricultural sector, where farmers were more affluent than in any other sector of the economy. They needed machines to work their farms and trips abroad to learn new farming techniques. When we left her, she reminded us that in China's long history, the people had endured great hardship. Her own troubles were but a part of that story, and through it all, China would endure and prosper.

Her story made me reflect on my own reactions to adversity in political life. Here was a woman who started again after

The four oldest McTeer girls. Maureen (3), Pat (18 months),
Colleen (4) and Pam (18 months). Winter 1955.

Maureen on graduation day, University of
Ottawa. May 1973.

My parents, Bea and John McTeer,
on their wedding day, October 8, 1949,
in Hamilton, Ontario.

Joe and I on our wedding day.
June 30, 1973.

Catherine and her happy parents on
her wedding day, the National Gallery
of Canada, Ottawa. June 8, 2002.

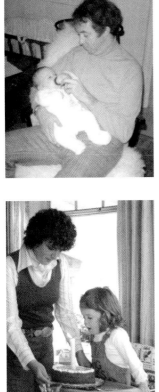

(top) Joe bottle-feeding baby
Catherine, Stornoway.
Winter 1977.

Christmas at Stornoway, 1981.
Our Great Dane, Taffy, was a somewhat
reluctant participant.

With Catherine on her third
birthday, at 24 Sussex Drive.
November 6, 1979.

Catherine welcomes former Prime
Minister John Diefenbaker to the
annual Press Gallery reception at
Stornoway. June 1978.

My first official picture as wife of the leader of the Opposition. Spring 1976.

Greeting guests at the annual diplomatic Christmas reception, Lester B. Pearson Building, Ottawa. December 1986. (inset) Reading to young students from my book on Parliament as part of the Parliamentary Spouses Literacy Program, 1986.

Joe addresses supporters after the defeat at the 1983 leadership convention.

Catherine and Joe at a Yellowhead constituency event in Alberta. 1984.

The first day of campaigning in my federal election bid. September 1988.

Greeting Prince Charles and Diana,
Princess of Wales, at a state dinner at
Rideau Hall. 1983.

An audience with Pope John Paul II. Also present are
Canada's ambassador to the Holy See, His Excellency
Pat Black and Mrs. Black. January 1989.

Speaking with former Quebec
Premier René Lévesque at the
Shamrock Summit,
Quebec City, 1985.

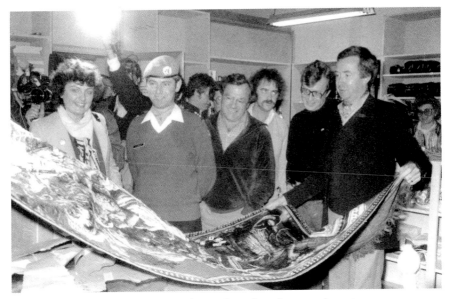

Receiving the gift of a rug from Canadian peacekeepers
in the Golan Heights. January 1979.

Joe and I with Nelson Mandela at a Commonwealth ministerial meeting on
Southern Africa. Abuja, 1991.

Catherine joins us for a caucus Christmas party on Parliament Hill. December 1999.

Catherine and Chad on the campaign trail during the 2000 federal election.

Catherine with me (above) at a Calgary campaign event in 2000; and with her aunt Jane McTeer on Catherine's wedding day.

being the victim of political zealotry and brutal repression. She could still find forgiveness and once again have faith in her future. I felt humbled by her strength and optimism. It was an important moment for me. I realized that I could not waste any more time lamenting deceit and underhandedness in politics and that I had to forgive and move on for my own sake and sanity. She had said it had been hard to forgive and I cannot even begin to imagine what that meant for her. She was an example of strength and inner calm, and I would always think of her whenever I felt my own lot in life was unfair or difficult.

I had always dreamed of seeing the Great Wall of China. I still have a picture of Joe and me on a sun-filled day as we struggled up the slippery stone road that tops the wall itself. I have seen different parts of the wall on subsequent trips, but climbing it for the first time, surrounded by students and soldiers from all corners of China, was an unforgettable experience. What struck me at the time was how we all behave the same when we are tourists. Bill Chambers was constantly being asked to take pictures of couples and groups as they, too, marvelled at the sites and saw their own architectural and historical monuments for the first time. The Great Wall was one such monumental engineering feat; and I thought of the work and planning that could create this road, which served as both a barrier to China's enemies and a transportation link across its vast geography.

On another night we were offered toast upon toast of maotai, a clear 150-proof Chinese liquor that seared our throats and fogged our minds. I kept passing my full glass to Bill Chambers until it was obvious that he could drink no more. I remember seeing the waiter pouring water into the host's glasses while he then poured liquor into ours. I took our host's glass and handed him mine just before the next round of toasts. He looked at me and smiled; he knew the jig was up. He spoke to the waiter and I was brought a glass of Coca-Cola. Just before we left Guangzhou we had another dinner, where Joe was introduced as "the Bright Honourable Joe Clark." Just as he rose to speak, fireworks started on the street below. We were all surprised and giddy. Upon thanking our hosts for the special fireworks, our translator whispered to us that they had been for a wedding dinner in the banquet room next door.

When you are in a foreign country and cannot speak the language, you are totally at the mercy of local translators. One night Joe and I talked about what we had learned that day and felt we had missed a lot in the translation. We decided that the main problem with our translator had been his youth. Born during the Cultural Revolution, he knew no other history of his country than what he presented to us, since the goal of that terrible period seemed to have been the denial of knowledge and learning. Discussion was limited to pat answers and political thought to simple slogans. Our young guide just did not know the answers to most of the questions Joe had asked him. His mind was rigid, stunted by an education that filled him with pre-set certainties at the expense of real thought. (I would see this in other closed societies, too, when I travelled with Joe later in the 1980s.) A week later in Shanghai, we were assigned another translator, who acted as our guide during the rest of our trip. She was an older woman who had been a child during World War II and had witnessed the years of the Cultural Revolution through the eyes of a discerning adult. Her education was formal, extensive and had been enhanced by her own experiences over the years as a translator to foreigners. She told us about the history of what we were seeing, not just the physical dimensions of the sites. She was sensitive to our lack of context as foreigners, explaining why people wore what they did, and what stories were important to the people we met. When we left her, I offered her a scarf I had brought from Canada as a gift. I thought it would brighten up her grey suit. She looked embarrassed and explained that she could not accept it; there would be questions. At the last minute, I went to a store in Shanghai and bought her a Chinese scarf and tried again. She accepted, telling me she could wear this scarf, as she would not stand out.

We had been advised by China hands to start in Beijing and end in Hong Kong, and we decided to take the train between Guangzhou, formerly Canton, and Hong Kong and stop in Shenzhen along the way. As we travelled south, I took pictures of the countryside dotted with water buffalo and parade lines of ducks waddling along in single file. Within the next decade, the entire landscape would change and there would be construction everywhere. In Shenzhen, thousands of young people from the far-flung provinces worked in factories by day and boarded in huge dorms by night. For the first time since our arrival in China, we were able to watch television, which apparently the young people could do too, as part of the nightly entertainment in their dorms. If it is true that open communications and television are the great equalizers, then an entire generation was learning about the greener pastures that lay just beyond its borders.

Just before we left Shenzhen, I went shopping at a huge store with Brenda Yates, one of our travel companions that trip. Wherever we went, Brenda's blond hair and blue eyes attracted a crowd. We felt like the Pied Piper as we were followed by young and old alike through the mega retail store. At one point we stopped to look at little clocks that we thought might make good gifts for family and staff back home. As we stood at the counter, three people deep, I felt something pecking at my leg. Looking down, I was startled to see a big red chicken in a mesh bag. Beside it hung a large dead carp, speared through a wrought-iron hook. The two old men who were carrying them were looking curiously at clocks, discussing them in some detail. Sent to buy lunch at the local market nearby, they had obviously taken a detour through this new Western-style store to see the many products on display.

After the rigours of travel within China, Hong Kong was a marvel for us all. We splurged and stayed at the Mandarin hotel. When we weren't sightseeing, we shopped. Terry Yates organized a wonderful surprise fiftieth birthday for Brenda, and we danced and enjoyed ourselves all evening. We all insisted that we would celebrate together ten years hence, and promised to come back to see how the country had changed. Of course, we all have made such promises over the years and we never did manage to make a return trip.

I realized that this had been one of the first trips of my married life during which we were unconcerned about domestic politics or academic deadlines. Later, when Joe was Canada's foreign minister, I would have a chance to see many countries in Asia, and to learn about their varied histories and several distinct cultures. But for me, this first trip to China will always be the highlight.

We returned to Ottawa in late May with the election frenzy in full swing. Catherine had two more weeks of school and I prepared for our move out of our house on John Street. Our belongings would be put in storage over the summer and we would live in a friend's cottage on Lake Edith in Jasper. An election call was expected within weeks and Joe began to campaign immediately, first in his own riding and then in ridings where former supporters were running. On our wedding anniversary, the newly elected Liberal leader John Turner became Canada's Prime Minister. While he had almost another year before he was required to call an election, he decided to capitalize on all the publicity and press attention from the leadership campaign that month. A general election was called for September 4.

I resigned myself to a summer without Joe. While he was campaigning across Canada, I would be campaigning in his Yellowhead riding in Alberta. In early July I was joined in Jasper by Susan Baxter, who came over the university holidays to help care for Catherine. As in previous elections, Joe's brother, Peter, joined me campaigning door to door, at country fairs and at public events in the riding. Joe volunteered to help the national campaign in any way he could and divided his time that summer between his own seat in Alberta and constituencies in the rest of the country. The national campaign was going very well. Brian and Mila were excellent campaigners and the momentum was building for a PC victory. There were no real issues that dominated the campaign to drag us down as had been the case with wage and price controls in 1974 or eighteen-cent gas in 1980.

While John Turner and the Liberal party enjoyed the usual blip in popularity that comes with any leadership campaign, they had serious troubles internally, especially in Quebec. There, many organizers for defeated candidate Jean Chrétien were content to sit out the campaign and lick their wounds. Brian, on the other hand, had crafted a coalition of federalists and nationalists in Quebec, which was unheard of in PC electoral history. It was one of his greatest strengths and gave him real depth of support there where others before him had failed. He was the only person who could have done this, and his success in Quebec would guarantee his victory. It was a bittersweet turn of events for Joe, who had tried so hard over the years to win the hearts and votes of Quebeckers.

While our election organization was important, two events during the campaign would boost Brian, and banish John Turner to opposition. The first was the leaders' debates. Brian scored a direct hit on the new Prime Minister on the question of ethics, when he condemned him for not overturning Pierre Trudeau's shameless last flurry of public appointments. An attack on Liberal patronage would help elect Brian Mulroney. The second was John Turner's famous pat on Iona Campagnolo's backside during the campaign. It showed not just bad judgment and poor manners, it came to symbolize an arrogant and out-dated party out of step with most Canadians, led by a man from another generation. At forty-five, Brian was much younger in age and outlook and ran as a leader of the future.

On September 4, Canadians gave Mulroney the largest victory in Canadian political history. On election night, the PCs won 211 seats compared with 40 for the Liberals and 30 for the NDP. For the first time since John Diefenbaker's 1958 election victory, the party had swept Quebec, winning 58 seats to the Liberals' 17. In Ontario, the province that ensures government victories, the PCs took 67 seats and the Liberals 14, one more than the NDP. It was a rout for Turner's Liberals and a clear demonstration of what happens to political parties when leaders stay too long in office. The Liberals had been defined by Pierre Trudeau and had let their political infrastructure grow weak. The PCs, on the other hand, gained new people, especially in Quebec, many of whom were good organizers.

Many of the new MPs were elected on the wave that swept Brian Mulroney to office and they owed their seats to him. The majority were political neophytes, but there was a core of seasoned parliamentarians, like Joe, Flora, Mike Wilson, Sinclair Stevens, Robert René de Cotret, Ray Hnatyshyn, Erik Nielsen, John Crosbie, Don Mazankowski, Jake Epp, John Fraser, Perrin Beatty and Elmer MacKay. All had been ministers in 1979 and knew how to run a department. Brian had a few people to pay back, including oldies like George Hees and Bob Coates, but generally his huge majority gave him free rein to name whomever he wanted and he chose a highly able team.

As we celebrated Joe's own re-election that night, I wondered if Brian would include Joe in the cabinet. I had urged Joe not to run if he would only be a backbencher, as that would be an untenable position for a former Prime Minister and party leader. He reminded me that his reason for running was to improve Canada and, while he could do that more effectively in cabinet, he would not seek to influence Brian's decision one way or the other. As it turned out, Brian asked Joe to join the cabinet as secretary of state for external affairs and Joe accepted. It struck me as a perfect solution for both of them. Brian had made an important gesture and Joe would be on the road a great deal, presenting Canada's face to the world in trade and foreign policy.

We returned to Ottawa the day after the election and went our different ways—Joe and Bill Chambers to the Westin hotel, within walking distance of the Parliament Buildings for Joe's first cabinet meeting the next morning, and Catherine and I to our new home near Aylmer, Quebec, where we camped out for the night in sleeping bags. The moving trucks were to come at eight the next morning, and my mother arrived early with coffee and muffins and stayed to wait for the movers while I drove Catherine to her new school. On that morning in early September, after all we had been through since 1976, I felt relieved for the first time in years. I could see that Joe would enjoy his new job and that I was free to move on to another stage in my own life. As I watched the television reports that night of the new cabinet, I felt it was the first day of a new and exciting decade for both of us.

14

WHEN JOE WAS CANADA'S FOREIGN MINISTER from 1984 to 1991, I often had the opportunity to travel with him. On these official trips, I was expected to attend formal events with Joe, and there was often a separate program for the wives. I had decided before starting to accompany him that unless I changed the role expected of me on these trips, I would weigh a ton before the four years were out. All spousal programs seem to assume that women's main interests are eating and shopping. Both pursuits are great in moderation, but I felt guilty overindulging in countries where poverty was endemic and women could barely feed their families. The question was, How could I politely do this and not insult host countries whose officials often wanted me to see only the new buildings and the urban success stories? I started by asking to visit community projects sponsored by the Canadian International Development Agency (CIDA) or by mission-administered Canada Funds from our embassy or high commission in the country in question. Many of these were in rural areas, which allowed me to leave the city and visit with women in their own villages. I could then see how women lived and worked in communities that often had few services and even fewer opportunities for women and girls to be educated. One thing that impressed me on these visits was the sheer force of women's innovation and determination in the countries of the developing world.

From the beginning, Joe's department helped me set my own schedule in each country. Before leaving Canada we were given expert written and verbal briefings on the countries we would be visiting, their political system and leadership and the current issues they faced. After our arrival in each country, I was guided in my own meetings and touring by the ambassador's spouse or by a member of our embassy or high commission. As I carried out my own role on behalf of Canada during these years, I had several interests and goals. As well as seeing how women lived in the countries we visited, I wanted to better understand each country's legal system. These would give me an idea of how, if the country was interested, Canada might help them achieve legal changes that would enhance their population's human rights and achieve greater equality for women. I wanted to indulge my love of art and culture by visiting their national museums and galleries. Finally, I wanted to speak with the opinion leaders in each country to learn more about their challenges and public policies. This was for my own education, but it also gave the embassy staff who accompanied me access to senior government officials and ministers and a contact for their work in the future.

As Canada's foreign minister, Joe focused on how Canadians were making a difference in the world. We learned about the role Canadians were playing as missionaries, doctors, aid workers and businesspeople, and I thought of ways I could contribute, too. Joe made a point, whenever he could, of travelling outside the major centres to broaden his understanding of the issues that affected the lives of real people in each country. It also gave him a chance to see Canadian foreign aid projects in action, and to assess their success directly. During these travels, I was always impressed with the intelligence and perceptiveness of Canada's foreign service officers. As a rule, a junior officer was assigned to accompany me to meetings and into the countryside to visit Canadian aid projects for local women. These officers were often young and willing to share with me their perspectives on a country. Most had insights born of direct experience, for unlike the ambassador or high commissioner, they were not chauffeured around and received at the highest levels. They stood in line for services and dealt with mid-level bureaucrats, local shopkeepers and acquaintances, and had the education and the savvy to analyze what they saw. I remember particularly the Canadian ambassador's spouse offering a lunch in my honour in Belgrade during a meeting of non-aligned countries in the late 1980s. There seemed a real tension among the guests whenever the conversation turned to the government, and I remarked on this to the young embassy staffer who was with me. She replied gravely that all her local friends told her that ethnic tensions in Yugoslavia were extreme and would likely erupt into civil war.

I often spent time with the ambassador's spouse, usually a woman. As a rule, she would host a lunch in the official residence for me to which women writers, journalists and artists were invited. This gave me a chance to speak with people whom I would rarely meet otherwise. My hope was to see the country through eyes not directly involved in politics. In each country I learned what was unique to women living there, and what bound them to women everywhere else.

A pattern emerged that troubled me and challenged me to respond. Joe had assumed his position as minister just after the Beijing World Conference on Women in 1984. That conference had stayed in the minds of many women I met in the seven years he was minister. I remember visiting the Middle East with him around that time and joining women at our embassy in Riyadh, Saudi Arabia, for lunch. I had had my share of excitement by the time I arrived, as on the way over to the residence my car had blown a tire and the driver would not stop until the tire rim had been destroyed and the car could no longer be driven. At my insistence, the protocol officer reluctantly agreed to flag down a passing car, and we were driven to the embassy by two men and a four-year-old boy with a red ball. He stared at us shyly the whole journey. At the residence I greeted my guests, who all arrived wearing black abayas, their heads covered in black scarves. It occurred to me suddenly that the stares from the little boy had been in part because we were strangers, but mainly because we were uncovered and wearing our brightly coloured spring suits. After lunch we spoke about women's roles and rights in the region, and I speculated that perhaps the Beijing conference would begin to break down barriers to women's equality in each of our countries. One guest looked at me askance and asked if I had not seen their delegation in Beijing. I told her that I had not attended and suddenly realized that their representatives at that conference had been men. "It is unlikely major changes towards women's equality will come here in my lifetime," the most activist among them remarked. They all agreed that the Beijing conference had served a symbolic role but that it would have little impact on the daily lives of women in most countries of the world.

This statement would be echoed in every country I visited during those seven years of travel. Yet the women I met always wanted change for themselves and their families. Women whom I met alone or in groups lamented the lack of social and economic policies to improve their lives and resented their lack of political and economic influence. The depth of their anger and frustration at being excluded from power pervaded even the most ordinary social event I attended. The intensity of their emotion varied depending on the country, but women's equality and rights remained potent and emotional topics wherever women gathered to greet me. Many had decided to forget about influencing national decisions, turning instead to their local communities, where they could more readily address issues like education, health care and jobs for women. I met hundreds of women who had been denied an education but fought all the harder for their daughters' opportunities to learn. I met women in Asia who had been denied bank loans and had banded together to create co-operatives to invest and borrow among themselves. The resourcefulness of these women was a powerful lesson to me and opened my eyes to my future commitment to women's health. I remember reading a speech by Margaret Catley-Carlson, a former head of CIDA, who wrote: "Educate a woman and you educate a community." After visiting as many countries as she had during her tenure as Canada's senior aid official internationally, I saw that this was more than a tidy slogan. It acknowledged her discovery that all countries, including our own, are better served when women are encouraged to play a full and mature role in the running of their communities. It is a goal that I believe we must achieve, even though I know it is still far beyond the reach of most women in the world.

My own direct observations of the development projects sponsored by CIDA showed me some of the ways Canadian tax dollars were achieving that goal. One of the most productive involved micro-credit. Women long denied credit from banks could find funding through co-operatives and small loans from funds set aside through our aid money. The loans rarely exceeded one hundred dollars but they worked miracles in the hands of women used to thrift and hard work. I remember meeting with women in one Indonesian village where they told me their stories of entrepreneurial success. One woman had borrowed ten dollars to buy a sow. She had bred it, raised the litter and sold half the resulting piglets at market. She paid off the loan and borrowed more money to buy other sows. Soon she needed help and more land. After three years she provided all the pork needed in her village and employed all her sons-in-law. Another woman told me about how she had started her corner store. She used a hundred-dollar loan to buy cases of goods to sell outside her house. This meant she did not have to buy each item individually as she had previously had to do. She paid off her loan and after a year added a new room to her house to use as a store and employed her daughter and her grandson. Prior to receiving such credit assistance, these women had been forced to rely on moneylenders who charged usurious interest on the money they lent. They could now depend on low- or no-interest micro-loans and Canadian officials told me that the repayment rate neared 100 percent.

The ambassador or high commissioner and their staff also had access to Canada Funds to support special projects. Although minuscule by Canadian standards, the amounts distributed in this way are significant in many of the world's countries and fund every kind of project, from culture to education and health care. I remember a special health care project Canada funded in the "Garbage City" in Cairo where more than a million people live and make their living as human recyclers of the tons of garbage that city generates each day. Here, a small amount of money given by Canada to two Belgian nuns was used to buy clean razor blades for the maternity clinic they ran. This small gift saved the lives of countless babies who would have died otherwise of septic poisoning when their umbilical cords were severed with glass from broken bottles found in the garbage heap that was home to their mothers.

And so it went on, project after project, women offering their families and each other a better chance at health and opportunity. Some days I would return to my hotel exhausted by the passions of women who still fought for fairness and equality despite all the obstacles set in their path. It was at moments like these that I so appreciated my own good luck. I had never really seen my own country through the eyes of others abroad, and I now understood just how special a place Canada is. From this awakening came a personal need to give more than I had before, and I began to think of how I might do this. My commitment to that point had been unformed. I decided to focus on women's health and legal-institution building.

I understood early on that the financial needs of women and children in the many countries we visited were overwhelming and unending. Reluctantly I had to accept that I could never answer all the pleas for help that I received as I travelled with Joe. Nor was there a guarantee that my efforts would have any impact at all on changing political systems and inefficient bureaucracies. I did not have enough money of my own to give endlessly to every request, so I decided to dedicate specific amounts from my writing and speeches to special projects that would directly benefit the daily lives of women and children. I tried to encourage others I knew to help where they could.

I remember visiting Central America with Joe in the late 1980s and touring a daycare centre run by nuns for the children of women who worked in the market. These women sold trinkets or even themselves in order to feed their families. Before the nuns opened this centre, the women had been forced to leave their children alone during the day, tied in their cribs or in the care of children barely old enough to look after themselves. Now, for a very small sum, the nuns received the babies, toddlers and pre-school-age children each morning, bathed and fed them, gave them a set of clean clothes and washed the soiled ones. They had breakfast, lunch and a snack before their mothers picked them up at the end of each day. When I toured this daycare centre, the babies were lying on plastic mattresses in the heat of the day. Their clothes, although very clean, were old and tattered. As a woman and a Roman Catholic, I deeply admired these nuns. On my way out, one of them noted that they could use some help, and I promised to do what I could. Later that trip I met two other missionary nuns who lived in a place with a corrugated roof. They suffered from extreme heat in the summer and the roof leaked during the rainy season.

When I returned home, I gave two speeches and sent the money to both places to help them with their work. I then decided to activate my own network of women friends and gave a little talk to several of them about the children's need for clothes and bedding. Many of them immediately cleared their cupboards and gave cotton crib sheets and baby clothes that their own children no longer needed. From then on, I tried to do two things when I met with women in the developing countries we visited. I asked what materials they needed and upon my return to Canada sought contributions from friends. And I always tried to involve as many of my friends as possible, urging them to widen the circle to their own friends. I knew that while many of them could not give cash, they had other items of use to donate.

Some people may say that this seems like a very "female" thing to do as a political wife. But while such small efforts are rarely noticed they affected the daily lives of women and children in a direct way in countries where war and poverty often reduce them to misery. I was not at the high-level meeting tables on these trips, but that did not mean I had no role. That is one of the most rewarding parts of helping out internationally—no matter how small or large your contribution, it is always needed and usually very welcome.

In the developing world, it is typically women who carry the heaviest burdens, as they are forced to do so much with so little. Women and children in the countries we visited benefited from the gifts offered by Canadians more fortunate than they were. My friends and I gained a chance to learn and to contribute to the bettering of their lives.

These efforts served a more subtle purpose as well. In speaking with community and political leaders wherever I went, and by seeing so much of these countries myself, I was able to round out Joe's perspective of places. This was particularly important as his ministerial schedule was usually full of high-profile diplomatic meetings, leaving him with little time to see the social, legal and cultural landscape for himself. I also had the luxury of being received with less formality than he did, and that gave me an access and insight that was easily missed when Joe arrived in his official capacity. Both of us were committed to women's equality and saw the main way to improve women's lives was through the work of CIDA and other NGOs. We understood that women would strive to ensure stability and prosperity in their country if given a chance, and that was what we tried to help them achieve.

One of the best decisions Joe and I made during this period was to bring Catherine with us whenever we could. When she was ten she joined me in Thailand to visit a school in a slum near Bangkok. She followed close behind me as we crossed the planks that formed bridges over open sewers in a slum where over a million people lived without water, proper plumbing or electricity. Families lived side by side in huts, and the smells of their cooking pots mingled with that of the open sewers in the humid heat. When we arrived at the school chosen by the ambassador for a gift of some two thousand dollars, we were met by children who sang for us and shyly surrounded Catherine to look at her fair hair and blue eyes. She sat on the floor with them and the children giggled and whispered to each other. Their teacher had just won a prestigious award from Thailand's king for her teaching work. A child of the slum herself, she had become a teacher through correspondence courses and had chosen to stay and teach there with her husband.

This visit was Catherine's first to a slum and it made a real impression on her. The Pope had visited Canada earlier, and at the time Catherine had asked why he bent to kiss the ground when he arrived in Ottawa. "He is thanking God for bringing him safely to his destination," I told her. Upon our return to Canada Catherine asked if she and Joe could go outside at our stop at the Vancouver airport. I told her that we were in transit and confined to the lounge, and asked why she wanted to go out on such a hot day. "I want to kiss the ground," she told me. "I want to thank God for making me a Canadian." I had sometimes felt that we took Catherine out of school too often while Joe was foreign minister, but after this episode I saw that all these experiences were themselves an education and made her a more compassionate and caring person, aware of her own good fortune. That Christmas, we decided to contribute to PLAN, an international development NGO, to sponsor a child in Asia, and Catherine sent a card to all her cousins announcing her "little sister." Since then we have continued to sponsor children and have watched PLAN use the money to educate these children and support their communities with schools and hospitals.

During the years that I travelled with Joe, and later when I was helping as an election monitor in Africa and the Caribbean, I was always heartened by the imagination and energy of Canadians working to help developing countries. It is a vocation for them and they give up their own comforts to live in countries where poverty and war are commonplace. I doubt if I could do this kind of work, but that does not mean that I cannot help in other ways. These years gave us both a chance to see Canada through the eyes of the world, and the world through Canadian eyes. We found them among the most rewarding years of our public life together, and we see ourselves now as citizens of the world, not just Canada.

15

HILLARY RODHAM CLINTON WAS HAILED as a trailblazer when, while her husband was President, she ran successfully for the U.S. Senate. But some Canadians were there first. Joe and I broke political tradition when we became the first couple to run for Parliament at the same time, during the 1988 federal general election. It had been done provincially before by couples in opposition parties, but not in federal politics and never when one of them was in cabinet. Running in different seats, in different provinces, was a real challenge. Naturally, it would have been more satisfying if we had both won. But the very initiative had a lasting impact and, among other things, redefined the role of political couples in Canada. Now, no wife of a cabinet minister or Prime Minister will be prevented from pursuing her own career because that is "not her role." Examples abound in Ottawa today of women married to senior politicians who are enjoying active careers in business, the public sector and the professions. Unfortunately, I cannot think of any who are also involved in politics.

As 1987 was drawing to a close, I began to think about running for Parliament in the election expected the following year. It had been something I had planned to do for a long time, but other events always intervened. It was time to act. In late January, several friends urged me to consider running in the newly formed riding of Carleton-Gloucester, east and south of Ottawa. It was a riding marked by considerable urban-rural splits and by a real French-English tension. During the early months of 1988 the question of what it would mean for our family if I were to run for Parliament was very much on my mind, and Joe and I spent many an hour discussing it. He had assumed that I would run one day and felt that if ever there was a time, it was now. It was a new seat, there was no incumbent and the PC Party was in power and able to help with organization and manpower. We discussed how Catherine, then twelve and entering the teen years, would handle it and decided to ask her opinion. She was very excited. Catherine had grown up in politics; it was the only life she knew. She understood what was involved and had been too young to really remember the very bad times in 1980 and 1983. I had not forgotten them, though, and wondered whether it was the best choice for the three of us. I called my sister Jane, who said that if I decided to run, she would take a month's leave of absence from her job at the Ottawa Children's Aid Society to travel with me full-time. Susan Baxter had finished university, was married and lived nearby. She and her husband, David, said they would help with Catherine's care and the campaign. My mother was reluctant to see me run. She knew what it meant and did not want to see me hurt. But, like Jane, she committed her help if I made the decision to run.

There were some political issues in the riding that could hurt my chances, including government cutbacks to the federal public service and the Medical Research Council, situated within the riding's boundaries. Free trade with the United States was another issue. It was popular in Quebec, southwestern Ontario and the West, but not in eastern Ontario, and I wasn't sure if it would be a winning issue or an albatross around my neck. Of greater concern was the voting history of Ottawans. Most Ottawa ridings traditionally voted Liberal in federal elections, but in the 1984 sweep we had won several ridings.

I had many contacts in the new riding and had grown up on the edge of its eastern boundary. I was fluently bilingual, able to debate and speak effectively in public and enjoyed a high recognition among voters. I had an enthusiastic group of supporters who wanted me to run. I was a prominent woman married to a man who was liked and respected. Interest in the outcome would be high in the media and among the public. After consulting my family and friends in the party, I decided to run for the nomination set for April 1988. I let the Prime Minister's office know of my plans to seek the nomination. While I did not expect his endorsement, I felt I owed him the courtesy.

At the PC national general meeting in Edmonton in 2002, Kim Puddister of Newfoundland noted that women and men consider becoming a candidate from opposite starting points. Men, flattered, ask themselves, "Well, why not?" and look for reasons to run. Women start by listing all the negative arguments, real and imagined. That process of worrying doesn't stop when a woman decides to run.

Three factors in particular weighed on my mind. Joe was a senior minister in the government, and I wanted to be certain that my presence, if elected, would not undermine his status there. While his professional relationship with Brian Mulroney was cordial, I had no doubt that it would be hard for me in caucus were I to be elected. I also feared that his political opponents in his constituency would argue that in the case of a conflict about government policy, he would give in to the interests of eastern Canada rather than those of the West in order to help me and to keep peace in our marriage. That was particularly worrying, as Preston Manning, the head of the Reform Party, was running against Joe in Yellowhead. It was an argument that the Liberal candidate in my riding used against me.

My concern about Catherine had been resolved by her enthusiasm about my possible candidacy. But I knew the teen years were difficult and felt that my task as a parent was only half complete. No one knew better than I did the price a family pays for one parent in active politics. I wanted to be sure she would not suffer if my pursuit of a parliamentary seat meant that both her parents were politicians. I decided that her enthusiasm and the fact that I would be running in a seat close to home outweighed the possible drawbacks of two political parents.

It would be expensive for both of us to run. It costs a lot for one person in a family to run for Parliament, let alone two. The cost of Joe's serving the public in Parliament had led to significant personal debt over the years. To meet this concern, I enlisted the help of Alex Siversky, a friend of my late father's, who put together an excellent fundraising team. With the help of other close friends, like Stella Torontow of Ottawa, the necessary funds were raised from contributions from across Canada for both the nomination and election campaigns. My national profile was to be a real blessing in terms of this election effort, as so many people, especially women, sent contributions. I spent one hundred thousand dollars to win the nomination and run in the election. This is peanuts in the American context, where it costs millions even to run for mayor of a large city. But for women in Canada, even this lesser amount can be prohibitive.

In running for Parliament in 1988, I hoped to achieve several things. I wanted to see first-hand what it was like to present and pass the laws by which we are governed. I wanted to put my legal training to work for all Canadians. I felt that I could be an effective voice for my constituents and for women and other equality seekers in developing and setting public policy. And I wanted to build upon my own national and international experiences to be an agent of cohesion and change. I had met too many Canadians who felt excluded or unrepresented in our parliamentary system, and I thought that I could help overcome that distance between government and the "governed."

I first had to win my party's nomination against two other candidates. One was a young Ottawa lawyer and the other an older doctor representing the local pro-life groups. Joe helped me put together a top-notch nomination team and came with me to meet the key PC supporters in the riding. I knew many of them from provincial politics and valued their help as I sought the nomination. At nomination meetings, the people who sell the most membership tickets and get their vote out win. My team went to work, and I asked Mike Calnan, a retired colonel and supporter, to take charge of the logistics for the nomination meeting. That night, we were very organized, and our supporters turned out in large numbers. It seemed strange to be back in the Civic Centre where we had lived through such highs in 1976 and such terrible moments during the 1983 leadership convention. As my name was placed in nomination, Joe and Catherine hugged me and I went down to give my speech. Our roles were reversed, and later that night Joe told me how odd it was for him to sit in the audience cheering rather than being on stage speaking. I gave a good speech, setting out why I wanted to represent the new riding and why I thought I would be the best candidate to do so.

Then we voted and waited. It took longer than expected, and I was beginning to worry that something had gone wrong. We had agreed that if we had to go to a second ballot, our lead scrutineer, Scott McCord, would not wear a tie as he left the room where the votes were being counted. If we had won, he would don the loudest one he owned. Scott emerged without a tie, and Mike and his organization team launched into action for a second ballot. It turned out that Scott had simply forgotten to put on his tie! I had won on the first ballot. All my supporters were delighted and, after their initial scare, were ready to celebrate. I returned to the stage and thanked my opponents, inviting them to support me and the party. The young lawyer had come second and moved to make the vote unanimous. The pro-life candidate refused. I could see that this issue would continue to dog me throughout the election.

I campaigned all through the summer and knocked on thousands of doors between my nomination and election day on November 21. I had an excellent campaign team, with David Small, a well-known local PC political strategist, as campaign manager, and the late Tim Ralfe, a former journalist, handling the media along with freelance journalist and friend Kelly McGillis. Lawyers Bill and Rosemary Simpson handled policy and legal matters, and the late Fran Kelly took charge of my schedule. Anne McDougall was the office manager, and my sister Jane travelled to every event with me. Four people ran against me that election—a municipal councillor for the Liberals, a young university student for the NDP, a lawyer for the Heritage party and a singer from Newfoundland for the Rhinoceros party.

It seemed strange at first to be campaigning for myself and not for Joe. But I was a seasoned campaigner and knew what was expected of candidates. What was difficult was not having Joe there every day to give me guidance and support. I had taken for granted that I could handle campaigning, but underestimated how lonely it was to be without him, only able to talk to him on the phone each day. He did come into the riding to campaign with me. At the first door we put both out our hands and introduced ourselves at the same time, forcing the surprised voter to put out his two hands in response. We burst into gales of laughter.

Our polls showed that the number-one issue for the all the candidates in eastern Ontario was free trade with the United States. The Liberals had very cleverly done two things on this issue. They had raised the concern among dairy farmers throughout the region that free trade would mean an end to their milk quotas. For most farmers this was the most valuable asset they owned. Second, the Liberals had insisted that free trade would end medicare, requiring Canadians to pay for their health care. To make the point, they had their candidates pull out a credit card in a crowd of older people and shout, "Do you have a credit card? Well, you'll need one if the FTA is passed. You'll have to pay for your health care." People were frightened by this tactic and later voted to protect their interests. Of all the people I met during the campaign only two had read the Free Trade Agreement documents. Yet by the end of the campaign, more than 65 percent of those who responded to an opinion poll carried out for my campaign declared their opposition to the agreement. I spent the entire campaign trying to appease constituents' fears that the Mulroney government would give too much away to the Americans in the negotiations, and that it was impossible for Canadians to ever win against the Americans, even if the agreement was a good one. The Liberals played it well, solemnly promising to abolish free trade the minute they were elected, a promise they did not keep.

A second election issue was a sleeper, raised near the end of the campaign. As part of its economic platform the Mulroney government had hinted at making the tax system fairer by eliminating the manufacturers' sales tax and replacing it with what would become the infamous GST. The Liberals opposed it vehemently and, as with the Free Trade Agreement, promised to abolish it the moment they were elected. (Of course, they never did.) They had raised the GST issue as a national campaign issue very late in the 1988 election, and in eastern Ontario it seemed to take hold. It became the final straw in all but two of the twenty-four campaigns in the region.

While it was not a significant factor in terms of actual votes in Carleton-Gloucester, I was dogged by the abortion issue during the entire campaign, at the instigation of the pro-life candidate for the Christian Heritage Party. My views on abortion had been public for many years and I repeated them frequently during the campaign. I believe that the decision to terminate a pregnancy must be taken by the pregnant woman herself and not the state. While I oppose abortion personally and would not counsel it, I do not believe that the solution lies in forcing pregnant women to carry an unwanted pregnancy to term or risk their health and safety at the hands of illegal abortionists. I met with the Archbishop of Hull (in whose diocese we then resided) before the election was called and explained my position to him directly. He raised no objections, and I thought the matter was settled. Tragically, the Archbishop drowned in a nearby lake during the summer of 1988. When he died, it was as if our meeting had never happened. During the campaign, I was subject to continuous attacks from pro-life supporters at all-candidate meetings. This abuse reached its peak just before election day, when I had to threaten an auxiliary bishop in Ottawa with legal action for libel and slander for publicly misrepresenting my position. He retracted but the damage had been done. I learned to my regret that there is no middle ground possible on the abortion issue, nor is there respect for the views of others by many of those who call themselves "pro-life."

I remember campaigning one evening with some of my team in an affluent suburban neighbourhood. Catherine was with me, running back and forth to the car with a volunteer to get pamphlets for our canvassers on the street. I had instructed my workers that for security reasons, she could not come to the doors. Unfortunately, a new campaign recruit was with us that night and was persuaded by a well-dressed and pleasant woman to bring Catherine to the door to say hello. I arrived at the door, annoyed that this was happening, just as Catherine was shaking the woman's hand. The woman said to her, "Hello, Catherine. I've always wanted to meet you. I've always wanted to tell you how happy your mother would have been had she aborted you." I was stunned. Catherine recoiled, saying, "You're sick." I grabbed her and left, struggling against my desire to level the woman on her own doorstep.

That night Catherine and I sat together at home. Joe was in his riding and I had called him to ask his advice. He suggested I speak to her frankly about what was happening. As we sat there, Catherine asked, "What's abortion, Mom? People keep talking about it, saying you want to kill babies." How, I thought, does one explain to a child the complexity and the pain of this kind of personal tragedy? I decided to take the next day off and we stayed home together, talking endlessly about the issue and why I was being targeted by those who wanted the laws changed to make abortion a criminal offence again. By the end of the day, I felt she knew where I stood and saw that it was both a very personal and extremely complicated issue. I then finally addressed the doubt and fear that this nasty woman had raised in Catherine's young mind. I told her that I could never have considered an abortion, not just for religious reasons, but because I had so wanted a child. I told her that she was the light of my life and of her father's and that her presence made our lives happy and whole. I told her that neither her father nor I could imagine life without her in it. The two of us sat there together on the couch with Mickey, our German shepherd, nuzzling our legs. Dogs always know when something is wrong, and had she been allowed, she would have been on the couch with us. That night Catherine and I slept together surrounded by the regular cast of stuffed toys from her own bed. We even let Mickey sleep beside the bed rather than at her normal place, guarding the top of the stairs. We awoke the next day stronger and ready for the remaining weeks of the campaign.

The coming days were very difficult. On the weekend before the vote, there were calls for my excommunication and electoral defeat from many pulpits. While polling showed that fewer than six percent of those who voted did so on the basis of the abortion issue, it became one of the most upsetting parts of the entire campaign. Ironically, its sheer ugliness did two positive things. It mobilized my support and increased the number of women and men who, angry at my treatment, came out to support my campaign. And more important to me personally, it brought Catherine and me closer as she started her teen years.

There were threats sufficient to require the presence of the RCMP while I campaigned. While it concerned me that anyone would want to hurt me for campaigning for what I believed in, I was more concerned about Catherine's safety. There are few things more devastating to a mother than to know that her professional choices might endanger her family, and it was a blow to my sense of self that I could not protect Catherine. With a few days left in what was becoming a very bitter campaign, we agreed that I would send Catherine west to be with Joe. While I rode in a parade in the riding the Saturday before the vote, Jane put her on a plane for Edmonton. There she was kept busy with her cousin Andrew, and was protected by her father and his security. I finished the campaign without the two of them. My older sister, Colleen, took time off from teaching and came down from her home in Haileybury in northern Ontario to be with me the last weekend of the campaign, a welcome support.

Election day always seems to drag on for a candidate. While the campaign team goes into overdrive to ensure that the vote gets out, the candidate is limited to calling key voters, travelling around the riding, delivering box lunches to workers in the polls and, if you are a female candidate, having your hair and nails done for the evening's events. My campaign had rented a suite at the Westin hotel downtown and, after going home to rest and change during the late afternoon, I arrived there around six. The polls closed shortly after in Newfoundland, where we lost two seats to the Liberals. Then came the results from the Maritimes, where in each Nova Scotia and New Brunswick we lost four seats to the Liberals and were wiped out in Prince Edward Island. Free trade was a problem in more places than eastern Ontario.

There were few smiles among my circle of family and friends. As the Quebec results started to appear, Bill Neville and his spouse, Marilyn, and Jodi White and Donald Doyle, experienced political advisers to Joe and the party, arrived to offer me support and counsel. I called Joe to see how he and Catherine were and he then spoke to Bill about what might happen in eastern Ontario. Even with new seats under redistribution, we needed to win in Ontario. As always, Joe was not as worried about his own results as the party's. As more results came in, it looked good in Quebec, where free trade was a popular issue and where we actually increased our number of seats from fifty-eight to sixty-three. Ontario was another story. After the votes were all in, the government had lost twenty-one seats, most of them in eastern Ontario. As the evening wore on, it became clear that twenty-two of our twenty-four candidates in eastern Ontario would be defeated, including Flora MacDonald, a political role model of mine. She had said to me once that if young women wanted to build upon her legacy in public life, they had to ensure that never again would the hopes of all women rest on the shoulders of only a few. I was bitter and sad at the news of her impending defeat, as it would be a loss to Parliament, the country and, most important, to women. Jodi called Joe to report the bad news, and Donald kept in constant touch with David Small at my headquarters. I went to the other room to speak to Joe privately about my remarks to my supporters. "Be calm and direct," he advised. "Say what needs to be said and no more. If you're scrummed by the press after your remarks, make sure Donald and David are there to back you up. You don't need to do any media tonight." I thanked him for the advice and wished him luck with his own election, as the polls had just closed in Alberta. As we said goodbye, I so wished he and Catherine were with me.

When I returned to the other room, I saw that CBC had declared me defeated. My mother objected. "How can they say that when not all the votes have been counted?" she demanded indignantly. But she was the only one who thought the numbers would change for the better. "I think it's time to practise the other one," said Bill as he handed me the concession speech to replace the victory notes I had been holding hopefully. My campaign team was trying vainly to find the winning Liberal candidate so I could congratulate him on his victory. We never did find him, and the next day I just sent a note to the address I had for his home.

At around nine-thirty we prepared to leave for the golf club where my supporters were waiting. "Okay," I said, "let's just do this." There was a slight hesitation among the group and Marilyn Neville, ever the humorist, said, "I like the outfit, but stockings and shoes would really pull it all together!" In my preoccupied state, I had almost left the hotel in my bare feet.

We went directly to my campaign headquarters where there was a large crowd of supporters and a significant contingent of journalists. My mother, my sisters Jane and Colleen and my brother, John, joined me on the stage, and I thanked my team for their support and help during the previous months. After these remarks and a brief press scrum, I left the stage and spoke with as many of my supporters as possible. I invited the key ones to join me in my hotel suite later, and went to the Château Laurier hotel downtown, where all the candidates from Ottawa and the surrounding ridings were to "celebrate." I stood beside David Daubney, who had just been defeated as the MP for Ottawa West, and we talked about how his daughter, Jennifer, one of Catherine's girlfriends, was taking his defeat. "Not well at all," he said. I remembered my own father's defeat in a municipal election when I was twelve and could commiserate with her. The whole event was depressing and gloomy, with small groups of people discussing what had gone wrong and others just wandering around looking lost.

After the speeches, I returned to my suite at the Westin, which was still packed with my supporters. "Joe's won," said

Jodi White, and I went directly into the bedroom and placed a call to congratulate him on his victory. He had defeated Preston Manning, the leader of the Reform Party, whose campaign theme had been that Joe was a great member of Parliament—just not for Alberta. But Joe had worked hard for his constituents for sixteen years and they respected him, even when they disagreed with him on issues like capital punishment. For the sixth straight election, the voters of Alberta had elected Joe to represent their interests in Ottawa. Unfortunately, this would not be the last of Preston Manning and his Reform Party.

As I was preparing brief remarks to offer to my closest campaign members in the room next door, Jane turned on the television. They were covering Joe's headquarters and I saw Catherine putting up numbers on the voting tally board, all decked out in campaign buttons and stickers and looking happy and useful. Her father had won and she was enjoying the excitement of campaign night. I felt terribly lonely without them but I was glad she was with Joe and not me. She called around eleven Ottawa time to tell me not to worry, as she would be home the next day to take care of me. A lump stuck in my throat as I heard these adult sentiments in a child's voice. She really was wise beyond her young years.

At about 3 A.M., as the party was ending and we were all promising each other that we would keep in touch "for the next time," I decided that I wanted to go home. Jane quickly packed our things and we left the hotel to return to Aylmer. My first adventure as a candidate in a political campaign was over. I would join the senior team for a post-mortem the next day, but other than that, I was free from campaigning. The Mulroney government had been re-elected with a reduced majority, but for a PC government, re-election with *any* majority was historic. Free trade had proven our undoing in eastern Ontario and parts of Atlantic Canada and I had been caught in its tide. I knew I had run a good campaign. As I lay alone in bed that night, looking forward to having Joe and Catherine home, I wondered if I would ever have the courage to run for Parliament again. Perhaps, I thought, but that decision would be for another day. I had proven to myself that I could stand the pressure and had enjoyed meeting so many people in their homes and at meetings. I had been part of democracy in action and felt that my contribution as a candidate was worthwhile. I was deeply disappointed that I had lost, as I believed I could have made a significant contribution to the House of Commons. At that moment, though, as dawn began to lighten the late November sky, I was overcome by the fatigue and relief that come to all candidates after an election. Win, lose or draw, it's finally over.

16

AFTER THE ELECTION our lives returned to a semblance of order. We went to Rome after Christmas and stayed for a few days with Canada's ambassador there, our old friend Alan Sullivan. We attended the Papal Mass in St. Peter's on New Year's Day and were granted an audience with the Pope the following morning. That meant a great deal to me after the trouble I had had with the Church during the campaign the previous fall. My own faith was renewed by the Holy Father's blessing and I was delighted to meet Mother Teresa as we left the papal audience. As we spoke through a translator, she reminded me of the works of charity that were being done by Catholics who lived their faith. Her two young assistants had attended a pro-life rally on Parliament Hill in Ottawa the year before and knew who we were. They tried to move Mother Teresa away and into another room but she seemed oblivious to their urgings and genuinely interested in talking to Joe about European security.

After our few days in Rome, the three of us went to Paris, where Joe was to join other foreign ministers at a conference on chemical warfare put together by the Organization for Economic Co-operation and Development (OECD). While he attended the conference, I re-introduced Catherine to the Louvre. We walked until our legs ached and spent three days together enjoying the sights. During these two weeks abroad I recuperated from the campaign and its defeat and thought about what lay ahead. I decided that I would return to university that fall for a master's in law, concentrating on issues of ethics and health. In the meantime, I agreed to accompany Joe on a tour that spring to the Soviet Union, East Germany, Poland and Hungary.

That trip inspired me to establish a program that would have a lasting effect on the lives of young lawyers and judges in some of the former Eastern Bloc countries. It had been a fascinating trip, beginning in Moscow, where the feeling of monumental change was unmistakable. Even the translator with me whispered that she thought that the country was about to change. Our ambassador was convinced that at the general meeting of the Communist Party that May there would be a major announcement by President Mikhail Gorbachev. When Joe and I said goodbye to Foreign Minister Eduard Shevardnadze and his wife at the Moscow airport, he admitted to us that he saw a time of great turbulence coming. He had walked right to the door of our plane without his guards and officials, and as he bade us farewell, he confided that we would very likely never meet again. He was right. Shortly after the convention that unleashed the massive changes that mark Russia even today, he left Moscow to run for the presidency of Georgia. In the coming years, he would survive several assassination attempts.

From Moscow we went to Hungary and saw that many officials there were already preparing for change. One evening at a formal dinner, I sat beside a young cabinet minister and we discussed his predictions for his country. As they moved away from Soviet control, they would need help in establishing an independent legal system and judiciary. He spoke at some length about his own education and the American Soros Foundation, which had funded a business school in Budapest. There, a new

generation of Hungarians had been educated and were ready
to move Hungary towards an open market economic system.
"If Canadian lawyers could do anything at all to help in this
period of change, what would that be?" I asked. His answer
was simple. "Take the best of our young lawyers, who have not
been tainted by cynicism or corruption, and let them see first-
hand how law is practised in a democratic society." Suddenly I
knew that this was something worth doing and turned my
attention to creating such a program. From that dinner conversation came the idea for the Canadian Bar Association's Eastern
and Central European legal programs.

As soon as I got back to Canada, I set to work finding the
funding and support to make this idea a reality. I met first with
John Jennings, the president of the Canadian Bar Association
(CBA) and with George Boros, a CBA staffer. George had fled
Hungary years before as a young child and had a special interest in being involved in this project. From John Jennings
through to the Honourable Paule Gauthier, four years later, I
received total support and co-operation for this innovative project. We began in 1989 with funding from both the federal government and several law firms for a pilot project involving
Hungarian lawyers. Events were moving rapidly in the region,
and the program was urgently needed to help governments re-
establish the rule of law and an independent judiciary.

That first summer in 1989 I went to Budapest with George
Boros, Senator Gérald Beaudoin and other experts to interview
the lawyers who had applied. We chose twenty lawyers to come
to Canada that September. I remember walking with George
one night across the bridge that links the Buda and Pest sides of
the city while he tearfully described the night he and his family
had escaped Hungary in the 1950s. This was his first trip back
since that flight as a child, and I knew that his commitment to
the program ran deep. While he had escaped to freedom in
Canada, so many of his friends had been forced to stay behind.

As the volunteer chair of this project, I knew I needed the co-operation of Canadian lawyers and established a large board of directors from within the legal and judicial communities. George and I phoned contacts and friends in law firms big and small to urge them to host a young foreign lawyer for three months between September and December each year. The commitment of each law firm was significant. Not only did they have to pay ten thousand dollars to cover board and expenses for each young lawyer, they also had to rotate them through their articling system and report to us on their progress. In the second year, we widened the scope of the law experiences to meet a wide variety of interests among the candidates, and placed them with municipal legal departments, Crown attorney's offices, environmental groups and both federal and provincial justice departments.

I urged the young lawyers who came to Canada to become involved in Canadian life, as their professional status would require them to play a large role in their community when they returned home. Many were interested in how elections were run and they followed provincial and municipal campaigns. One young Polish lawyer even ran successfully for a municipal seat back home while he interned in St. John's! His sponsors gave him many political tips, including how to carry out a sophisticated direct mail campaign to raise awareness and funds for his first foray into Polish politics.

In 1991, we added a judicial program for Polish judges who were then twinned with a Canadian judge from a court of similar jurisdiction to study judicial interpretation Canadian-style. They learned to draft their judgments directly on laptops, which of course meant that we had to find them each one to take home, and many later kept in touch with their judicial mentors by e-mail. Those who wanted to bring their families with them for the three months they were in Canada could do so, but they had to pay the extra costs themselves. Most of their spouses were professionals, too, and we started similar programs for them with accountants, dentists, doctors and teachers. The children who accompanied their parents were placed in Canadian schools and learned English or French. Many made lasting friendships. Many of the lawyers we received in Canada had never entertained foreigners in their homes and were surprised by Canadian informality and hospitality. When we went to their countries, many returned the favour and even held Canadian-style barbecues.

In those early days Canadian board members and other legal experts were actively involved in the exchange. They travelled to the participating countries to choose the following year's recruits each summer, to present professional development courses and participate on legal panels. It was a genuine two-way street. We were not just coming over to tell the "poor locals" what they should know about modern society. We had a lot to learn from them too, and the panel discussions allowed us to see the gaps and issues within our own system of law, and to undertake a real dialogue among equals. The program has changed since that time to meet different national needs but it lives on.

When Joe began his term as foreign minister, the world was as foreign to me as his title. By 1989, five years later, I was a committed internationalist, keen to play my part in the transition to democracy that was beginning in the countries of eastern and central Europe. It was exciting for all of us who joined in making the CBA program happen. Through our work we helped to shape the new generation that must now take their countries the next step towards democracy and prosperity within the European Union. This commitment was rewarding and worthwhile for me—personally and professionally. I made new friends, travelled on my own and chaired a significant international project with an important aim. It overcame any lingering hurt at my election defeat and enhanced my self-confidence and my standing within my profession.

Few things in my professional life have touched me more than the response of the young lawyers who wrote to me after their stay in Canada. Their sojourn changed their lives. The fall of the Berlin Wall had set them free, but their experience in Canada gave them a sense of how that freedom might be used. One of these young lawyers said to me one night in Budapest in 1993, "I did not know such a world even existed. Thank you for bringing me to learn about law and life in Canada. That is what I want to build here in my own country." She had taken me to mass that afternoon to celebrate the withdrawal of all foreign troops from her country. An elderly woman beside me wept openly throughout the service and then, as we all stood for the playing of their national anthem, I looked over at my friend, to discover that she was crying too. She told me later that the old woman reminded her of her late grandmother who always told her stories of the great Austro-Hungarian Empire, and who had insisted that one day they would be free again.

These human sentiments were thanks enough. But I was deeply touched when my legal colleagues honoured me with the Canadian Bar Association's Rt. Hon. Louis St. Laurent Award for legal achievement in 1993. The Canadian government had awarded me a Canada 125 medal the year before. Then, in 1995, the Hungarian government awarded me its Cross of Merit for contributing to the establishment of the rule of law and an independent judiciary. My own modest efforts had made a difference to a new generation of young lawyers and judges at an important time in their countries' modern history.

17

WHEN WE LOOK BACK ON OUR LIVES, most of us can identify unanticipated events that shaped our future. In the weeks after the 1988 election, I received several requests to speak to groups across Canada. After I'd made one such speech to the Manitoba nurses' association, my attention was drawn to a set of issues that preoccupy me to this day. In the serendipity of events that mark our lives, my speech went on longer than planned and I missed my plane. I stayed for lunch to hear Dr. Margrit Eichler, a respected sociologist, speak about the coalition she headed to demand a Royal Commission on new reproductive and genetic technologies. I was fascinated by her description of the revolution in medical science in these fields and approached her to see how I could become involved. We flew back to Toronto together that night, and the next morning I began to study the fascinating issues raised by our developing power to create, manipulate and alter human life in the laboratory. What I discovered troubled me deeply. These new technologies, like in vitro fertilization (IVF) and genetic testing, then as now raise so many ethical questions. What is the status of the embryos created in fertility clinics, and can a child born using donor sperm ever know who his or her father is? Why are so many embryos created each cycle, and is IVF a therapy or really an experiment using the bodies of women desperate to have children? One development in this field always leads to another. For instance, freezing embryos leaves the parent couple with a surplus of embryos, which are then stored in clinics for future use. What happens to these embryos, and to whom do they belong? Is surrogacy for pay a good thing for women? And as the Mary Beth Whitehead case in the U.S. showed, we need to amend the law on who a mother is. In 1989, I saw that science was forging ahead without input from the wider public; and law and public policy were light-years behind.

I had had briefings on medical research from experts as part of my run for Parliament the year before, and have always supported scientific research. But I saw that reproductive and genetic technologies created real challenges to human rights and the very definition of what it meant to be human. I came to the conclusion that Canada needed to address these issues swiftly to balance the needs of science and the interests of our society.

In late March 1989, while Joe and I were holidaying in Florida over Easter, he told me that the government was looking for a significant social policy item for the upcoming Speech from the Throne, the first since the 1988 election the previous fall. He suggested that I draft and send a letter to the Prime Minister outlining why the government should create a Royal Commission on reproductive and genetic technologies. On March 29, I wrote to the Prime Minister asking that he consider creating such a Royal Commission, arguing that the legal, ethical and social issues these technologies and practices raised required a national response only he could initiate. I argued that a Royal Commission would be a better forum than a ministerial or parliamentary committee and ended by saying, "I realize that the Speech from the Throne is in its final stages of preparation and hope perhaps this item may be included."

The Canadian coalition continued its lobbying efforts to have a Royal Commission established, and as I sat in the Senate that spring listening to the Governor General read the Speech from the Throne, I was delighted that the government had decided to act. The coalition immediately sent a list of some fifty names as suggestions for commission members, and I urged the government to select from among that list. None of those suggested were chosen.

Then one day shortly after the parliamentary session began, the Prime Minister called me at home and asked if I would agree to serve as a member of the Royal Commission on New Reproductive Technologies. I refused his request initially, insisting that I wanted Margrit there instead. He asked me to reconsider, saying he would call the next day. When I spoke to Joe about the call, he urged me to accept, insisting that I had a great deal to offer as a lawyer who knew about public policy and about the issues raised by the commission's mandate. Joe was as surprised as I was about the invitation. Brian had not spoken to him about it. I felt this revealed a healthy regard for both the independent identity of political spouses and the avoidance of conflict of interest. I appreciated the Prime Minister's confidence in my ability. Since the Winnipeg meeting in 1983, we had kept our distance, although he had attended the launch of my Parliament book in 1984 and brought Mila and the children to a barbecue in my riding the year before. But generally, our paths rarely crossed. No one could suggest that he was appointing one of his "friends," in the conventional sense of that term. Indeed, in the climate of the time, he was taking a risk appointing a pro-choice feminist. After a great deal of discussion with Joe, I decided to accept the appointment.

I was not at all privy to the considerations that led to the other appointments, and can only speculate as to why they were made. But here is what I think happened. The issues raised by new reproductive and genetic technologies are significantly different from those of the abortion debate. But they both involve questions about human life: when it begins, its status and who makes critical decisions. The Canadian Parliament was as deeply divided on the abortion question as the Canadian public was and could not even come to a decision on a new law to regulate abortion when it was tabled several months later. In that charged context, it was inevitable that the emotions of the abortion debate would influence the choice of members of the Royal Commission. As the decision to establish a Royal Commission was made, I heard through the political grapevine that some of the members of the PC caucus were concerned that my presence would bias the commission away from the pro-life stance they wanted. I volunteered to withdraw in favour of one of the candidates from Margrit's list, but the Prime Minister held to his position. The Roman Catholic Church and the "family values" group of MPs were, in the end, each granted a position on the commission. In one of life's bizarre developments, it turned out that the "family values" nominee was a lesbian, which I understand the Prime Minister found hilarious when he was told later.

Given the concerns flowing from the abortion debate, it is surprising that the government went ahead with this commission at all. It could have easily handled it some other way, including within a parliamentary committee controlled by its majority, with a much narrower mandate. It is worth noting that after the commission issued its final report in 1993, the Chrétien government shelved it. Ten years later, Canada had not yet passed legislation to regulate fertility clinics and oversee controversial research on human embryos, including stem cell research and reproductive cloning.

From the beginning there were real problems within the commission. To protect its independence, Margrit Eichler's coalition had insisted that the chair should be someone not directly involved as a legal or medical practitioner currently working in any one of the technologies or practices under study. I don't know what factors led the Prime Minister to name Dr. Patricia Baird, a Vancouver doctor and geneticist, as chair.

During my first meeting with her, I was startled at how oblivious she seemed to the dynamic of working with non-medical professionals in a team setting. I urged her not to call a first meeting of the commission until all commissioners could attend. This was more than a mere courtesy. She would risk jeopardizing our work from the start if she excluded anyone from this crucial first meeting. But she decided to hold the commission's first meeting on a day when she knew that commissioner Louise Vandelac was speaking at an international conference in Europe. That soured their relationship from the beginning. I had also suggested to Dr. Baird that our meetings include simultaneous translation as was the custom for all such national bodies. It was essential in this case because the chair was unilingual, three of the other members spoke little or no French and the two francophone Quebeckers preferred to speak in French. Dr. Baird did not require simultaneous translation at that first meeting and, surprisingly, the bureaucrats on staff did nothing about her decision.

The commission's first meeting was held at a Toronto airport hotel and was a disaster. Martin Hébert, a Montreal lawyer specializing in medical law, began his intervention in French. Dr. Baird insisted that he speak in English, as she and three others knew no French. Martin looked up from his notes and said to me in French, "What is she saying?" To which I replied, "Speak white." That wasn't very diplomatic, but it indicated to Martin that he would have to speak English as it was the language of the majority and the chair. Shaken by Dr. Baird's demand, Martin pulled out a pack of cigarettes and lit one. Another commissioner, Suzanne Scorsone, went into a pantomime of protest about cigarette smoke and Martin just pushed back his chair and left the room. We were only minutes into the first formal meeting of a difficult new Royal Commission and already two members had been totally alienated. They were both Quebec nationalists who had agreed, against their better judgment, to serve on a federal body because of their concern about the seriousness of the issues. There had been silence when Martin left, and then I followed him into the hall. I encouraged him to return and promised that this was just an unfortunate mistake that would be resolved. I reminded him of the Prime Minister's commitment to bilingualism, and to a full pursuit of the commission's mandate. We both returned to the meeting, although little was achieved after this dreadful beginning.

After this meeting, I called Marjory LeBreton, the senior staffer in the PMO responsible for appointments. I knew her and wanted this handled delicately, before the whole thing got out of hand. I mentioned that I did not see ill will, just insensitivity, and urged Marjory to have the clerk of the Privy Council, Paul Tellier, speak privately with the chair to help her understand that this was a national commission with protocols that she would need to follow. Her colleague commissioners, whether or not she happened to like them, were her equals and it was in a spirit of collegiality, not confrontation, that she would get the best out of everyone. If the commission was to meet its mandate and respect its deadline, these growing pains would have to be overcome, and soon. I was confident that they would be, and focused on briefing myself on the issues at hand.

Royal Commissions are established under the federal Public Inquiries Act, which provides for two types of commissions. One involves appointing a single (usually well-known and respected) person who sits alone and has complete authority to act. This kind of a commission is chosen when someone like a judge, for instance, is asked to investigate a train or plane crash and to recommend how to ensure it does not happen again. It could also be used in larger situations of concern, as in the case of the Romanow Commission that reported in late 2002. The second type of commission involves appointing several people, often from different backgrounds and professions, to tackle controversial issues like the ones that were the subject of our work. In such cases, there are rarely right or wrong answers, and the government benefits from several professional views and experiences as it prepares to legislate or change public policy. In such cases, the questions are far reaching and no one individual would be able to address them alone.

Our group of commissioners was diverse, which I saw as a strength. If we could produce a final report, the government would be well served. In spite of the bitter atmosphere, I could see some consensus already developing, especially about the role of an oversight body and the need for legal rules to govern fertility clinics and the research to be carried out on human embryos. Other areas of common ground were appearing, including on donor anonymity, the commercialization of women's bodies and surrogacy, the policies governing fertility drugs, the safety of experimental IVF procedures and genetic diagnosis for eugenic purposes. If we could manage a lively debate, followed by a report that included several opinions and options, we would show the diversity of views that existed among commissioners, as well as across the country. Then, with top-notch research and analysis, we could give the government the evidentiary tools it needed to draft a law to regulate the use of IVF and related reproductive and genetic technologies.

In a Royal Commission like the one I served on, all commissioners have equal legal responsibilities and rights. One of the members is chosen by the government to act as the chair and assumes additional responsibilities of an administrative nature. For this, the chair receives extra money and the administrative rank of a deputy minister. In our case, Dr. Baird took that to mean she was the boss and we were her underlings. We had no role unless she gave us one. She assumed she had the right to act unilaterally and to make all decisions alone. For whatever reason, the government supported her in this erroneous view of her power. In doing this, she effectively denied some of her colleague commissioners their rightful and legal role. But we were required by law to provide a report and failure to do so could lead to legal sanctions. In an attempt to resolve the issue, I urged Dr. Baird to divide the total budget on a pro-rated basis. That way each commissioner could proceed alone or pool individual budget allocations to work in a group. We would travel together for the public hearings across Canada and edit our work to form an integrated whole for the final report. My request was denied.

By the end of the first few months, commissioners Bruce Hatfield, Martin Hébert, Louise Vandelac and I were frustrated and marginalized. The chair allowed us no role in determining what research we would undertake. No research director had been hired and no research plan had been drafted. Decisions about the commission were taken without our input or involvement. Out of the blue, one day in late 1990, at the end of the first year, Dr. Baird advised us that she had unilaterally sought an extension from the government to complete the report. Moreover, her request had been granted. We were stunned. Out of basic respect for all of us who had signed on for two years, could she not have asked our opinion on an extension? We were all busy people and had other personal and professional commitments. I, for instance, had decided to begin a master's in law program at Dalhousie University's Health Law Institute during the fall of 1991, on the basis that our final report would be completed by then. Bruce, Martin, Louise and I felt that given the state of existing research and legislative options around the world, the commission did not need an extension. What we needed was a work and research plan, and a whole year had slipped by with neither.

After this unilateral announcement of the extension, all semblance of trust among commissioners evaporated and the commission broke into two conflicting groups, with the majority demanding a vote to adopt a plan of action and draft a final report within time and budget. The chair advised there would be no votes on any matter, and that while she would listen to other commissioners, she and the bureaucrats in her office would determine the course and the conclusions of the commission. We asked what kind of research personnel and budget we had to work with and were refused an answer. Minutes of our meetings were rewritten and sanitized. During a particularly bitter meeting, Martin Hébert asked that all tapes of the contentious meetings be kept for use in any possible future public inquiry or legal proceeding. The tapes were not kept. Trying to keep all this out of the press, we asked the clerk of the Privy Council to intervene directly, and a special mediation session was set up. When we arrived we were told that the chair did not plan to attend, as it was the commissioners who were the problem. The year passed and the four of us continued to be denied the tools to do the work required of us under the law.

———

In September 1991, I started the course work for a master's degree in law at Dalhousie University in Halifax. My thesis would analyze the legal issues surrounding reproductive technologies in Canada and, if needed, it would become my contribution to the final report of the Royal Commission, of which I was then still a member. Joe was busy with his parliamentary duties and work as foreign minister, and Catherine was doing well in school. My own commitments to the Royal Commission were part-time and I worked at their office on Monday and Friday. I flew to Halifax each Monday evening, attended classes from Tuesday to Thursday and returned that night to Ottawa. I was chair of the Canadian Bar Association's Eastern and Central European legal programs during this period, but left the bulk of the administrative work to CBA staff, who briefed me on it each week. I knew the year would be very busy, but in the past had found that deadlines and structure forced me to focus. They also provided me with an excuse to be absent from the many social events that mark the daily life of a political wife. Joe knew how frustrating the Royal Commission had become and was enthusiastic for me to start something that would be both stimulating and rewarding. If I had to attend official dinners or receptions during the week, then I would, but he agreed that classes would have priority that year. My mother volunteered to care for Catherine, and by extension Joe. When I asked Catherine what she thought, she simply told me, "Go for it, Mom!" She was almost fifteen and agreed to attend official functions with Joe if he needed her.

All went swimmingly the first week I was away, but when I arrived back the Thursday night, it was as if I had entered a hurricane. Catherine had an asthma attack, the septic tank erupted at our home in the country and just as we prepared for bed, our delinquent German shepherd, Mickey, picked a fight with a skunk. Three cans of tomato juice later, Catherine and I gave up cleaning her. We each took a shower and crawled into bed. "That's it!" I told my mother the next morning. "This experiment has failed. I am not going back next week." My mother disagreed. "Try it for one more week," she insisted. "I will miss my little darling if you don't. I love staying with her." And so, after a weekend of relative calm, I returned to Halifax as storm clouds gathered at the commission in Ottawa. All fall I would leave the commission office on Monday night drained and tense and return to face more problems on Friday.

Before I started classes that fall, Martin, Louise, Bruce and I had tried yet again to address the serious problems of research and resource allocation to commissioners. Roles and rules had not been clarified and intrigue was everywhere. I felt particularly vulnerable, and Joe was not immune from the intrigue. During this time, he was asked to sign an Order-in-Council concerning the commission and refused. He was startled at the request and criticized the public servant involved for his lack of concern over conflict of interest. His lame answer was that Joe was the only minister in town that day, an unlikely story. I saw this as a not-so-subtle attempt to sow division between us and to threaten Joe to make me conform. I did not want Joe to be bothered in any way in his official duties, but as a lawyer I knew my legal responsibility to produce a report, something for which we were all being paid a daily fee.

Throughout 1990–91, there had been several acrimonious and unproductive meetings. Martin, Louise, Bruce and I had even walked out of a meeting in Nova Scotia that summer when we discovered that several of the invited guests there had been awarded contracts for research. We had not been involved in any of these decisions, and when some researchers raised their work with us, they could not believe we did not know they had been hired. In Ottawa, staffers told us that they could not talk to us and had to report to their superiors when we tried to talk to them—even to say hello in the washrooms. We again asked Dr. Baird about the research plan—what work would be done and by whom. At the end of the summer, she told us that we would be able to see and critique research proposals in the future and some were given to us with great fanfare for our review. We disagreed with the quality and scope of several of these proposals and reminded Dr. Baird that excellent work on these questions had already been done in other countries and should be used to reduce cost and save time. A week later, by chance, we learned from one of the staff that Dr. Baird had already given researchers the go-ahead to do the work. We asked her for an explanation and were ignored.

We again requested a meeting with the clerk of the Privy Council and he told us that we could always leave if we didn't like it. The health minister, Benoît Bouchard from Quebec, became involved, and we appointed Martin to be our contact with him. He insisted that we be patient as all would be resolved, but nothing happened. We were being treated like naughty children, being punished for misbehaving. At one point, for instance, during the fall of 1990, Martin, Louise and I were censured by Dr. Baird for speaking to the French-language press at a meeting in Quebec City. We were told that speaking to the press was her exclusive prerogative. We protested—Dr. Baird spoke no French and the reporters had specifically asked for Martin, Louise or me. In those French-language interviews, the press were very curious when we could not answer even their most basic questions about cost and research plans.

Naturally, I wondered who was at fault, and more particularly whether I was. I am known to speak my mind, and my strength is often in my candour. I am told, though, that people often find this threatening. But the breakdown on the commission was not about the six others against me. It was four against three, and I was part of the majority. Of the other members of that majority, Louise Vandelac, if asked, would acknowledge that she is at least as outspoken as I am. But among Martin Hébert's strengths is his ability as a skilled conciliator, and Bruce Hatfield is one of the gentlest and most affable people anyone could meet. The problem was not that the four of us were inherently unable to work with others. Nor did the fatal divisions on that original commission have much to do with the questions we were convened to consider. There were different approaches to the issues raised by new reproductive and genetic technologies, and different interpretations of the facts, as is bound to happen in any serious inquiry. But other Royal Commissions before us had been divided on the issues and were able to continue their work together. Sadly, in our case, the fundamental issues that divided the majority and the chair was whether we were to work as a team of equals, each bringing our different strengths to the task at hand, or whether she was to run the show as she wished. In the end, for reasons that have never been made public, the government and its bureaucracy made a decision not to conciliate but to support Dr. Baird by building a new

majority within the commission that would support her completely. Two new commissioners, Susan McCutcheon and Bartha
Maria Knoppers, were named in 1991, and the original majority thus became the minority.

All this tension was weighing heavily upon me. Political
"friends" attacked me for rocking the boat. Some even accused
me of a vendetta against the Prime Minister as a way of getting
revenge for his defeating my husband in the 1983 leadership convention. I was labelled a poor loser and told by these "friends"
that I was embarrassing the government. I heard rumours that all
I really wanted was to be the commission's chair. I had fought for
two years to be allowed to do the job I had originally refused and
had then agreed to do out of sense of duty and recognition of the
urgency and importance of the issues. Instead I was embroiled in
endless intrigue that made no sense to me at all and threatened
my reputation and professionalism.

Martin, Louise, Bruce and I were being left with but two
choices—submit to Dr. Baird's view or quit. We wanted neither
option. We knew the stakes involved and were convinced that
our critical perspective was essential to the commission's work.
We had legal rights and responsibilities to meet and were not
interested in writing a little add-on to the final report that
would be conveniently labelled as a "dissent." In October 1991,
we decided to place the matter before the Federal Court of
Canada for resolution. We sought legal advice from several
sources and asked the Toronto lawyer John Laskin to prepare
and present our case to the court. We would then have two
options—either we would be able to fulfill our legal mandate to
produce a final report or we would resign. At least all the issues
would be in the public domain and could be addressed.

On December 6, 1991, we filed a statement of claim with
the Federal Court, asking the court to clarify our situation and
offer guidance on the roles and responsibilities of the commission's members. We argued that a decision in this case would

assist all future Royal Commissions by ensuring that the same problem did not happen again. We did not have to wait long for an answer—on December 16, the four of us were fired. That morning I received a letter over the signature of the clerk of the Privy Council, Paul Tellier, telling me that my appointment to the Royal Commission was being revoked. In his letter he wrote: "I want to take this opportunity to thank you for your work and express my best wishes in your future endeavours." I then received a press release by fax from Barbara Uteck in his office, which advised me that "the decision to revoke the appointments of the four commissioners was taken to ensure the continued viability of the Commission and its ability to fulfill its mandate."

By firing us, the government ensured our case would not be heard by the Federal Court. There would be no independent investigation into the workings of the commission, no lessons learned for future commissions and no criticisms levelled at anyone but the commission's original majority of members. In short, it was business as usual for the commission even though the national coalition that had called for its creation and the National Action Committee on the Status of Women both asked that the commission be immediately dismantled and the research and report preparation transferred to the Canadian Humanities Institute Research Council. A panel of eminent scientists from around the world wrote the Prime Minister, protesting our treatment, but they had no impact on his decision. Normally this kind of major controversy would have been the stuff of parliamentary questions, but the House had already adjourned for Christmas, and there seemed little press interest except for its political spin that Joe Clark's wife had been fired by his opponent, Brian Mulroney. In yet another twist of deceit, when the report was finally published in November 1993, our four names were omitted, as if the entire ugly experience had never even happened.

As I left the Supreme Court building in Ottawa on that cold, snowy morning in mid-December 1991 and tried to absorb what had happened, I felt betrayed and despondent. I spoke briefly to the friends who were there to support us, said goodbye to Bruce, Martin and Louise, hugged them all, started my car and drove slowly home. Later that day I issued a press release in which I responded to the firing and ended with this paragraph:

> Like hundreds of other individuals and groups, I worked hard to have this Royal Commission established, and was very encouraged when the Government chose a large and genuine inquiry. The last two years have been agonizing for me, and have raised important questions about the conduct of public inquiries. But right now, the real issue is not procedural but substantive: How does a responsible modern society respond to developments raised by science, which challenge our basic realities and assumptions about morality, ethics and public policy? I am truly sorry to be off this Royal Commission, but intend through speeches, writing and other means, to continue to play an active role in this fundamental debate.

In the following years I would keep that promise.

—

After this experience, I could barely write my Christmas exams. I believe that a person has only so much positive energy to go around each day and that it must be preserved carefully. Facing the saga of the Royal Commission had sapped every ounce of this energy from me and left me debilitated and depressed. My regular excitement at Christmas preparations fizzled, and I could scarcely find the enthusiasm to attend public events such as the annual diplomatic reception Joe and I held each December in Ottawa.

That Christmas we went to Hawaii, where we had a chance to relax and reflect on what had happened. Joe had been deeply troubled by my treatment and knew that I felt betrayed by his cabinet colleagues who had been willing to go along with my firing. Always wanting to put the best face on events, he encouraged me to put the commission fiasco behind me and to focus on my studies and the CBA program that I enjoyed so much. He argued that by writing my thesis, I could learn a great deal about reproductive technologies and could put that knowledge to work to change public policy. As our holiday concluded, I suddenly realized that not having to worry about the Royal Commission anymore actually freed me. I returned to classes in January much more optimistic about the future and eager to complete my thesis for that September.

18

In the years following my father's death, my mother often travelled with us. She is an easy person to love. Giving and kind, she lived through a number of tough patches with us all before becoming a widow at fifty. She now has nine grandchildren and one great-granddaughter to worry about, plus hundreds of honorary grandchildren all over the world who go to sleep at night under one of her beautiful baby quilts. There has never been a doubt that "Mother Bea," as friends and colleagues alike call her, is always on call no matter what the charitable cause or family need. She still lives in the house we built along the Ottawa River as our family's Centennial project in 1967, and the four of her six children who live in the Ottawa area make a point of seeing her as often as possible. I try to have dinner with her once a week when I am in Ottawa, and I cannot imagine not having her there at the end of the phone line when I call each day.

In the summer of 1992, Mom joined us for a holiday on Nantucket, an island off Cape Cod. Upon her return, she began to exhibit symptoms of fatigue and listlessness. She looked ill but, as always, insisted she was fine. All August she was "not herself" and even refused to come with me to a friend's home for the Labour Day weekend. I was staying there for a few days to finish my thesis, due later that month, so that I could graduate from the master's of law program that autumn. "Just go alone," she said. "It will be easier if you have no distractions." Then, on Labour Day, my sister Jane called me in a panic. She had just returned home from her holidays to find that Mom was in the hospital with a high fever and was incoherent and in pain. In fact she was so sick that she had let an elderly friend drive her to the hospital even though this friend was legally blind. We were all away somewhere and she had not wanted to bother us. As a sign of her determination to be diagnosed and treated, she had told the emergency room nurse she was not leaving until the doctor told her what was wrong. I rushed back to Ottawa and met Jane and Pat at the hospital. No one had any answers for us and her situation was becoming worse. Initial blood tests had revealed nothing in particular, but they were doing more. My sister Pamela came from her home in Oakville, near Toronto, to help provide nursing care, and we all took turns watching over Mom. Two more days went by and her fever was so high that we were now changing her sheets five times a day. We brought clean bedding and clothing from home, and Pam bathed her continually to try to bring the fever down. She was delirious and seemed unable to fight the infection and fever.

Sometimes when things are going wrong, they just don't stop. The week my mother was burning up in hospital, I still had to finish my thesis. I knew very little about computers and had asked a friend a few weeks earlier to take all the various parts from several disks and integrate them into one whole, which she had successfully done. I had worked on the text night and day for two weeks to finish it on time. I had risen at 4 A.M. on a Wednesday to work on it one last time before sending it to Dalhousie by courier for the Friday deadline. My heart wasn't really in it but I was almost there. As I tried to save the document, the disk failed. It just seemed to be eating itself from within. As the noise whirled on and on, I felt as if someone had punched me in the chest. I managed to turn off the machine and pull out the disk before I was physically sick. A neophyte in computers, I had no backup except the original scattered pieces on disks, some of which I had erased to use for other things. Computer experts could not help me, and by the end of the day I had to admit defeat. My thesis would not be completed on time—if at all. I vowed I would not look at it again. It is difficult to describe the sheer feeling of panic and pain that comes from such an incident. I saw this erasure of data and words as a mirror of what was happening inside my mother. I wanted to help her; to make her better; to find the problem and fix it. What could this illness possibly be?

I am not sure how I came to think of Lyme disease and make the link between its prevalence on the eastern seaboard of the United States and our trip to Nantucket earlier that summer. Lyme disease is a blood ailment carried by ticks that can be fatal if untreated. Usually, an infected person has a red circular rash at the site of the bite, and flulike symptoms and fatigue should raise alarm bells. Mom certainly had some of these severe symptoms. I rushed to the hospital and my nurse sister, Pamela, told me that her body was not producing white corpuscles, leaving her vulnerable to fever and other infection. The doctor called us all together to tell us that if she did not rally she would be unlikely to live beyond the weekend. I asked him if he had tested for Lyme disease. He hadn't. Pam and I suggested antibiotics and a blood transfusion. The doctor did not want to do a blood transfusion, but we insisted. It seemed to make little difference in Mom's condition. "Do another one," Pam insisted.

On the first day Mom was in hospital, I had started a diary to serve as a record of what had been said and done about her illness. Each of us kept a complete record of what happened on our watch, in part to keep the other siblings informed and in part to save the staff from having to repeat themselves when we changed shifts three times a day. This terrible day I had written to remind Pat to insist on a blood transfusion as Pam had requested earlier. When Pat went on duty, she read my entry and told the young doctor what I had asked for. He refused. Pat looked at him in surprise and said, "Do as you please, but if you think I'm tough, wait until my sister Maureen arrives." At that, I came in the door and asked why he was hesitating about acting. "We'll sign away our legal rights if need be," I said, "but I remind you that no one has ever been sued for trying to save someone's life at the request of the family."

After half a day of watching my mother suffer, we noticed that her condition seemed to be improving and she began to rally. Over the next couple of days, her fever abated and her strength started to rebuild. Within two weeks she was home again, very weak and frail, but on the mend. Our prayers and supplications had been answered. Jane had promised to quit smoking if God would only spare Mom—a measure of the kind of bargains people are willing to enter into under extreme stress. She held to her promise. "After all," she said, "I haven't talked to Him in a long while. It wouldn't be a good idea to start to rekindle the relationship by breaking my promise on this one!"

We realized during this crisis that we had no idea at all what Mom wanted us to do in such a situation. We were fortunate that she rallied and that no heroic interventions were needed. God was watching over us and her, and it was not yet her time to leave us. But there had been a period during those terrible two weeks when she was unable to make any decisions or choices and we could not reach her in her delirious state to seek guidance. I kept thinking to myself, Would our mother ever want to be kept alive on a machine? Then other worst-case scenarios played themselves out in my overactive mind. What if she was confined to a wheelchair or bed for the rest of her life? She was so active and full of energy. She loved to travel and visit all of us no matter where we were in the world. I could not imagine losing her. But this brush with death forced me to face the fact that we were all aging and that soon we might have to cope with these kinds of situations again. I decided that we had to broach the subject of death and disease with her when she was stronger. What really mattered to me was what *she* would want if we ever had to deal with a similar crisis in the future.

In the years since then, I have given many speeches and lectures on how we can keep control at the end of life. I have an entire section in my last book on issues of living wills, the donation of our organs, assisted suicide and euthanasia. As a lawyer I think about these matters narrowly, through the lens of law. It is easier, then, to analyze medical options and suggest legal solutions. But from my own experience as a daughter facing the possibility of my own mother's death, I know how hard this is for each of us on a human level. When my mother was sick, I saw how much we resist asking the tough questions and confonting the worst of all nightmares—losing someone we so dearly love. In my family, none of us had ever raised the matter of death with our mother. Only once had I spoken about it to my father as he lay in the hospital dying from lung cancer. He had been categorical and refused all heroic interventions. He made that clear to his doctor, and I was pleased that the doctor respected my father's wishes. But Dad's cancer was inoperable and swift, and he had chosen palliative care over chemotherapy. He had been competent to consent to treatment and to refuse it. He could talk and he did. There was no doubt what he wanted from us and from the medical staff. He wanted to die with as little pain as possible and, while pain management was not as well understood and monitored then as it is now, he was nonetheless granted his wish.

But my mother's illness took us by surprise and, at the critical times, she was not competent to decide. Further, my siblings and I had found it difficult to agree on how she should be treated. Once she was better, we talked it through during a family meal and Mom agreed to a living will. Preparing these documents for my mother was difficult but meaningful. It forced me to face the fact that she would die one day, and to confront my own mortality. Why do we leave every major decision about our leave-taking until the last minute, sometimes until it's too late? I remember a doctor telling me in frustration how we spend huge sums of money and several months preparing for a wedding and then pretend that we will never need to plan for our death. His job would be a lot easier, he insisted, if more people made time for this major "life" event.

As a result of this crisis with my mother, I have often spoken to groups and hospice care workers about the importance of having a living will. In preparing it, I suggest that people write down a list of what they value most in their life, how they want to live and what event or handicap would make living unbearable. This focuses their thoughts and gives them a chance in a quiet moment, while still healthy, to contemplate their future. One thing I have found is that older people are a lot more realistic about life and death than younger people. They refuse to pretend that they will live forever and accept that there are some pretty gruesome and awful ways to die. No person I have ever spoken with has wanted to be kept alive against his will or when her life serves no purpose. Many value their physical and mental independence so much that they cannot imagine life without either. For others the biggest fear is unbearable pain. They have seen friends drugged and forced in many ways to live a living death. They have spent time visiting or volunteering in a seniors' home and have seen what life can look like near the end.

Years later, when I was touring across the country promoting my book *Tough Choices,* which deals in part with these particular subjects, I spoke to seniors' groups. I was surprised at the vehemence of those who stood up and insisted that it was their right to end their lives and not to be required to go on living when there was neither hope nor purpose. Of course the law disagrees with them on this point. Assisted suicide and euthanasia are criminal offences in Canada and in most of the countries of the world. A Canadian parliamentary committee has studied the issues surrounding palliative care, assisted suicide and euthanasia, and recommended that there be no change to the current law. However, as medicine develops, and so many of us age and face our own illnesses and death, these questions will continue to be an insistent part of the public agenda. I personally believe that we must not allow euthanasia where we decide deliberately to kill a person at or near the end of life. But there are so many in-between situations and our laws need to offer options on how we handle these.

The Supreme Court of Canada gave us some excellent suggestions in the case of Sue Rodriguez, which dealt with a request by a mentally competent but physically incapacitated woman for assistance in killing herself when she was totally disabled, felt she could not go on and could not manage it herself. Remember that it is not illegal to commit suicide in Canada, and her argument was simply that her rights under our Constitution were being violated because she was being denied the chance to do what every able-bodied Canadian can choose to do—end his or her own life. This was a very different situation from the Latimer case, where a Saskatchewan farmer killed his severely handicapped daughter, arguing that it was an act of mercy and not murder. Even if our laws were to change to allow assisted suicide in certain situations, cases like this would rarely be affected. That is because historically, certain classes of people, especially children and those vulnerable through mental handicap, have been excluded and specially protected by the courts.

But if my own observations are anything to go by, there is a significant interest in the question of assisted suicide. That interest will grow as the baby-boomer generation moves from middle age and sees parents and friends forced to live with serious or chronic diseases—often in great pain. Most of my generation are educated and highly independent. We are used to having our say and our way. We have barely started to see the impact on our health care system of keeping people alive in a persistent vegetative state or in hopeless situations. It seems that people are not as afraid to die as they are afraid to be forced to remain alive in a state of pain, or mental or physical incapacity. They are comforted when they know they have options and that it is they, and not the doctors or others in their own families, who will have the final say in their lives. Most Canadians with whom I have spoken about this know that they have the right to commit suicide. But most also prefer to have the option to do so quietly and in their sleep, rather than by following the example of Ernest Hemingway. Concern about those who must deal with the consequences of a suicide weighs heavily upon many people.

My mother and I spoke several times about a living will, and I drafted one for her based on her own life choices and preferences. It is tucked away safely where we can refer to it, if and when that time comes. It is comforting for me and my siblings to know what she would want done if she were ever unable to speak for herself, and it is equally reassuring for her to know that she can count on all of us to respect her decision and to follow her directions. What it really allows us to do now, while she is well, is focus on living and enjoying each other as we move through all the big and little events—good and bad—that make up our family's life.

1 9

IN 1991, BRIAN MULRONEY CALLED JOE and asked if he would leave foreign affairs and become constitutional affairs minister. When Joe told Catherine of his decision she looked at him in surprise and said, "Well, so long, Paris; hello, Moose Jaw." Quebec had not signed the 1982 Constitution; and after his election in 1984, Brian decided to use his influence and mandate to try to negotiate a constitutional agreement with Quebec. The Quebec government had five conditions for signing. It required recognition that it was a distinct society; the creation of a constitutional veto available to each province on constitutional matters; a commitment that the federal government would appoint the three Quebec Justices of the Supreme Court of Canada from a list provided by the province; the right of any province to withdraw from certain federal programs with full compensation; and greater provincial control over immigration. Quebec Premier Robert Bourassa negotiated on behalf of Quebec, and the bargaining process was difficult. What made the agreement possible was the desire among the Premiers to bring Quebec into the constitutional fold. After much discussion the federal and provincial governments signed the Meech Lake Accord on June 3, 1987, at O'Brien Cottage beside Meech Lake in the Gatineau Hills north of Ottawa. Each had until June 23, 1990, to have their legislatures ratify the agreement. Parliament and eight of the ten provincial legislatures proceeded to ratify the accord, but when the deadline arrived, Newfoundland and Manitoba had not. One year later, in 1991, the lingering bitterness and anger among the provinces and within Quebec made negotiation and consensus almost impossible. Despite this, the Prime Minister wanted to try one last time to make the Canadian constitutional family whole. He asked Joe to take on this monumental task.

Some friends worried that asking Joe to take on this suicide mission was a trap to tarnish his political star. While Brian was being criticized for unpopular policies like free trade and the GST, Joe was basking in the glow of a successful seven years as Canada's voice on the international stage. Whatever his reasons for assigning this task to Joe, Brian knew that no other minister had the reputation or ability to try to negotiate a new constitutional accord between the federal government and the provinces. He was respected within Quebec and known to be a leader who had always put his country first. As a former Prime Minister, he had the standing needed to negotiate with authority and the character to bring together the diverse group of Premiers leading the provinces at the time.

Joe knew this would be one of the most important yet difficult challenges of his political life. Critics of the Meech Lake Accord had accused the Prime Minister and the Premiers of hatching a deal behind closed doors. They were castigated as "the men in suits" and Aboriginal groups and women argued they had been left out. Joe was determined that this would not happen again. His first consultation was in Yellowknife and included Aboriginal people. At the same time, a constitutional subcommittee headed by MP Dorothy Dobbie and former Quebec cabinet minister Claude Castonguay began to hold public meetings. The first public meeting was held in Manitoba and was a disaster. No one showed up. Joe decided that only a radically different approach to public participation would work and suggested five regional meetings, sponsored by five different groups, each addressing different themes of Canadian federalism. A request was made later by national Aboriginal leaders for a sixth meeting dealing specifically with Aboriginal issues, and that meeting was held in Ottawa. From these six conferences a report was prepared and used as the starting point for discussion between the federal government and the provinces.

Joe could see that the legitimacy of the final outcome was inextricably linked with the openness of the process that created it. He decided to try two things. For the first time in Canadian history, so-called ordinary Canadians would join representatives of business, labour and governments as equals in the regional sessions. Joe drafted a letter that was carried in all the daily newspapers asking Canadians who wanted to participate to write him, setting out their reasons and qualifications for being a part of these meetings. Three thousand people replied, and many of them attended one or more of the regional meetings held in Halifax, Montreal, Ottawa, Toronto, Calgary and Vancouver.

I attended three of the six meetings as an observer, and was fascinated by what I saw. There was a mood of seriousness and co-operation. It's often the same people who are invited to such meetings, either because of their competence or position. They are used to being there and expect some deference. Joe had insisted on round tables, which were used at all but one of the regional sessions, and there were two "ordinary Canadians" at each table. At a round table, every person there can pretend to be the leader of the group. I remember watching a table in Halifax, where two men representing different groups were dominating the conversation debating some ancient conflict between them. "Excuse me," said an older woman who had been chosen to participate because of her essay. "We have an important job to do and not much time, so maybe you two gentlemen could continue your discussion later." She then took out her notebook and suggested they each write down their answers to the questions before them so they would not just waste the morning "talking with nothing to show for it."

The second point of note was a memorable moment in Toronto. All day people had discussed, debated, agreed and disagreed. They were all talked out by the time the buffet dinner was over and Kashtin, a rock group of young Montagnais from in northern Quebec, began to play. To my surprise several people got up to dance and within a few minutes the dance floor was packed. As I watched the growing crowd, many of whom had met for the first time that morning, the band started into a medley of Beatles songs, ending with John Lennon's "Imagine." Perhaps it was the song's sentiments or maybe it was no more than the emotion of the moment among people gathered to find a common path to their country's future, but suddenly couples stopped dancing and stood still, swaying to the music. Then slowly, they linked arms, formed a big circle around the dance floor and began to sing the words. It was a poignant moment. That night, for the first time, I thought that there was hope at last for the process and its positive outcome, and that the deep divisions between English Canada and Quebec could be healed.

These six regional sessions led to negotiations involving the federal government, the provinces, the territories and, for the first time, representatives of the four main organizations representing Canada's Aboriginal peoples. Joe had always argued that public opinion had turned against the Meech Lake Accord because of the groups Meech excluded rather than the provisions it included. The symbol of exclusion had been one Manitoba MLA, Elijah Harper, who had prevented Manitoba's ratification of the accord because it did not deal with Aboriginal issues. To succeed, any new negotiation needed to win the confidence of the Aboriginal leaders and that could be done only by their direct participation. That was just one dimension of a negotiation that was much more complex and inclusive than any that had ever occurred before.

Despite the enormous complexity of the task, in June the committee that Joe chaired reached agreement on issues ranging from Quebec's status as a "distinct society" to a triple-E Senate (equal, elected, effective) and Aboriginal self-government. Modifications were discussed through the hot and humid Ottawa summer, and a final meeting of first ministers and Aboriginal leaders was held in Charlottetown. On August 28, 1992, in the birthplace of Confederation, an accord was signed.

That, it turned out, was the easy part. The accord had to be approved by voters in a national referendum. That referendum campaign drew together startling alliances. For example, Pierre Trudeau and Preston Manning united to oppose aspects of the Charlottetown Accord. It drew out both the anger that had been accumulating against the Mulroney government and the endless tensions and misunderstandings that lurk beneath Canada's quiet surface. It was a long and discouraging autumn for Joe. As the vote drew near, he watched as his successful consensus-building among Canada's political leaders disintegrated into confusion and nasty debate. On October 26, 1992, the Charlottetown Accord was (as Joe put it) "enthusiastically rejected" by Canadian voters. He was not sanguine on the night the votes came in, however, and, almost alone among the commentators and participants, he argued that the defeat of Charlottetown would cast a long and dark shadow over Canadians' future ability to agree on common constitutional goals.

Joe laboured on in Parliament throughout November and early December 1992. That Christmas we went again to Hawaii, and I hoped a long rest would improve his outlook and rekindle his optimism. But the rejection of the Charlottetown Accord by Canadians had had a profound impact on him. He had dedicated his entire life to building Canada and saw the rejection of Meech Lake and now the Charlottetown Accord as a serious threat to Canada's future. We returned to Ottawa in mid-January, but even after our time away, he could still find little enthusiasm for his work. He raised for the first time with me the question of leaving politics, and we discussed what else we might do in private life. Catherine and I both told him that we would support him in whatever decision he took. At the beginning of February he decided to retire from politics. Later that week, Catherine and I stood with him in front of a press conference as he announced his decision. After twenty long and exhilarating years in Parliament, Joe Clark was leaving politics.

—

When Joe decided to leave politics in early 1993, a world of possibility opened to us. Since our marriage twenty years earlier, politics had been an integral part of our life together, controlling our schedules and often dictating our personal choices and family lifestyle. I knew it would take quite a while for us to adapt to this change, but I was excited about what the future could offer both of us. After Joe's announcement in February, we discussed options and decided to make a real break from federal politics by spending a year living and working outside Canada. Joe's tenure as foreign minister had made both of us committed internationalists, and we intended to stay involved by offering our expertise to institutions like the Carter Center in Atlanta, established by former U.S. President Jimmy Carter, and the National Democratic Institute in Washington, D.C., for election-monitoring programs in developing countries. During the coming years, I was asked to serve on election-monitoring teams in Ghana, the Ivory Coast and the Dominican Republic. Joe served on others with the Carter Center, including in Mexico, where Catherine used her fluency in Spanish to advantage as one of Joe's assistants.

On the academic front, we accepted an invitation to be visiting scholars at the University of California at Berkeley, where

Joe was in the Canadian Studies department and I was in the School of Public Health. Catherine enrolled in a school near Berkeley to finish grade twelve. Meanwhile, other opportunities came Joe's way, and during the summer, he was asked by the Secretary-General of the United Nations to serve as his special representative for Cyprus. His mandate was to see if the conflict between the Greek and Turkish Cypriots could be resolved. He accepted the invitation. The position would require him to spend many weeks in the following two years flying to and from Cyprus, with stops in New York in between.

—

A month after Joe's announcement, Catherine and I joined him on an official trip to India and China where, as the most senior-ranking cabinet minister, he would begin the renormalization of relations with China after the events four years earlier in Tiananmen Square. While in China he was to attend a meeting of the Asia Society in Guangdong province, and we stopped for a day in Hong Kong after our India trip before going into the countryside south of Guangzhou.

Our plane had not arrived until 4:30 A.M. and I awoke around 10 A.M. at our hotel in Hong Kong feeling nauseated and with a terrible pain in my side. I begged off a walk with Joe and Catherine and went back to bed, but the pain only worsened. After an hour of vomiting and unbearable pain, I called Roseline MacAngus, Joe's senior staffer who was travelling with us, and asked for a doctor. Roseline came to our room and had to help me back to bed, as I could no longer walk unaided. She knew something was terribly wrong and called the hotel doctor who advised her to call an ambulance. Within minutes I was being pushed through the lobby in a wheelchair on my way to the waiting ambulance that was to take me to a local hospital. Joe and Catherine were just returning from their walk, and Joe came with me to the hospital while Catherine ran upstairs to collect my personal items and purse, and followed. Fortunately we were met at the hospital by a senior surgeon, Dr. Wong Kar Mau, who just happened to be there handling another emergency case. Within a few minutes he had conducted an ultrasound, and I was signing a consent form for surgery to remove a large benign ovarian cyst and the ovary to which it was attached.

After surgery that night I finally regained consciousness, but it would be weeks before I would overcome the effect of the anesthetic. As I opened my eyes a nurse said to me, "Hello, my name's Maureen too, and I'm from Edmonton. I'll be your nurse while you are here; welcome back." Her husband was with the Alberta delegation, and when she had heard I was in the hospital, she came to my floor to be there when I awoke. In my mind, Florence Nightingale would have her face. Sometime later Catherine and Joe arrived, and I refused to let Joe cancel his trip into China. I insisted that Catherine go too, as all I would be doing for the next three days was sleeping.

The following morning, my first visitor was Shelley Lau, the deputy minister of health in Hong Kong, whom I was to have met the night before at an official dinner. That afternoon an Ottawa friend, Elizabeth McDougall, who was working in Hong Kong, showed up with flowers. Apparently a Canadian reporter covering Joe's trip to China had been in the hotel lobby as I was being unceremoniously bundled into the ambulance and had sent the news back to Canada, where family and friends were startled to learn I was ill. Elizabeth's mother, Anne, had called her from Ottawa and she had tracked me down. That evening, the Canadian High Commissioner to Hong Kong, John Higginbotham, and his wife, Michèle, came to visit and invited me to recuperate with them at their residence. The next day (after paying the ten thousand dollars for my care on my only credit card), I moved to their home for five days. To show I was well and that the reports of my illness were exaggerated, I attended an official lunch at the end of the week with John and

Michèle; and a few days later, although I was still in considerable pain and rather weak, Joe, Catherine and I flew home.

Back in Ottawa, I got to work. After having lost my thesis because of a faulty disk the previous September, I had decided in January of that year to piece it together from various files so that I could graduate from Dalhousie with a master's in law that spring. The aftereffects of the surgery slowed me down, and I had trouble focusing and sitting at a desk longer than an hour at a time. Still, I knew we would be starting a new life in California away from politics that fall, and wanted to have the thesis behind me as soon as possible.

That May I completed my work and handed in the six required copies to the graduate studies secretary at the university. Two weeks later I received my degree as the first graduate from Dalhousie's Health Law Institute, as Joe, Catherine and Mom sat proudly in the front row. After a salmon barbecue at a friend's home, Mom and I left for a five-day trip around southern Nova Scotia, a treat I had promised her months before. I had hoped to rest for a while, but no sooner had I returned to Ottawa than I was caught up again in politics.

20

SHORTLY AFTER JOE ANNOUNCED in February that he would not run again for Parliament, the Prime Minister followed suit. There was always a suggestion at the time that Joe and Brian were playing a cat-and-mouse game about who would leave first. That was certainly not the case with Joe, and I have no idea why Brian decided to leave when he did. Serving Canada had been Joe's life, and politics and Parliament had been the means through which he had participated and sought to make a difference. After twenty years in Parliament and a lifetime in politics, Joe had come to the decision that he had accomplished as much as he could as a parliamentarian and that it was time for him to move on to other challenges.

Brian's resignation triggered a leadership race to replace him as party leader. Whoever won would be Prime Minister. The convention date was set for early June 1993 in Ottawa, but to my surprise, few ministers decided to run. It was a new experience for me not to be the wife of one of the candidates, but I knew I could not just watch from the sidelines. I studied the field of candidates and decided to support Jean Charest, a young cabinet minister whom I had known for years and whom I respected as an able politician and superb campaigner. A week later, Joe joined me on Jean's team. Jean had worked for Joe during the difficult leadership campaign in 1983, and I thought Jean offered what we needed at that time for the election race that lay ahead. One of his key workers, our friend the late Denis Beaudoin from Quebec, whispered to me at a rally just before the convention, "*Tu sais, Maureen, Jean est le dauphin de Joe*" (Jean is Joe's natural heir.) In many ways he was right. There were differences, of course, among them the fact that Jean was a Quebecker and, if successful, would start his leadership as the Prime Minister of a majority government, with strong representation from both Quebec and Ontario.

Despite his youth, Jean understood the complexity of governing and had a lot of parliamentary experience as a cabinet minister. I chose to back him because he had a combination of political skill and parliamentary ability that no other candidate in the PC Party's 1993 leadership race possessed. He was young, politically experienced, could hold his own seat and was an excellent campaigner. He was a fluently bilingual Quebecker, something that could not be underestimated. It was clear to me, given the antipathy towards the government and the departing Prime Minister, that the winner would have to hit the road running. Walking on water was a precondition of even being in the race. After eight years in office, the government had an activist yet unpopular record to defend, and time would be short for the new leader to set his or her imprimatur on the position. At most the winner would have four months.

Kim Campbell was the frontrunner and her campaign brought together many of the best women in the party. Many had backed Flora in 1976, and this time they wanted a woman to win. I was criticized for not joining her campaign, a difficult decision that I made after considerable thought. I wanted a woman to be Prime Minister but I did not want her to be a sacrificial lamb. I had seen what was needed to be the leader in a national election campaign and I did not believe that Kim could do it. Other factors affected my decision, too. Since the

1988 election, I had watched with growing concern the rise of two regional parties on the federal scene—the Bloc Québécois, a separatist party from Quebec, and the Reform Party in the West. Brian had used consummate skill to build an unlikely alliance among many factions and points of view in Quebec. Without him, all bets were off. Indeed, maintaining that coalition was one of the main arguments for his staying. It was crumbling all around him as the political star of the Bloc's leader, Lucien Bouchard, was rising. (Bouchard, a former Mulroney cabinet minister, had been part of that government's effective coalition of federalists and nationalists.) Our new leader would have to use his or her own credentials to either hold what we had or forge strong alliances with both federalists and nationalists in Quebec if the government was to maintain its seats. I firmly believed Jean Charest would be the only one with even a chance of doing this.

The PC Party had been strong in the West throughout Joe's parliamentary years. But since the previous election in 1988, the Reform Party had been eating away at those roots, making us vulnerable on two fronts—in Quebec and across the West. That would not be fatal if we could rely on winning big in Ontario—just as the Liberals do now. Historically, the federal PC Party had been the beneficiary of a well-oiled provincial organization in Ontario. But in 1993 those glory days were both in the past and the future. The lack of a provincial organization or a powerful Ontario leadership candidate left us in limbo in the province that would decide our party's electoral future.

By the time the convention started, Kim Campbell was the candidate to beat. She started well ahead of her opponents in the race, but despite that lead she began to lose support during the campaign. The decline continued at the convention, and had the leadership vote been taken a day later, I am not sure she would have won it. That was not just due to Jean's ability as a platform speaker. It was also due to Kim's failure to extemporize and reach out to the audience. As the convention went on, I was increasingly optimistic that Jean could win. There was a real mood of excitement and anticipation among delegates and his supporters, and there was no doubt Kim was not performing as well as she needed to. As I went out the door one night into the parking lot at Lansdowne Park, several young students, seeing my campaign button, ran up and told me that they had seen Jean on television and wanted to sign up to help. An informal poll was taken among the ministers' drivers after the candidates' speeches that night, and one of them came over to tell me that Jean had won hands down. Even the press seemed to be more favourable to Jean. The afternoon of the vote brought back memories of conventions past. I looked out at the sea of delegates on the floor in front of me and saw that while the colours of the campaign hats had changed, the thrill and enthusiasm remained the same from one convention to the next. I sat back to wait for the final results and knew exactly what Jean and Michèle Dionne, his wife, were feeling. On the last ballot in 1976 Joe and I had only dared to dream that he might win. In 1983, we both dreaded that he might lose. Sitting near them, I could see that Jean and Michèle were overwhelmed by both these feelings.

It had been an odd campaign. As the establishment of the party had gone early to Kim, many candidates, like Perrin Beatty and Barbara McDougall, had decided that they could not organize a winning team. Jean had been the exception, the one candidate who had decided to take his chances and throw his hat in the ring. He had ruffled some feathers in preventing a simple coronation for Kim, but it had been good for democracy and the party that he had run such a vigorous and successful campaign. I wondered what Jean would do with his victory if he won, and what Joe and I could do to help him. For all their attempts at civility and the successful working relationship they had established since 1984 on many matters, I knew that Brian and Joe had never had much in common, and it would be even less now that both were leaving politics. We owed it to Jean to work with him if he won the leadership, and decided we would return from California and campaign full-out for him when the election was called. I was roused from my speculation by the voice of the convention chair, who droned on for interminable minutes about various party voting rules. I reached for Joe's hand—as I had done twice before in similar moments—and listened for what really mattered, the number of votes. I held my breath and hoped, Please let him win. Kim Campbell . . . Jean Charest. . . . By the time the last number was out, Campbell's supporters were alive with screams of excitement. I turned to Jean and Michèle and muttered some word of consolation. Catherine, a veteran of defeats as well as victories, consoled their crying young daughter Amélie. Then, as Joe had done before him, Jean began the descent to the stage to shake the winner's hand and ask that the vote be made unanimous. As I watched Jean and Michèle on the stage, I thought how painful such political moments could be.

That June, I completed my duties as chair of the CBA's Eastern and Central European legal programs, and left for Warsaw with the team of CBA lawyers just as Kim named a new cabinet. Former ministers, like Joe, who were not planning to run again, were not included. Kim's supporters wanted to be sure they moved quickly to establish themselves in the Prime Minister's office. I could understand that, but time was running out and she was required by law to go to the polls within four months. Every political party enjoys a jump in the polls after a leadership convention and Kim was no different. She had the added bonus of being the first female Prime Minister in Canadian history, whose appeal to women was real initially and could grow. In the immediate aftermath of the convention, I was delighted that her victory might improve the party's chances of winning a third mandate. But under all of this veneer, I knew that the 1993 election would be the most difficult we had faced in many years. Many in the party had wanted a star, as they felt Brian had been, and there was no doubt that, at first, the press found Kim new and fun. But these are just extras in a candidate, like icing on a cake. When all is said and done, a national campaign is a finely tuned event, requiring the party leader to manage not just the gruelling weeks of non-stop campaigning and travel but to present the party's policies well and to respond to the unexpected. In this case, Kim was also Prime Minister, which meant she was defending the Mulroney government's record while presenting her own plans. Part of her strength was her willingness to say what she felt. But in a campaign, as I had learned from personal experience years before, that can be a fatal luxury. Still, as we left Canada at the end of August, Joe and I stood ready to help if asked, as we had always done in the past.

At the end of the summer, Kim Campbell set election day for October 27. Joe went back home to campaign for former colleagues, and was concerned about what he saw. He was sure we would lose many seats in the West to Reform and he worried about our lack of electoral support in Ontario. Jodi White, who had been Joe's chief of staff at foreign affairs and Jean Charest's leadership campaign manager in June, had reluctantly agreed to come back and help with the election organization. She called Joe frequently to bring him up to date and seek advice. While she seemed optimistic in public, we could see that she was very worried. In early October Joe came into my den after a long call with Jodi and said Kim might only be able to scrape by with a minority government. Two weeks later, he returned from Alberta worried that we might lose all our seats there. A friend called from Quebec and said the situation looked grim. The Bloc Québécois was showing remarkable strength and Brian's legendary coalition there was in tatters. The polls were bad and Kim seemed unable to get out the daily messages, defend the Mulroney government's record or define her own agenda for governing. The weekend of the vote, Jodi called one last time. She was prepared for the worst, including losing Kim's own seat. Joe came into the living room, where I was reading, and said pessimistically, "There's a chance we will lose every single riding in Canada." I looked at him in disbelief and thought of all our friends whose futures were at stake. I remembered the long and exhausting days of political campaigning, of the victories and defeats that had marked the first twenty years of my married life, and despaired.

I was due to deliver a speech on women in Canadian politics in Hong Kong the following week, two days after the election, and I had just finished writing it. The prediction of our party's political annihilation seemed too ridiculous at first to even take seriously. Still, I thought, Jodi and all the other friends with whom Joe had been speaking were not prone to exaggeration. On election night, Joe went over to UC Berkeley to watch the results. I stayed at the house to pack for my trip to Hong Kong and China the next day and watched the results on C-SPAN. I was stunned and shaken. By the end of the counting, we held only two seats in Parliament.

In fairness, the devastating vote in 1993 was not all Kim's fault. The Mulroney government had been in power for nine years and the public's perception of its failures cast a long shadow over the new leader. Kim was never able to move free of it, nor did she have much chance to set her stamp on a new government. In the few weeks between her election in early June and the time she was required to call a general election, she had no time to build her own team or set her own theme. I remember wondering at the time why Brian had left it so late to announce that he was stepping down. What surprised me more was that more senior ministers did not run to replace him. I know that several people had encouraged Perrin Beatty to run, and I believed that he had looked seriously at that. I urged

Barbara McDougall to run and would have supported her, as several others in the party would have, including colleagues in cabinet. But I think both discovered that the financial and organizational support they needed was already committed to Kim. The leadership campaign that spring cut into the time needed to prepare for the election that had to be called by fall. At the very moment we needed to organize for the toughest campaign in a decade, we were preoccupied with choosing a new leader. Kim's victory mended some of that, of course. She was not just a new leader but an intelligent woman, and that brought some real political opportunities. But, like any new leader, she needed time to learn the ropes. Unfortunately, time was the one thing no one could give her.

Election night 1993 did more than end nine years of an activist national Progressive Conservative government. It almost eliminated one of only three national political parties and left the PC Party without official party standing in the House of Commons. A once-powerful voice of moderation, of socially progressive and fiscally conservative views, was nearly silenced. In the coming years, when all was so bleak for the party, that role was seized by an excellent team of PC parliamentarians in the Senate. The 1993 election changed the very composition and comportment of the House of Commons, and when the final results were counted, the Official Opposition was the Bloc Québécois. It proposed Quebec's independence from Canada, and its sole purpose was to represent the interests of Quebec in Ottawa. Snapping at their heels was the other new regional movement, the Reform Party, carved from the right wing of the PC Party and remnants of the old Social Credit Party of Alberta. Its leader, Preston Manning, had won on the slogan "The West wants in."

Kim Campbell lost her seat but Jean Charest had the misfortune of holding his and, in December 1993, reluctantly accepted the role of party leader. For four long years his only parliamentary dancing partner would be Elsie Wayne, a new MP from Saint John, New Brunswick. The House of Commons Joe had joined in 1972 was unrecognizable in 1993. A place of national debate had become a hive for local grievances. We both watched gloomily on election night and went to bed sick at heart, wondering what lay ahead for our party and the Canada we loved.

21

THROUGHOUT OUR MARRIED LIFE, Joe had been away half of most every month. Part of the excitement of leaving politics for me was the expected change in that pattern. Yet no sooner had we arrived in California than he had to leave for New York for a briefing on Cyprus with the Secretary-General. From there he flew to London and then Cyprus for his first meetings with the leaders of both the Greek and Turkish Cypriots. I felt my initial optimism about a new lifestyle for us as a family fading as Catherine and I completed the move and started to settle into our new home. As the days passed that September, we both felt a little lost. I went with her to her school on the first day of classes and realized that she was the only one who knew no one there. The first three weeks were very difficult for her. One night in early September, as the two of us made supper, she burst into tears and insisted that she wanted to go home. I was going through a similar moment of doubt, and we just stood there hugging each other and having a good cry. In the little time we had been in California, I had been befriended by Kay McNamara, whose husband, David, was Canada's trade commissioner in San Francisco. Kay had two teenage boys and had moved several times in her life as a diplomatic spouse. She sympathized with me when I called her one night, but insisted that the first few weeks were the hardest and that soon we would feel right at home. She was right. By early October, Catherine had a new set of friends and I had met several colleagues at the university.

Joe was rarely with us during September and October. He went to Canada frequently in those months to campaign for friends worried about winning their ridings in the general election. By Christmas, he had been away more than he had been home, and I realized that leaving politics would not necessarily mean we would start a different and calmer life. We both hoped that the coming year would allow us to enjoy California as a family, and started the new year travelling with Joe's brother Peter and his sons to the southern part of the state. By the beginning of February, our spacious California home had become a bed and breakfast for two kinds of Canadian friends—those escaping a particularly brutal Canadian winter and those recovering from their blistering political defeat. Joe and I had left Canada on a high and had been spared the worst of the humiliation. But we had both experienced electoral losses before and could commiserate with our friends who had been thrown out of politics after years of serving their constituencies. I like to think that after a week with us in California, eating good food, drinking excellent wine and talking with close friends "who had been there already" they were able to better face their own futures.

My position in the School of Public Health at Berkeley allowed me to pursue my interest in law, science and public policy. I joined a discussion group of doctoral students and professors who addressed the ethical and legal issues that genetics raised in the American context. I shared with them, and with the students to whom I lectured, the lessons I had learned in Canada. Soon after my arrival, Dr. Patricia Buffler, the dean of Berkeley's School of Public Health, asked me to coordinate the school's part in an international conference on genetic engineering to be held the following April in San Francisco. That gave me an opportunity to use my organizational skills and to include several respected Canadian, European, Asian and American academic experts working in the field.

While I had specific commitments at the university, I also had time to pursue other interests, especially in women's health. When Joe was foreign minister, I had met a Vancouver pediatrician, Dr. Wah Jun Tze, who had founded the Canada China Child Health Foundation. Among many objectives relating to mother and child health, the foundation twinned children's hospitals in China and Canada. He had come to Canada alone from China as a teenager and against the odds had learned enough English to enrol in medicine at Dalhousie University. From there he had practised pediatrics and married Dr. Theresa Chaing, a pediatric dental surgeon. They lived in Vancouver with their two children. Dr. Tze was a very special person, with a vision of health that included bridging the gap between traditional Chinese and Western medicine. He thrived on challenges and was a tireless fundraiser. In the late 1980s he had raised money to ensure that all children in southern China were inoculated for childhood diseases following a devastating flood. In 1993, the foundation purchased 150 specially fitted trucks built as mobile health clinics to serve even the remotest communities in China. Joe and I attended the special event for their inauguration in Tiananmen Square. The trucks (painted grey with a Canadian flag on the front) were parked side by side, and one by one a representative from each region came forward to accept the keys from Joe before driving out of the square to make the trip to the many villages and cities across China that would benefit from them. It was a wonderful sight and I was so committed to Dr. Tze's work that I even missed Catherine's birthday that year—the first and only time in her life.

Dr. Tze enjoyed wide support among all political parties across Canada for his work, and in May 1994, Governor

General Ray Hnatyshyn agreed to attend a national conference on mother and child health that Dr. Tze had organized in the southern city of Guangzhou. The Governor General and his delegation of Canadian businessmen and bankers were scheduled to arrive the morning of the conference after they finished a business trip to Hong Kong. I was to give a speech in the morning and was delighted that Ray Hnatyshyn, an old friend from political days, had accepted to attend. Before I left California, a group at UC Berkeley who were working in maternal-child health asked me to deliver a proposal for a project with China they had drafted. I agreed to deliver it to the minister of public health, who was also a speaker at the conference.

On May 1, I flew to Vancouver to join a delegation of nurses and doctors from the B.C. children's hospital who were travelling to China for the conference and for site visits to the children's hospital in Guangzhou. The federal government sent one of its ministers, Vancouver MP Hedy Fry, to speak at the conference. It was quite a crew. This trip was in sharp contrast to my first trip there ten years before. We all flew from Vancouver to Hong Kong and then transferred to Air China for the trip to Guangzhou. There is something discombobulating about flying through bad turbulence in China in a Russian-made plane to the music of 1970s American pop songs. As we disembarked, the plane rang with the lament for a cowboy and his dead dog. The following day I learned that the former mayor of Guangzhou, who had hosted a dinner for Joe and me in 1984, was to be my host again. He met me at breakfast with his shy five-year-old granddaughter in tow. He remembered that we had talked about opportunities for women and he wanted me to see that he was already grooming his granddaughter to replace him!

We were staying in the White Swan hotel, remarkably changed since I had been there in 1984. The lobby was full of Chinese families dressed in different shades of Western-style clothing. Given the cost of our rooms in this four-star establishment, I assumed they were from the new business class, and many were. But I learned from my translator that a huge wedding reception was taking place in our hotel that evening and that many of the guests were staying there. A grandmother leaned self-consciously against a brass railing, directed by many contradictory commands on the pose she should strike for her grandson's camera, while on a sofa nearby, an entire family (with children piled on the grandparents' laps just to make room for them all) smiled happily for another camera. Modern Western hotel furniture vied with traditional Chinese pieces to create an eclectic and sometimes incongruous look in the hotel's massive lobby, and there was bustle and optimism everywhere.

After a while I decided to go to the convention room to help with the last-minute details of the next day's conference and, on my way, looked out at the river filled with boats and floating garbage. As I watched, a woman threw waste over the side of her houseboat while another on a smaller boat nearby lowered her basket on a string into the river to bring up the same water for her personal use. Neon signs advertizing cigarettes, cameras, film and restaurants competed for my attention on the far shore. The next day the weather cleared, and I joined some of the doctors and nurses for a visit to an open market to see the stalls where Chinese traditional herbs and medicines were sold. The sight of dog, rat, snake and deer carcasses hanging from hooks before me that morning made me feel nauseated. The smells of the market's wares were heightened by the intense humid heat and by an open sewer with a stream of black sludge that trickled past us. Garbage was everywhere. I wondered how on earth the Chinese miracle of economic growth could possibly lead them beyond the problems of resource use and management that bedevil us in the so-called developed world.

The next day, I arrived early at Dr. Tze's conference, where I could already feel the excitement among the audience, even though no one knew the Canadian Governor General but our own group. All the seats were filled in the early morning for his afternoon arrival, and I was very pleased for Dr. Tze. At the head table sat the minister of public health, the Governor of Guangdong province and the Mayor of Guangzhou—all ready for an important occasion that even the misspelling of the Governor General's name would not dampen. Finally, after lunch, the Canadian vice-regal delegation arrived. As I saw them march in I thought that the Chinese in attendance could be forgiven for thinking that all men in Canada wear navy blue suits and that only men are in business and banking. The Governor General spoke, was his charming and humorous self and was promptly ushered out the door by the protocol officers, followed by every single one of the men in navy blue suits. The crowd was deflated, as all crowds are at the end of the show, but with consummate discipline they stayed and finished the conference. That evening at the dinner offered by the Chinese in our honour, the dessert was apple pie! Oh well, I thought, from the Asian vantage point, Canadians and Americans probably all look the same. The hotel chef was European, so it was really a type of apple strudel, but all of us went back for seconds. Hedy and I managed to hail the dirtiest, smelliest and smallest taxi in the entire city and rattled our way back to our hotel. Having left in a white Mercedes earlier in the day as part of the GG's entourage, we felt like Cinderella rolling home in her pumpkin coach. We even had to show ID before the doorman would let us past the front doors. Hedy was surprised, but I told her jokingly that this was what she could expect when she was out of power.

I continued my volunteer involvement with Dr. Tze until 2000, when his charitable foundation held an international mother-child health conference in Vancouver. It was a huge success that was bought at great cost to Dr. Tze's health. Halfway through the conference he collapsed from exhaustion, a warning sign that he ignored. In December 2001, he died of a heart attack; but his vision and commitment live on in his projects in China.

—

When I arrived at Berkeley in September 1993, I assumed that Canadians and Americans were cut basically from the same cloth and had taken for granted that shared views and academic interests would help me fit in with my colleagues and neighbours. That worked generally within the School of Public Health, where several colleagues had studied and worked in Canada and, among other things, applauded Canada's universal health care system. But this view of Canadians and Americans as cousins merely separated by the forty-ninth parallel was severely tested as I learned just how different a culture and country the United States is from Canada. The most telling contrast came in the field of health care. That year, the Clintons introduced a proposal to overhaul the funding of the American health care system—seen as a real challenge to private health care providers and insurers. For months, all I heard on the radio and television were horror stories about the Canadian "socialist" system of medicine.

Critics of Canada's model of publicly funded health care presented the most outrageous accusations, and I spent many an hour trying to set the record straight. One day, I was so outraged by a caller to an open-line show in San Francisco that I called the program and protested. The show's host insisted that our health care system was so bad that even our former Prime Minister, Brian Mulroney, had sent his mother to Miami to have heart surgery. I told him that the truth was that he had flown her home to Canada for surgery at the world-renowned University of Ottawa Heart Institute when she became ill in the U.S. No matter how I tried to counter them, the attacks on the Canadian system of universal health care continued unabated. Indeed, when the anti-reform groups finally defeated the President's proposal, they had spent billions of dollars on their campaign—enough money to insure every American's health care for a year!

I learned many lessons during my stay. But the most striking was how American policies and laws were influenced by commercial interests at all levels of the governmental process. On closer scrutiny, I saw that the same phenomenon was increasingly at play in my own country. The Canada–U.S. Free Trade Agreement, for instance, opened many markets for Canadians with our largest trading partner, the United States. Years before, the Mulroney government had argued that the FTA was essential to Canada's economic future. After 1993, the new Chrétien government abandoned its main election plank and passed the North American Free Trade Agreement (NAFTA). Canada prospered economically, despite considerable specific problems to those who could not or would not compete, and most Canadians seemed satisfied with the economic results.

My stay in California, though, showed the extremes of treating every public issue as a commercial problem. I had never witnessed this before and it gave me pause. Everything in the U.S. is viewed through the lens of commercial activity. I saw that most starkly while in California, as I organized the School of Public Health's part in an international conference on genetic engineering. Our American colleagues were promoting all manner of medical-scientific development—from private IVF clinics for all who could pay, to the buying and selling of human ova and sperm and women's reproductive capacity through the practice of surrogacy—under the umbrella of "personal choice" and "individual rights and liberties." Stories of how the laws of supply and demand worked in the reproduction field troubled me. Every university publication contained ads asking for ovum donors. Young women from Ivy League schools were in particular demand and could pay for a year's tuition by selling their eggs to wealthy infertile couples. The Human Genome Project, an international science project to sequence all human genes, was a popular topic at conferences in California that year, and its privatization through patents was treated as a given. "Why shouldn't the U.S. government and companies be able to patent human genes?" I was often asked. "How else would there be progress to help people with genetic and other diseases?" Mary Claire King, a scientist who had been instrumental in identifying the gene linked to genetic breast cancer, spoke at a conference I attended. She had learned the hard way how commercial competition and patents worked when she lost her own chance to patent that gene to another company. All around me that year, the talk was of how companies would conquer diseases by controlling the new frontier of human genetics. It was the first time that I saw science, law and ethics so willingly bent to serve the specific interests of commerce, and I worried about the trend moving into Canada. I returned home in August 1994, committed to maintaining our public health care system and addressing the issues raised by the commercialization of human life, the human body and all its parts and processes. I realized what could happen when a country's objectives and public policy were seen only through the narrow prism of economics.

The California experience was a unique one in my life. I had travelled a great deal when Joe was foreign minister, but this was the first time that I had lived away from Ottawa. I made lasting friendships and successfully moved from politics to private life. That did not mean politics was no longer of interest to me but it was no longer the main focus of my personal and family life. I was able to watch current events with a trained eye, but from a distant perch. For once, I knew that my life would not change if the government faltered or an election was called. I was delighted that my days were my own for the first time in two decades. I revelled in the change and was not sorry to abandon the adrenaline highs and despairing lows of political life.

Joe was thriving too. He had set a triple challenge for himself during our year away and successfully wrote his bestselling first book, *A Nation Too Good to Lose,* lectured on Canadian politics and government at Berkeley and travelled every six weeks to Cyprus and New York. He seemed happy to be away from the wear and tear of politics and ready to accept new options that were becoming available to him on corporate boards and in the private sector.

When we left Ottawa we had deliberately set aside the decision on a future home, happy to just use our year away as a bridge from public to private life. As our time in California drew to a close, we began to talk about where we would live in Canada. I had discovered in the early days of my time in California that I missed my mother, family and friends, and hoped that we could go back to Ottawa, where we still had a house. Joe, on the other hand, had his heart set on returning to his home province of Alberta. As we had done the year before, we decided that we would move to a place that allowed both of us to pursue our individual interests and work. On a scouting trip to Calgary during the spring of 1994, I met with the late Murray Fraser, who was then president of the University of Calgary. He believed that I could offer a new perspective on the legal issues raised by genetics, and we agreed to an appointment in the faculties of law, nursing and medicine for the following two years. As part of that position, I agreed to coordinate Calgary's bid to become a federal Centre of Excellence for Women's Health. That was important to me, as it meant I could keep my oar in on issues of women's health research. During that same trip to Calgary, Joe met with several people and decided that he would start an international consulting business in partnership with the law firm Milner, Fenerty (as it was then called) and the international accounting firm Ernst & Young. He would continue his work with the UN and lecture at various universities on Canada's role in the world. Our decision was made. In August 1994, we packed up our belongings again and moved to Calgary.

The only matter left to resolve was Catherine's university education. When we moved to California, we had planned that Catherine would start university in Canada in September of 1994. But I had underestimated Canada's provincial education fiefdoms and was shocked to learn that despite having graduated from an excellent American high school, she would still have to complete four additional grade thirteen courses to be admitted to any university outside Quebec. I fumed for a month until a friend recommended we consider a private school in Neuchâtel, Switzerland, where her daughters had gone years before. That September, while her American friends went off to college, Catherine travelled to Switzerland for six months to finish the Ontario grade thirteen curriculum. While it was not the happiest time of her life, it did give her a chance to see Europe again. Catherine had already travelled a great deal in Europe, but this would be the first time that she would live away from home. All three of us were in a state as she left us in early September, and she had not been in Switzerland three weeks before Joe managed to "drop in" to see her on his way back from Africa. Her asthma was a problem in the first house she was assigned to, so she moved out of the town to the hamlet of Cornaux and lived with a Swiss-Italian family.

After Joe's visit, I met her in Frankfurt in early October 1994 and we spent the weekend with our California friends, the McNamaras, in Bonn, where they had just been posted. Catherine was terribly homesick and we both cried as I left the train at the Frankfurt airport and she continued on to Neuchâtel. I was supposed to travel to China in early November, but decided to cancel the trip because it would mean I would miss Catherine's birthday on November 6. She and Joe had agreed to meet in Paris to celebrate her eighteenth birthday, and I surprised her by arriving with him. Even though the weather was grey, wet and cold, we had a wonderful time together. The night before her birthday, we went to a little restaurant on the Île St-Louis and had a long talk about our changed life. Catherine had grown up with politics and while we protected her from its vicissitudes, she continued to find it fascinating. We reminisced about the fun we had had over the years in different parts of the world and the times we had holidayed in France when she was a child. We realized that it was a relief to be away from the hurly-burly of political life but that it had given us all many exciting memories. As we walked back to our rented apartment, I asked Catherine what she wanted to do for her birthday the next day, and she chose the Paris Opera. Catherine and Joe stood in line in the rain a good part of the next afternoon for tickets to the *Marriage of Figaro;* and amid scolding from me that we would have to take out a second mortgage to pay for the treat, we celebrated Catherine's coming of age.

The following September, Catherine started an honours program in art history at the University of Toronto. At the end of her first year she returned to Paris to take two courses in art at the American University there. Her little walk-up apartment at 58 rue de Babylone in the seventh arrondissement had a bathroom the size of a suitcase and narrow steps to the attic. It became my home away from home that summer, and Joe joined us whenever he could. Many a night Catherine and I would talk until all hours, watching the stars through the little skylight above our narrow beds. When Joe tired of being alone in Calgary, we rented a farm near Pornic, on the Atlantic coast, where he and Catherine wheezed their way through the haying season, and my mother tended the absent landlord's garden. Unlike on our previous trips to Paris, Catherine became the tour guide and we spent many hours ambling together through the Louvre, the Musée d'Orsay and the Rodin Museum and travelling by train to Chartres to see the cathedral and Giverny to see the place that so influenced Impressionism. And of course, we shopped. Our time together that summer gave us the chance to relate to each other in a new way—as friends and not just as mother and daughter—and her growing maturity gave her a sense of independence and freedom as a student in one of the world's great cities.

When I returned to Canada that fall, I turned my attention to the Centre of Excellence for Women's Health project that I was coordinating in Calgary. In that work I was seconded by several organizations and individuals in Calgary, including Dr. Janet Storch, then dean of Nursing at the University of Calgary, and Kathy Grand, the former director of outreach services for the Salvation Army Grace Hospital in Calgary. We had put together an excellent project, but with the exception of MP Jan Brown, we had no support from Alberta Reform politicians, who viewed women's health as just another special interest. By the end of December, we learned that all our efforts had been for nothing. After two years and thousands of dollars' expense, we were unsuccessful in our bid to create a centre of excellence for adolescent girls' health. Edmonton's bid was also rejected, meaning that Alberta did not even have a share in this important program. I was furious when a few months later federal health minister Allan Rock announced a special project on adolescent girls without offering so much as an invitation to our Calgary consortium to participate. I was angry that we had lost our bid for this national project only to have our idea stolen by the government without so much as an acknowledgement of our work.

My years in Calgary were full of friendship and achievement. I was able to work with gifted women like the late Dr. Elizabeth Flagler, Dr. Penny Jennett, Dr. Billie Thurston, Mary Jane Cullen, Kathy Grand, Phyllis Kane, Linda Smith and Suzette Millar to establish a women's health research group at the university. I also started my involvement with the Osteoporosis Society of Canada and became their national spokesperson.

I have never been one to sit around and mope when things don't work out, and I always try to see the silver lining in every cloud. When my two years of work on the Centres of Excellence project did not meet with the desired results, I decided to redirect my academic interests. In 1994, I had created and taught a course at the university on law, science and public policy with an emphasis on reproductive and genetic technologies. Frustrated that there were so few organized materials for the course, I decided to write a book that would look at the points at which science and society intersect. It would take me a long time to research and write, as so many other events always intervened in my life, but I felt it was an important project and pursued it actively.

In the meantime, politics knocked on my door again. Although I had distanced myself from politics after 1993, I did keep in touch with Jean Charest when I could and went to see him in his Ottawa office in late 1994 to see how he was, how I could help him and what he thought of his chances in the following election. He was enthusiastic and focused, but realistic at the same time. He was very concerned about a future referendum on sovereignty in Quebec and he was being shunted aside by the federal Liberals, who saw him as a parliamentary rival to Prime Minister Jean Chrétien. In 1995, Jean confided to me that the federal government's strategy in the referendum was not working, and he was relieved when the Liberal organizers finally opened the door for his involvement in the dying days before the vote. I had not been involved in that battle, although Catherine had been helping to organize students from the University of Toronto to attend the final rally in Montreal. The day before the rally, I awoke convinced that I should travel to Montreal to show my support. Joe was away, but would be home in Calgary when I returned the next night. My mother had just arrived in Calgary and when I told her of my decision, she encouraged me to go. I flew to Montreal the night before the rally and the next day walked towards Canada Place, where the final speeches for the *Non* side would be given by several politicians, including the Prime Minister and Jean Charest.

As I made my way through the crowd, vainly looking for Catherine, I felt a cold numbness. In the shops earlier that day I had met with silence from French Canadians when I lightly raised the referendum vote, and no matter how well-meaning they were, I was embarrassed by the silliness of many Canadians from other provinces who had been bused in to show support. Their painted faces and beery breath seemed better suited to a soccer game or a rock concert than a rally the day before one of the most important votes of our country's history. I listened to the speeches of the *Non* side, and was delighted with Jean Charest's brilliant and passionate speech in support of Canada and of Quebec. But when I called Joe in Calgary from the Dorval airport to tell him how well Jean had done, I learned that no one had heard the Charest speech except those of us on the street in front of him, as an unexplained "technical problem" had deadened his microphone at the moment he started to speak. Political cynicism, I thought, seemed to know no bounds, even when a country's future was at stake.

That night I returned to Calgary and was dismayed that a gold fleur-de-lys brooch I had been wearing alongside a gold maple leaf on my jacket had been stolen during the flight. Joe had gone ahead to a dinner with senior oil executives nearby, and I rushed there to join him. My hostess supported the Reform Party and wanted to know what I thought about the rally and the next day's referendum-vote outcome. When I told her I feared the worst, she just sighed and said, "Aren't we lucky we live in Calgary!" I was flabbergasted by her response, yet knew she spoke for a large number of Westerners. In despair I felt that perhaps the divide in my own country was just too wide to bridge. The next night, October 30, 1995, the vote seesawed back and forth through the long and painful evening, and Canada was held together by a whisper. When all the votes were counted, 50.6 percent of Quebeckers had voted against sovereignty and 49.4 percent had voted for it. Some 93 percent of all eligible voters had cast their ballots. Fewer than 54,000 votes separated the two sides.

As we watched the coverage of the referendum results, I reminded Joe that on that date, twenty-three years before, he had been elected to Parliament for the first time. So much had happened since then, and yet so little seemed to have changed in the Canada-Quebec drama. The arrogance of the federal Liberals running the federalist side of the campaign had known no bounds and we had all paid a high price. Respected federalists, including Joe, had not even been asked to campaign for Canada during that crucial referendum. In spite of the result Jean Charest had become one of the most effective defenders of the federalist cause. In the months ahead, he became stronger in the House and challenged the Bloc Québécois for the right to represent Quebec's interests there. In Quebec, it would only be a matter of time before the push began to oust provincial Liberal leader Daniel Johnson. It is the price politicians pay for losing any important battle, and it was unlikely that Jean Chrétien or the federal Liberal Party would accept responsibility for the disastrous *Non* campaign during the referendum. But the question after that would be who could succeed Johnson. In the fascinating worlds of Quebec and Liberal politics, anything could happen.

Before that, though, Jean Charest had another federal election to fight. The Prime Minister called one for June 2, 1997. It had been my plan to avoid active politics, but after the referendum battle, I knew I had to do what I could to help Jean Charest, and I decided to work for the young PC candidate in my riding of Calgary Centre. After the heady years of power in the 1970s and 1980s, when all the Alberta seats had been held by PC members of Parliament, I discovered just what a wasteland the province had become for us. Still, many of the party faithful and a whole group of new young faces who were friends of the candidate came together to wage a very good campaign. It was odd to be campaigning with neither Joe nor I in the battle, but it felt normal to be knocking on doors, writing briefing notes, accompanying the candidate to coffee parties and dropping pamphlets around the riding. I thought our candidate, Rob Gray, was excellent and saw him mature politically as the campaign progressed. Jean Charest agreed to come to our riding in Calgary Centre for a breakfast campaign stop, and we had people lined up out to the street to meet him. I thought it a huge success and told one of my fellow workers how lucky we were to have Jean as our leader. "He is a really good leader," she replied. "Just too bad that he's from Quebec. Albertans will never elect another leader from Quebec." I was stunned by this remark and was surprised in the coming months to hear it repeated by many others. When the votes were in on June 2, the Liberals had won a clear majority with 155 seats. Jean had done better than expected, winning 20 seats in Parliament—one fewer than the NDP. Still, we were a long way from Official Opposition status. That went to the Reform Party, which at 60 seats had beaten the Bloc's 44. Flush with his victory, Preston Manning abandoned his plans to change Stornoway into a bingo hall, and, with his chauffeur-driven car, moved into the official residence. His blatant flip-flop added fuel to the accusations so often heard that all politicians lie and are out only for themselves.

When I next met Jean Charest after the 1997 election, he was pleased with the results but acutely aware that it would be a long and difficult road back to power for the PC Party. From my vantage point in Alberta, where we were once again wiped out, there were many in the party who criticized the 1997 campaign. Simple solutions were urged. The most persistent was the suggestion that the Reform and PC parties bury the hatchet and join forces—the beginning of the "unite-the-right" solution, as it came to be known. As a member of the PC Party since I was a teenager, I found the whole idea absurd. I had no interest in abandoning my support for a national party that advocated fiscal discipline and progressive social policies to marry a movement whose agenda was both local and limited. I hoped that the whole crazy and unworkable idea would just blow over.

Instead, the idea gained ground, especially in Ontario, where PC Premier Mike Harris adopted an agenda similar in content and tone to that advocated by the Reform Party and supported Reform candidates in many Ontario ridings. In such a climate, it was inevitable that there would be talk of change in the federal leadership. But I knew how hard it was for Jean to rebuild a party structure from nothing, with few human and financial resources. I also knew how any party in opposition, and certainly the PC Party, was difficult to lead and discipline. Throughout the fall, I continued to meet people across Canada who insisted that he was not the one to lead the federal party back from the political and parliamentary wilderness. These were hard months for Jean Charest in Ottawa.

—

During our four years in Calgary, Joe built an international consulting practice focused on the energy sector, joined several corporate boards, gave many speeches and travelled extensively in Africa and Asia. He built upon his standing among several leaders in Commonwealth Africa, with whom he had worked while Canada's foreign minister, to help end apartheid in South Africa. He gave freely of his time to help developing countries with regulatory and policy issues, ranging from education and training to basic security matters of law and order. We were happy in Calgary, where Joe's only brother, Peter, and their mother, Grace, both lived. If there was one person missing in Calgary, it was Catherine, who in the spring of 1997 had just finished her second year in art history at the University of Toronto. Joe saw her more often than I did, as he continued a hectic pace, travelling frequently to Toronto and Ottawa. In 1997, Joe's international consulting work required a greater presence in Ottawa, and we decided to look for an apartment for him there. It would be cheaper and more pleasant for him than staying in hotels all the time, and I would be able to use it whenever I needed a change or was lonesome for home.

One weekend in early May we met Catherine in Ottawa and looked at what was available in the rental market. At the end of three days, we had still not found what we wanted, when our friend and real estate agent, Judy Reid, persuaded us to stop at a house that she thought would "be perfect" for us. It had a sign that described it as a "California-style house," which intrigued us, and we agreed to take a quick look. As we entered the door, Catherine whispered, "Tell her we'll take it." It was the perfect mix of house and garden and we all knew immediately that this was the house for us. We returned to our hotel room and spent the next two days studying our options. The chance to see Catherine regularly finally sealed our decision. We put in an offer, bought the house and sold our condo in Calgary—all in less than two weeks! Shortly after, Joe opened an Ottawa office for his consulting company and I was elated that Roseline MacAngus, who had been with us for years while Joe was an MP and cabinet minister, agreed to take charge of our lives once again.

Joe's mother's health had begun to deteriorate, precipitated by a fall in which she had broken her hip. She had to be moved from her High River home to a seniors' residence in the city. Joe's father, Charles, had suffered a fatal heart attack in 1982 and she had been living independently since then. In early 1997, she began her final decline, and in August, just before our departure for Ottawa, she died. Grace Clark had been a formidable force who had exercised tremendous influence on her two sons' lives. A high school teacher in the Alberta foothills town of High River, south of Calgary, Grace had encouraged Joe and Peter to achieve, and both had reached the pinnacle of their chosen careers in politics and law. She had earned a university degree from the University of Alberta in the 1930s, at a time when few women even graduated from high school, and had taught an entire generation of young people from rural Alberta. Even today I meet her students, who tell me of the impact she had on their lives as a teacher and mentor. In late August 1997, after her funeral, I prepared to leave Calgary with promises to all my new friends that I would be back often. Little did I know what that would entail.

22

WHEN WE RETURNED TO OTTAWA, it was as if I had never been away. I was asked to join the clinical ethics committee at the University of Ottawa Heart Institute and then became a public member of the Committee of Accreditation of Canadian Medical Schools. I continued my volunteer work in women's health as the national spokesperson for the Osteoporosis Society of Canada, and helped them start their annual series of fundraising Bone China Teas across Canada each November. In that position, I travelled that fall to each provincial capital and met with the ministers of health to further the excellent awareness programs on nutrition and personal care that had been put together by Joyce Gordon, the association's national director, and by the scientific advisory team, staffers and community volunteers.

As the new year approached, I prepared to move to Vancouver for three months to lecture in reproductive law at the University of British Columbia. I had agreed to the position the year before, when we still lived in Calgary, and decided to carry through on my commitment even after we moved to Ottawa so I could finish the research on my new book about law and science. Still, I did not much want to leave my new home in Ottawa and was homesick from the moment I stepped off the plane in Vancouver on a dull, wet January day in 1998. To make matters worse, I soon watched helplessly as television reported the ice storms of the century in eastern Ontario and parts of Quebec. My own mother was without electricity for almost three weeks, and she survived by using her stove in the basement to keep her warm. She had candles and oil lamps that my father had bought at auctions thirty years before, which she cleaned and lit at night; she quilted during the day and kept the fire going through the night. She lived on the contents of her freezer, cooking for my brother, who moved in for the duration, and for everyone else who was without food and electricity. I relied on our neighbours across the street in Ottawa to watch over our place. Joe was unable to return to Ottawa from Edmonton immediately. I enjoyed my semester lecturing, writing and spending time with old friends in Vancouver, but I was eager to return to Ottawa, where I could quietly finish writing my book during the summer. By the end of the year, my idyllic dream would be shattered once again by politics.

It is hard to describe how I felt the day in 1998 that Daniel Johnson resigned as leader of the Quebec Liberal Party. I was driving to my lecture when I heard the news on the car radio and nearly drove off the road. I had been around politics for too long not to see how this incident thousands of miles away would affect my own life. I arrived in class distraught. "I'm sorry to be so upset," I told some of the students in my class before starting, "but Daniel Johnson has just resigned." Silence and blank looks from them all. I could see their brains working: Who is Daniel Johnson, and why does it matter? Of course, I thought, why would they know? So I proceeded to walk them through the possible consequences of Johnson's decision, including the likelihood that the list of proposed successors would surely include Jean Charest, the leader of the federal PC Party. I tried to explain that in the world of Quebec politics this would not only be possible but would make sense for the federalists, who were battling a strong separatist government and were saddled with ineffectual federal leadership. I spared them my lecture on the domino effect of political life, where the failure to include Quebec in the patriation of Canada's Constitution in 1982 coupled with the subsequent failure of the Meech Lake Accord and the rejection of the Charlottetown Accord had led us inevitably to this point. Most of them had been in diapers then and seemed more concerned about my own state of mind at that moment than about what perhaps lay ahead in federal and provincial politics half a continent away.

I ended the lecture early and drove back to my apartment to call Joe. As always, he calmed me down, telling me that while Jean might not have won the last election in 1997, he was deeply committed to rebuilding the party. There was no doubt that that was true, but I had seen him speak in Montreal just before the referendum debate in 1995, and had heard the passion in his voice when he defended his federalist views during the televised leaders' debates in the 1997 election campaign. The separatist threat in Quebec was real and he knew it. I was sure the Liberals would call on Jean's honour and patriotism as a proud Quebecker *and* Canadian in the coming days. It would be a brilliant political move for the Quebec Liberals to steal him from federal politics, and would remove yet another embarrassing reminder to the Prime Minister in the parliamentary question period each day that his constitutional policies were bankrupt.

Even if this pressure proved insufficient to move him, there were other elements at play that might. Since the 1997 election a few months before, there had been a dynamic in our own party that bothered me. Jean's failure to make any breakthrough in Ontario and the West weighed heavily on his shoulders and gave new life to the growing demand in these provinces for a union between the Reform and PC parties. The logic for those who wanted to "unite the right" went something like this:

Jean Charest is a French Canadian and a Quebecker and people in the West won't vote for him—witness the 1997 election results. In the weeks of decision for Jean, I could see that the strategy of proponents of a unified PC–Reform party was to encourage him to accept the provincial offer. They did not play the anti-Quebec card, but argued that he "owed it to Canada" to move back to Quebec. In the absence of any strong and respected alternative for leader, the unite-the-righters would have a green light to argue their case for unification, even if it meant a hostile takeover of the PC Party of Canada.

In the days that followed Daniel Johnson's announcement, I examined in detail these and other factors that would affect Jean's difficult decision. I knew that politics was very hard on one's personal life and that it had been a long and difficult four years on the road and in Parliament for him. I could only imagine how lonely and frustrating it was travelling around a country the size of Canada, day in and day out, trying to rebuild a devastated party into a national political force again. He was a young man with a beautiful wife and family and financial obligations to meet. I knew that no matter what he said now, it would be hard to resist the appeal to move from leader of a fifth-place federal party to the leader of the Opposition in his home province. I sent him a note from Vancouver urging him to stay. While I was greatly concerned for the party should he leave, I had another, more personal, worry about who would replace him. In the current situation, with Reform haunting our halls, we would need a strong and seasoned leader to take charge if Jean stepped down. Such people existed among the former cabinet ministers from the Mulroney years, but the question was whether any of them would run. If not, then I knew there would inevitably be pressure on Joe, as a former leader and party elder statesman, to take on the job again. I did not want that to happen.

I went home to Ottawa as soon as I could to discuss all this with Joe. He had been thinking about the many hurdles facing the party and he did not rule out running himself if it were necessary. I told him that he had done enough for the party and should urge others to come up to the plate. I approached Perrin Beatty, who was still young and had great experience as a minister in both Joe's and Brian's cabinets, arguing that many of us would build a strong campaign for him. He was head of the CBC and enjoying life, and declined my urgings. He was not alone. In the five years since 1993, most former MPs and ministers had moved on and made commitments elsewhere to jobs and families. Few of Joe's former cabinet colleagues had stayed involved in any way, and Jean had brought in his own group to help him in the rebuilding process. Added to this, most former members of Parliament had been devastated by the magnitude of their own and the party's losses in 1993, and were not willing to re-enter the demanding and all-consuming arena of politics.

In March, Jean Charest decided to leave federal politics and move to Quebec to lead the provincial Liberal Party. His departure left a very big void. Politics is about timing, and the timing for the federal PC Party could not have been worse. Since 1993, Jean had nurtured the once-powerful federal PC Party in Parliament and in the country and had ensured its survival and growth. He was young, energetic and politically experienced, and most of us had assumed he would be our leader for the long haul, with a real chance of being the leader of the Opposition after the next election. That did not seem a pipe dream. The Reform Party had failed to break through the Ontario border again in the 1997 federal election and remained very much a regional political party. Their leader, Preston Manning, was under pressure both from those who wanted him to boldly try to absorb the federal PC Party into the Reform Party, and those who wanted no truck and trade with the Tories, their ideological and political enemy. Preston had been looking actively for ways to become a force beyond the Manitoba-Ontario border and had enlisted the support of Ontario's Premier, Mike Harris, in that effort. Indeed, one friend told us that Manning and Harris had already met in March to discuss how they might work more closely together. For those of us who believed in a national PC Party, this was not the time to be leaderless. The stakes could not have been higher, as the party struggled for its very life. We could not afford to spend the coming months in a state of political and parliamentary drift without a strong and experienced leader.

By April 1998, I knew that Joe was receptive to the calls from many party supporters for his return as leader. The logic was simple. The party would not survive otherwise. I worried that I was fighting a losing battle in arguing against it. He had enlisted Catherine in his cause, and she was enthusiastic. By the time we decided to travel to Paris for a week in May, we had reached an impasse in our discussions. Our plan was to make the decision as a family, away from the media and all those helpful party friends. In a rented apartment in Paris, our discussions continued. I argued against Joe's running. There was the cost of a campaign, the loss of income, the party's small presence in the Commons and its heavy debt burden. There was its poor organizational and membership base and Joe's lack of a parliamentary seat. I also noted the public's seeming indifference to politics generally, Joe's age (though he was younger than both the Prime Minister and his finance minister and possible successor, Paul Martin) and the impact all this could have on our life as a couple and a family. On the other hand, I agreed with Catherine's view and his, that as leader he would bring status and stability to the party at this crucial moment. He would inject a different vigour and enthusiasm into the caucus and hopefully would keep in check the internal conflict between the progressive wing and those who still insisted that we had to join the Reform Party to beat the Liberals. Joe was convinced that his standing and reputation in the country would allow him to reach out and rebuild the party as a national force, and I agreed that no other opposition leader in Parliament understood Canadian politics or our nation's public policy better than he did. I was moved by his commitment to the larger ideal of service to his country, even though I felt he had already done more than any one else I knew to achieve that goal.

As the tense week dragged to a close, Joe and I went for a long walk and stopped at a little sidewalk café near St-Germain-des-Prés. He knew how upset I was by all that was happening and, for the first and only time, said that he would not run unless I agreed. It was a difficult moment. Politics and service to Canada had been his life's work and he had never really settled into our private life as I had. He insisted that it would likely only be for five years, but that seemed a long time to me, and I knew that if he was successful, we would be there longer still. Finally, I nodded my assent, unwilling to trust my voice to reply. The decision had been taken. One last concern remained to be resolved. I had to finish writing my manuscript during the summer and so I could not travel with Joe in the coming months. On our last night in Paris, we had dinner with friends Bill Chambers and Rona Waddington, and as we discussed this concern, Catherine volunteered to travel with Joe throughout the leadership race.

During that summer Catherine kept her promise and served as Joe's assistant and travel companion. Art Lyon, who had been the wagon master for several previous PC election campaigns, recommended that we hire Chad Schella to take charge of logistics, media and travel, and we did. Originally from Peterborough, Ontario, Chad had graduated from Bishop's University in Lennoxville, Quebec, and had worked for Jean Charest in his Ottawa office. It was during this campaign that Catherine and Chad fell in love. I was surprised when she confided this to me near the end of the campaign, but I understood

divided and wounded by years of neglect. A deep cynicism and anger against government and political leaders bubbled close to the surface among the public, their frustration stoked by broken election promises that led to polarization and strife. Our party had been on the receiving end of the public's wrath in 1993. As a result, Canada's political dynamic had been challenged and changed by several factors, including an official opposition with a limited and limiting agenda that could never form a national government. There were now five political parties in the House of Commons. That should have made it a more vibrant and relevant forum. Instead, without any new tools to encourage co-operation or achieve consensus, Parliament was a place of frustration bordering on irrelevance. Parliamentary reform had been at the heart of Joe's government's agenda twenty years before and remained a priority. The six goals he had set for his government then were as relevant and necessary in 1998 as they had been in 1979. We needed to build upon our regional strengths, restrain the growth of government spending, rely on the private sector as the prime generator of growth, jobs and wealth and build upon our cultural diversity as a singular national asset. We needed to put a fresh face on federalism by modernizing major public institutions, making individual members of Parliament partners in the shaping of government policies, sharing constitutional power with Canada's provincial and municipal governments and respecting provincial jurisdictions. Other issues had arisen in the interim and would have to be addressed, including those of the environment, sustainable development and energy, globalization, defence and peace-keeping capabilities, trade and a new role for Canada in the world. I knew that an effective leader for Canada in the new century had to understand our unique history and have the vision to build upon our sometimes common, oftentimes conflicting, stories. In describing Canada during his maiden speech in Parliament in 1973 as "a community of communities" Joe had identified our biggest weakness and our enduring strength as a country. The challenge of governing Canada is in striking an elusive balance between the interests of the whole country and the pride and dynamism of its regions. In supporting Joe's decision to run again for our party's leadership, I knew it was right for him personally, and crucial for the future of the country that I loved. Even knowing the price I would have to pay, I could not abandon my deeply held conviction that this was required of him and of us. I believe that we must all make our own futures, and with a daughter whose life is before her, I knew that I could not stand idly by when we had something to offer in the shaping of that future. When I sat in that Paris café and reflected on my family's future, I had prayed for the strength to see this burden through.

The campaign itself was fought under the party's new rules, which I still do not pretend to understand. "One person, one vote" was its thesis, although the votes in each riding were weighted and there was no convention site where people could come together and meet each other. I wondered if any of the architects of the new rules had really been involved in such a campaign before. Joe had a headquarters in Ottawa and several supporters volunteered to help. In the meantime, Joe, Catherine and Chad travelled the country.

By the end of the summer I had finished the manuscript for my book and I turned my attention to the campaign. I worked with Linda Oliver and Eileen Wilson to put together a women's committee to support Joe. In this I asked for advice from Toronto supporter Carol Jamieson, who had set up the highly effective Women's Connection for Clark campaign in 1983. I joined the national telephone campaign to boost interest and support in Joe's campaign at the riding levels across Canada. I discovered that most constituencies had no more than a skeleton of an organization, and without paid organizers we relied on volunteers during the long, tedious and exhausting months of the campaign.

The day of the first vote in October, Joe was firmly in the lead, although with less than the required number to win on the first ballot. Hugh Segal was in second place and, seeing that he could not win, withdrew from the race. We waited for word that David Orchard, who had placed third, had done likewise, but he refused, insisting on a second ballot two weeks later, a move that would cost the party and our campaign thousands of dollars. I saw his decision as petty and mean, and even those who had tolerated his anti-free-trade campaign were unforgiving in their criticism of him. While the outcome was never in doubt, we worked hard during the next weeks to ensure that party people voted again. On the Saturday evening of the second vote, we ate supper at home in Ottawa and awaited the results. It should have been a happy occasion for us, as Joe won the vote and became party leader again. Instead, the death of young Michel Trudeau in an avalanche in British Columbia cast a sad shadow over our celebration, and the images of his anguished parents and brothers haunted the television screen that week.

People who only see MPs attacking each other in the House of Commons can be forgiven for believing that they all hate each other, but that is not the case. While there was certainly a rivalry between Joe and Pierre and each disagreed fundamentally with the other on the nature and future of Canada, they respected each other. We had last seen Pierre in Atlanta the year before at Jimmy Carter's meeting of retired leaders of freely elected governments. He had seemed much older, yet friendly and charming as we talked about our children and their most recent youthful exploits. Catherine was near in age to Michel, and I still remember the boys and Catherine at the annual children's Christmas parties, oblivious to the political turmoil that divided their fathers. At those holiday events, Michel seemed like a little imp trailing along after his two older brothers. By 1998 our children had grown up and were seeking out their own adventures. Michel's took his life. On that grey and cold November evening, as we celebrated Joe's victory, my heart went out to Pierre and to Margaret, and I prayed that they could find the strength to confront the very worst of tragedies—the death of a beloved child.

23

THE NEXT YEAR WAS FILLED WITH DÉJÀ VU. Joe travelled the country, trying to rebuild the party and to set the policy course we would follow for the next election. I was sheltered by the fact that I had other work to do, including launching my third book, *Tough Choices: Living and Dying in the 21st Century.* I had several speeches, media interviews and other public appearances as part of its promotion, and with a little coaxing Catherine agreed to travel with me to act as executive and media assistant for my month on the road. Travelling with her during that book tour reminded me of how she had grown into a mature and able young woman, and I listened with pride as she handled telephone calls, set up interviews and liaised with the publisher.

The year was a frustrating one for Joe. After his election as party leader, he decided not to seek a seat immediately but to wait until the next election. He did not need to prove himself as a parliamentarian and believed that his time was better spent campaigning and preparing the party organizationally. I cannot overstate how changed the party and political landscape were upon Joe's return to politics as leader in 1998. In 1976 he had led a caucus of ninety-five members who had represented both depth and regional diversity. In 1976, the goal had been government; in 1998 the task was survival. Aware of the party's vulnerability after Jean's departure, the unite-the-right campaign was in full swing. In an attempt to broaden their base into Ontario and beyond, the Reform Party had held a national convention in May 1998 in London, Ontario, to begin re-creating itself. From my vantage point, all they were offering was more of the same. The effect of their political facelift was supposed to be magical and modern. It would fool very few Canadians.

Just after Joe became leader, Preston Manning had asked him to attend their upcoming meeting in February 1999, to describe how he—Joe—planned to defeat the Liberals. It seemed an odd request to me. I had watched Manning's speech in May 1998 and thought it was clear what his own plan was— "the creation of a governing party based on Reform principles under the great banner of Reform." I wondered if he thought we couldn't read. All through this period, Manning kept insisting that the Reform Party contained many former federal PC and provincial party members and he was right. But these people had left the PC Party for Reform because they did not support the PC Party's platforms, especially its progressive social policies. I, for one, was not a social conservative any more than Preston Manning and his supporters were social progressives. We were separated by a massive and unbridgeable divide on this principle, and could never agree on questions of key importance to most Progressive Conservatives, including those of women's equality and reproductive rights, public support for social programs, human rights laws that protect all Canadians and the belief that there is a role for government in Canada in ensuring social and economic well-being for all its citizens. Joe had declined Manning's invitation, but I could see that many in the Ontario provincial PC Party supported the Reform proposal to unite the right. I took this as a personal insult. I had been raised in the Ontario provincial party and my father had been a volunteer campaign organizer for years in eastern Ontario. I had never differentiated between the federal and the provincial parties and had worked on all their campaigns. I was dismayed that the provincial party would betray its federal cousins by actively working for the Reform candidates against us.

In late May 1999, after their second convention in a year, Preston Manning came over to our home in Ottawa for a meeting with Joe. He was determined to build his Reform Party beyond its regional base, and sincere in his view that all that was required was a marriage of convenience between the Reform and PC parties to defeat the Liberals. He seemed unable, though, to understand that his party's policies and views, especially on social policy and the role of government, were alien to those of the PC Party. I thought his insistence that we were all somehow brothers-in-arms against the Liberals disingenuous. At the same time I knew that his identification of the challenge to replace them as government was realistic. After he left our home late that afternoon I could see that their meeting had been cordial but inconclusive and I was not surprised. These two men, born into different parts and cultures of the same province, had visions and experiences so different from each other's that it was impossible for them to ever share common ground. Joe drew strength and insight from his Alberta roots, formed as they were in the big-sky country of the foothills of the Rocky Mountains. Alberta's history was in his bones, as it was in Preston's. But unlike Preston, Joe sensed that history defined him in a different way—as forward-looking, modern, dynamic. His Alberta was a place of the future where anything was possible if only you set your mind to it. Over the years, that "can do" spirit imbued him with the self-confidence needed to face political adversities that often seemed insurmountable and would have broken a lesser or weaker man.

Manning saw Alberta differently. To him, the West wanted in. He did not treat Alberta as the powerhouse that it was, but a place that needed to be protected—a political version of circling the wagons and pointing guns out at the world. His tone was one of complaint; if only we would understand him, we would love him. It is ironic and sad that at the very moment when he was finally able to see the shades of grey that define life as well as politics, his own people abandoned him. I could never have supported most of his political views but did respect his courage in trying to force his party to become moderate and modern. The following year, as I watched Preston and Sandra Manning the night his own party rejected him, I thought I knew how they felt as their political dreams and hopes were dashed forever. Given what happened next to his party, his defeat was a loss to Canada as well as to his party.

By spring 2000, there was increasing pressure on Joe to seek a parliamentary seat. The Reform Party had morphed into the Canadian Reform Conservative Alliance (known thereafter as the Canadian Alliance) and in June had abandoned their founder, Preston Manning, in favour of Alberta's former provincial treasurer, Stockwell Day. Joe announced that he would gladly meet Day in a by-election in Calgary Centre—winner take all. The offer was not accepted, as a safer seat was already being arranged for Day in neighbouring British Columbia. In the meantime, Joe was the candidate in Calgary Centre and campaigned there as often as he could. His audacity in challenging Day in Alberta—the CA's own backyard—might have surprised local organizers, but it gave many PC supporters a boost to know that their leader was so confident.

In July, as usual, we attended the Calgary Stampede, and Joe met with the local campaign organizers in Calgary Centre to ask them to prepare for a possible snap election. We then flew back to Ottawa to start our annual drive to Nantucket. We were both looking forward to a much-needed break and on the drive down to the Cape talked about whether Joe should try to create an opening among his caucus colleagues so he could run for Parliament as soon as possible. Manning's defeat had created

a new dynamic in the pre-election period and many were pushing Joe to run early. At least, I thought, we would have three
weeks of rest before deciding. But there was to be no rest for
either of us. Immediately upon our arrival Joe had to deal with
a flurry of long-distance conference calls from his caucus and
advisers, eager for a decision about creating a by-election. In
spite of his total lack of experience in Parliament, Day was
adamant that he wanted to be in the House by the fall and
announced that Alliance MP Jim Hart had stepped down to create a by-election. That night, Scott Brison and Peter McKay,
two of our best and brightest young MPs, offered to do the
same for Joe. Scott's riding was marginally better for Joe, and
after many more phone calls, Joe decided on Scott's riding of
Kings-Hants in Nova Scotia. Catherine and I sat on the couch
of our Nantucket cottage holding hands, lost in our own
thoughts as Joe called Scott to tell him. It was a big sacrifice for
Scott, who had remained loyal to Joe throughout this period of
caucus rumbling, and all three of us would remain in his debt.

After his short conversation, Joe put down the phone and
looked at us. None of us spoke, but we all knew what lay
ahead. The next day Joe asked if I would cancel the rest of my
holiday and go with him to Nova Scotia and I agreed. We left
our SUV on the island to be driven up to Nova Scotia at a later
date by a friend and flew to Halifax. The vacation we so needed
would have to wait for another time. We found a house to rent
and spent the summer in Wolfville, a charming university town
in the Annapolis Valley.

There was enthusiasm for Joe throughout the Kings-Hants
riding, but real confusion and concern about what would happen to Scott. To put an end to the rumours, Joe suggested that
he and Scott stage their nomination meetings at the same time.
Joe was elected as the candidate for the by-election at the beginning of the meeting and then Scott was nominated for the general election right after. This reassured his supporters that they

would not lose their excellent young MP for long. In introducing Joe at the press conference that first week upon our return, Scott insisted that he and Joe were a double bonus for Kings-Hants. "Meet Batman and Robin," he quipped. As we burst into laughter at his sheer irreverence it occurred to me that this might actually be the beginning of a fun campaign. In late 1999 I had begun to host a weekly Internet interview program on science in Ottawa, and during the summer I had to return to Ottawa for one day each week to tape the show. While there, I would check that our house was still standing, but after the second week I gave up on the garden, resolving to look after it in the fall.

Workers came from all over the riding—indeed, the country —to help Joe in this important by-election. Scott travelled full-time with Joe and his young assistant, Kurt Beers. Catherine joined us at the end of the summer for the last big push. It looked as if we were on our way to a big win on September 11, when we were alerted by a call from Joe's Ottawa staff that the government had struck a deal with two of our Quebec MPs to leave us and join the Liberals. One MP, André Harvie, had already done so earlier in the year, insisting that it was better for his constituents to be on the government than opposition benches. It seemed two of his colleagues shared his view. Joe tried in vain to change their minds. He argued that they owed him at least a meeting in person before bailing ship. But the Liberals are no fools, and part of the deal was that they would announce their move the day after the by-election to reduce the impact of Joe's victory. I was furious at their callousness and angry that the press did not condemn the government for this shameless act. I tried to imagine what would have awaited us if, while in government, Brian Mulroney had tried such a trick. After this, I had no illusions about how low the Prime Minister would stoop to get his way.

On the weekend before the vote, we all returned to the campaign with as much enthusiasm as we could muster and left the media spin to the Ottawa office. Most of the caucus were in the riding for the vote, and Nova Scotia MP Gerald Keddy was hosting a smoked salmon barbecue at his farm. We had agreed to drop by before going to the election night event to watch the vote in Wolfville: during an election, you work until the last poll is closed. As we drove to Gerald's event the evening of the by-election vote, Catherine, Scott and I sat in the back of the campaign's minivan using cellphones to call our list of supporters to be sure they had voted. Joe sat in the front seat preparing his remarks for later that night. Out of the blue, Scott's cellphone rang. We were stunned to hear the voice of one of the defectors, Diane St. Jacques, explaining her untimely departure from the caucus to join the Liberals. She wanted him to understand that she had a mortgage to pay and a child to raise. She needed to be sure she could get re-elected, and the Liberals had promised her that they would help her do that. The clincher was that she hoped that she and Scott could still be friends. We had all stopped to listen to this most incredible conversation, and I could see Scott's jaw tighten as he replied, "If you need a friend, get a dog," and slapped his cellphone shut.

That night, Stockwell Day won an impressive victory in B.C. and was planning to move into Stornoway and his Centre Block offices as soon as possible. The betrayal by Joe's two former colleagues would give new life to the calls for Joe to fold the PC Party into the Canadian Alliance and to unite the right against Jean Chrétien. Worse, coming when they did, the defections would inevitably call his leadership into question and limit his ability to mount an effective national election campaign. That night, as the voters of Kings-Hants gave Joe a ringing endorsement as their member of Parliament, it was a bittersweet celebration in Wolfville. But as I walked through the crowd I was heartened to see friends who had come from other provinces to be with us, including Irving Gerstein, head of the PC Canada Fund, who with his wife, Gail, had celebrated good and bad election nights with our family for two decades. His presence reminded me that loyalty and friendship still existed in politics.

We flew home to Ottawa amid the defection stories. Joe did his best to answer reporters' questions of what he planned next, although what was there to say? After the excitement of the by-election victory, it was a great disappointment to spend time on the defensive. Later that month Catherine and I sat proudly in the gallery of the House of Commons to watch Joe be escorted to his parliamentary seat. The House was unusually alive with excitement and anticipation as political friends and foes welcomed him back to Parliament. I felt it natural as he was the most accomplished and tenacious parliamentarian of his generation—something the government would learn in the coming months. He went to his seat, bowed to the Speaker, looked up at and smiled at Catherine and me as we applauded him with pride. Each of us was relieved that this stage was over for now, even as we suspected what lay ahead. During our brief spell in Nantucket in July, Joe had called Jean Chrétien to ask him if there would be a general election that fall. There would be little use running for a by-election in the summer if a month later the whole country would be going to the polls.

Joe had known Chrétien since 1972, and he wanted to hear directly from him that this effort to return to Parliament would not be a waste of time and taxpayers' money. Chrétien had been noncommittal, but insisted that he wanted all the party leaders in the House of Commons for the fall session of Parliament. After this conversation Joe decided that his lack of candour could mean anything but that there was a better-than-average chance that we would be facing a general election as early as the fall. There was no evidence for this, just his gut feeling. The Prime Minister was barely starting his third year of a majority government, and there was no reason for him to even consider another election for another year and a half. But the polls showed him significantly ahead of the opposition parties and he wanted to stay there—something he could not really control with both Joe Clark and Stockwell Day in Parliament.

In July, even as he prepared for a by-election in Nova Scotia, Joe had moved aggressively to prepare the local riding association in Calgary Centre for a fall election. I cannot really remember how I felt when the Prime Minister called the election that October. I had just returned from Quebec, where I had launched the updated French-language version of my book on science and law and was on my way to another series of speeches. I lay in bed the following morning, unable to move, yet knowing the frantic pace that was required for the election ahead.

I had no illusions about the outcome; the Liberals would win. My concern was with our party and my husband's future. Where would we end up, with the newly renamed Canadian Alliance well funded and with a leader whose circuslike antics the media appeared to adore? How could this be happening? It was the worst possible time for the PC Party to be going to the polls, for in spite of Joe's insistence on election readiness, much remained to be done. He continued to top the polls as a favoured political leader, but the party was nowhere. We had a few strong local candidates at the time, but if we were to avoid a repeat of 1993, Joe would have to take the entire campaign on his shoulders. That is exactly what he did.

John Laschinger, a prominent Tory political strategist and organizer, came to our rescue at party headquarters to run the campaign. He managed to cajole others into joining him, and people like former MP Jean-Guy Hudon took over responsibility for Quebec—an electoral wasteland for us. Irving Gerstein and his team worked to find the money to rent a plane and mount an effective national campaign tour for Joe. In all of this activity, there remained the leader's own riding in Calgary. One of us had to be in Calgary to campaign full-time. Once again, Catherine volunteered to set aside her own career and campaign

that we were further behind than we should have been when I
arrived in Calgary two weeks into the campaign and understood
that unless we did something dramatic, the numbers would not
be there for Joe to win. During the summer, I had joined Joe in
urging the local organization to build on his strengths as a former foreign minister because a large part of Calgary Centre is
multicultural. I felt it was ludicrous to try to be more conservative than the sitting Alliance member. Our vote lay elsewhere than
with disenchanted Alliance supporters. Reaching beyond our base
to Liberals who wanted someone of Joe's stature to represent
them in Parliament, and to uncommitted voters, was the best way
I could see for Joe to win in Calgary. Our hope was to situate
ourselves where we belonged, in the middle of the political spectrum. This became a key part of our message at the door in those
parts of the riding where we knew the campaign could grow.

In addition to our hard work on the ground and Joe's own
standing in Calgary, three events would give us the momentum
and the numbers we needed to win the Calgary Centre riding.
The first was Joe's showing in the televised national leaders'
debates. He was brilliant in his attacks and scored a direct hit
when the Prime Minister could not name one achievement of his
seven years in office. The leaders' debates became the turning
point for us in terms of press coverage and support in Calgary
Centre. The second was the Liberals for Joe Clark Campaign, in
which well-known Liberals, led by Donn Lovett in particular,
threw their support and excellent organizational skills behind
Joe. Many of the Liberal members were women who became
real supports for me personally and key members of my door-
knocking and scheduling team. No Liberal had ever been elected
in Calgary Centre, and Joe was a person many Liberals were
willing to support as their member of Parliament. The third
milestone along our road to victory in Calgary Centre, was the
decision by members of the gay and lesbian community to support Joe. I campaigned actively with Brian Huskins, who later

ran for the provincial Liberals, to gain the support of gay and lesbian Calgarians. We would later be condemned by the Bishop of Calgary for participating in Calgary's annual Gay Pride Parade, but I think people have always known that for Joe Clark there are no second-class Canadians. It was a natural role for me to play, too, as I have been an advocate for human rights in Canada since my days in law school.

For all of these breakthrough events, Stephen Carter arranged press conferences that made national headlines and gave credibility to our claim that Joe had broad support in his chosen riding. The press and the party finally began to believe that he could win in Calgary Centre. Joe's huge risk was paying off, and he was demonstrating that Calgarians from all parties and walks of life supported him, challenging the boast by the Canadian Alliance that Joe could never win in the West. In the end, though, while our campaign team did a superb job on the ground, I believe that Joe won Calgary Centre because his constituents saw in him a man of integrity, intelligence and experience, whom they respected and wanted to have in Parliament as their elected representative.

As in all elections, the last week was frantic, and when Joe and Catherine arrived the day before the vote, we all campaigned furiously across the riding. Finally, late in the evening, after a pep rally in a local restaurant for our supporters and workers, we went home. It was the first time we had all been together for weeks and we tried to catch up on what was happening. We had few illusions that we would do as well as we wanted, but we had two goals—to maintain party status in Parliament and to win Calgary Centre. We achieved both.

Winning in Calgary Centre answered once and for all the question of whether the PC Party could ever win in the West again. It showed the importance of organization and it proved Joe's popularity as a leader among the people of his home province. But in barely maintaining party status in the House of

Commons, the party had failed in its bid to become the official opposition. Of course, the leader accepted public responsibility, but there needed to be a lot of accounting at all levels of the organization for why the party was not ready for the election. No leader will be able to deliver a future victory for our party unless essential party rebuilding takes place. It is in the ridings that elections are won. Had we had that kind of infrastructure in 1997 under Jean Charest, or in the 2000 national campaign under Joe, we would have seen very different results. When Joe aced the leaders' debates in 2000, there was no way he could translate that success at the local level into electing members. When you put half your candidates in the field on the eve of the election call, without financial or organizational support, nothing short of a miracle will elect a national government. That fact is as real today as it was the day after the 2000 election campaign.

24

IN JULY 2001, CHAD ASKED CATHERINE to marry him and she accepted. It is hard to describe how you feel when your only child tells you that she is planning to marry. In our case, we had been a threesome for so long that it was hard to think how we would fit Chad into the family. No doubt his mother felt the same way about Catherine. For days after she told us, I went through moments of real happiness that my only child had found her life mate at such a young age, followed by teary moments of deep sadness that somehow I was losing my only daughter. I thought she was so young to be making such a huge decision, only to realize that by the time I was twenty-five, I was a mother, a lawyer and the wife of the leader of the Opposition. Seeing my child prepare to marry reminded me that I was old enough to have a child who was old enough to marry. That was a severe blow. Joe is thirteen years older than I am, and for a long time when we had attended the weddings of his friends' children, I was always somewhere in age between the children and their parents. Now I was to be the mother of the bride.

As veterans of the process will tell you, planning a wedding requires many subtle exercises in diplomacy. We all knew that because of our public life we had two options. We could have three hundred or three thousand guests, but not really any number in between. Our bank account suggested three hundred, and we stuck with that number in spite of hurt feelings and requests to include people who felt that we owed it to them after all their efforts on Joe's behalf. We narrowed the list to our immediate families and to friends who had made a difference to Catherine's and Chad's lives. After all, I reasoned, it was their wedding.

Catherine had graduated in art history from the University of Toronto, and she wanted her wedding reception at the National Gallery in Ottawa. We decided on an evening wedding ceremony at Notre Dame Basilica (my parish in Ottawa) with the guests walking across Sussex Drive to the National Gallery for a reception, dinner and dancing. It was particularly poignant to have the Parliament Buildings as a visual backdrop for the dinner in the Great Hall of the National Gallery.

Any woman who has planned a wedding knows the hours and patience required to handle all the intricate details. I thought ironically that I was lucky to not be losing any sleep over it all as I had reached that stage of my life where sleeping through the night was a distant dream. That is one of the benefits of menopause for a mother of the bride. As I sat up reading or worrying in the middle of the night in the months before the wedding, I often reflected on the unfairness of a woman's life as it relates to sleep. When I read a recent news article about freezing our ova as teenagers so we can have children when it suits us later in life, I wondered why the medical profession was not focusing its research attention instead on changing our biological clocks to suit our current lives better. For instance, why can't a woman go through some of the menopausal symptoms earlier in her life? I was never more tired than during the first year after Catherine's birth. What if I was already awake waiting to soothe or feed her? One night during that first year at Stornoway, as I was sleepwalking from our bedroom to hers, I ran into a solid door frame. I never woke up, but the next morning, I had a black eye and a broken toe! During the same winter, Catherine and I often sat huddled under blankets in Stornoway's family room—one of the coldest spots on the planet. Imagine how a hot flash would have improved my life.

A daughter's wedding day is one of tumultuous emotions and lasting memories. Catherine was a beautiful bride. All that day, we had a steady stream of people in and out of the house; and while I am an organized person usually, I felt as if I was running behind the whole day. The best part of the afternoon was when the bridesmaids opened champagne as they waited in line to have their hair and makeup done downstairs. The afternoon flew by, and in a panic I finally had to call my own hairdresser, Pauline Clarkson, to rush over after work to do my hair. As we went out the door I dabbed on some lipstick and pulled on the beautiful royal blue dress I had made by Ottawa designer Richard Robinson. Rather than leave it to chance, I had bought Joe a couple of ties for his tuxedo the week before; I had heard too many stories of races to menswear stores at the eleventh hour. I tried not to look at him as we left, for fear I would burst into tears of joy for our only child—our little Muffin. Catherine glided down the stairs of our home with her four lovely attendants in tow, and as she opened the door, the sun broke from behind the clouds and shone on her path to the car. It was a magic moment in an already wonderful day. Some say that even the homeliest woman is radiant on her wedding day, and there is no doubt that most brides look very special. But Catherine seemed to glow with happiness as she and Joe walked down the aisle towards Chad, and I knew then that this had been the right choice for her. She was in love and confident in her decision. From then on, I just relaxed and enjoyed every minute celebrating with our families and close friends.

———

The year 2002 turned out to be another one of change for us. When we had started the year I did not think too much could happen beyond the wedding. I was wrong. First, I celebrated my fiftieth birthday in February. That event forced me to think about both my future and my past. Along the way I had let myself be talked by my literary agent into writing this book, and my publication commitments would require time to write throughout the year. In February, I decided that we should change condos in Calgary, and in the spring I put our Ottawa house on the market. Joe and I had discussed doing this after Catherine married but it was a difficult thing to do. We downsized and bought a new townhouse in the community of New Edinburgh nearby. In early April, I acted again as a spokesperson for the Osteoporosis Society of Canada and signed a "Call to Action on Osteoporosis" on their behalf in Lisbon, Portugal, with ten other women from around the world, led by Queen Rania of Jordan. In that international effort, we urged governments to address this serious debilitating bone disease that affects one in three women and one in eight men over the age of fifty every year.

During the weeks after Catherine's wedding, we went away for a holiday in Hilton Head, South Carolina, and while there, Joe pondered his own future, and decided to step down as party leader. This was a most difficult decision for him, as it required accepting that he would not lead the country again. The recognition of this fact was made more poignant by the knowledge that age would deny him the chance to ever try again. It was a decision that took a great deal of courage, but he wanted to make it soon enough to allow for a generational change in leadership long before the next election.

As I looked forward to the years that lay ahead, I decided that I wanted to take time away to study and start doctoral research, and accepted a position as a visiting research fellow in law at the University of Sheffield in England. While there I would complete a second master's degree, at the Sheffield Institute of Biotechnology, Law and Ethics, writing my thesis on gene patenting. The issues raised by biotechnology are vast and complex. For instance, will we allow stem cell research or human embryo cloning in our search for cures to disease? Will tissue engineering and the creation of whole organs in the lab, using our own cells to avoid rejection, actually solve the current organ transplant crisis? Will our children choose, change or enhance our grandchildren's genetic traits before birth with the ease of making a purchase at a grocery store? In a world where everything can be bought, bartered and sold, can we protect the human body from becoming no more than another commodity? I knew early in 2002 that no matter what course Joe chose for his future, I wanted to put my own years of research and experience to work addressing these issues. This change in academic focus and country would give me an entire year of privacy and anonymity to complete my degree, and also to reflect on my past and on my future plans.

—

Like everyone, I have a personal life—who I am, what I feel, what I think—and a public life—what I do and how I am seen. What I do in my public life has been largely in two realms: first, politics and, increasingly, the intersection of law and science. In both realms, I have wanted absolutes—justice, truth, "the answer"—and I have learned how hard it is to be certain, and how often we have to settle for the better rather than the best. That lesson has sometimes been painful but, more important, it has also been exciting. I have seen things change. I have made things change.

What fascinates me about my work in law and science is how dynamic it is. There are no absolutes. Every day, science discovers new things, and the law has to integrate the new into the known to keep the community orderly and whole. These scientific changes are happening every day in the laboratories, but their integration into the culture occurs a lot more slowly, and usually with the help of the courts. Ironically, some of the more traditional voices in politics argue that the courts are too activist in responding to the undeniable changes that science makes possible, and they insist that the courts should wait for the legislatures. Well, that would be a long wait. Because the problem is not activist courts.

The real problem is that the legislatures and the ponderous machinery of government are not activist enough. Bureaucracies are built to deal with the expected—they are slow to respond to change, often afraid of surprises and always determined to protect their own authority. Legislatures and parliaments usually contain some courageous and outspoken individuals but, as institutions, they are more often captives of conventional wisdom. Ironically, that may be even more true in a populist era such as our own, when petitions from aroused constituents, polls and focus groups are more compelling to politicians than hard evidence from experts. The field of law, genetics and reproductive technology, in which I have been immersed, dramatizes the difficulty. It is now fourteen years since the Mulroney government named a Royal Commission on New Reproductive Technologies. As I write today, no law has yet been passed to regulate these revolutionary technologies and practices—despite the cloning of sheep, the potential cloning of humans, other transforming advances in genetic research and the patenting of human life forms.

What is so disquieting about contemporary politics is how static it is, how reluctant to change, how slow to respond to new realities. That is the real reason why young people are not voting and older citizens grow more cynical about politics and more detached from the essential processes of democracy. Politics is simply not relevant to the ordinary lives of most people, or the fascinating challenges of our times. Yet society can't function without organized leadership, which, in a democracy, means politics. So politics must be made relevant again.

—

Political and parliamentary systems can be likened to our houses. They often need repair, but there comes a time when changing the rugs and the wallpaper is no longer enough, and we have to concede we need an entirely new house. That's where we are now with our systems of government—we have to move beyond renovating and remodelling how we are governed, and make the house of politics new again, in style, in substance and in relevance. There are plenty of structural ideas about how that might be done, from proportional representation in the electoral system, to minimum quotas for women in party candidacies, to restoring Parliament's ability to shape government priorities by controlling how money is spent, to reforming the Senate. But more than structures have to be changed. What is at issue is nothing less than the purpose and relevance of our political institutions. Other elements of our society—science, business, the courts, local governments, social agencies, individuals living their lives—know they can't hide from the changes transforming our world. National political institutions, including government bureaucracies and national parties, are dragging behind. That is what we have to change. The purpose must be a new house, which will both welcome the people who have been kept outside and let their ideas and experience connect public policy to real life.

I cannot speak with confidence of our young people, except to say that I have witnessed their passionate commitment to social and environmental and community causes and the high standards they set in their personal lives—which leads me to believe that they are a generation eager to be engaged.

I can speak with more assurance of women. It is common knowledge that politics is a blood sport. It can destroy men as easily as it gobbles up women. But since the 1970s, when women started to enter politics in Canada in increased numbers, the popular wisdom has been that our feminine (or at least our female) nature would alter how politics is played. That has not happened—at least, not in Canada. The Scandinavians, and some other societies, have changed both rules and, what is more difficult, attitudes to make their political systems and legislatures more welcoming to women. In Canada, one of the main reasons women still avoid politics, after years of being encouraged to run for office, is that they are convinced that politics is a hostile game of little real relevance to them. So we all lose. Women can bring a different perspective to politics and the running of governments, because many of our life experiences are so different from those of men. Look at most women's lives today. Look at what's on our plates, and how much juggling we have to do just to make it through another day. I'm not talking about time management, but about the inescapable pressures and priorities of most women's lives, in a society that still distributes domestic responsibilities unequally. I know that women can be as selfish as men—but few of us can be as selective about the pressures we respond to or ignore. When we leave our paying job each day, the realities that await us at home create another immediate set of responsibilities. Children do that to you, as do ageing parents. As does a broken stove, or a leaky roof, or being out of milk. Women's lives revolve around real people who don't stop needing, and practical details that can't be put on hold.

Through Canada's first century well into our second, men set the agenda for public policy. Their focus has been too narrowly on economic issues, with social needs treated as a poor cousin. What would happen if we made social equity a priority equal to economic growth in setting Canada's national agenda? What would happen if all new laws and policies were judged first for their impact on the practical responsibilities that most women can't escape? One result would be that we would be forced to accept and witness how social priorities—child care, for example, or elder and hospice care—fit into the scheme of our lives. Another would be that we would have to check some of our assumptions about who carries the burden as governments cut back services that were previously public. Specifically, there is an assumption that women—traditionally, the "caregivers" in society—will take up the slack in our public health and social care delivery systems. Yet if—as I profoundly believe—there are fundamental differences between the life experience and thus the perspective of women and men, having a significantly larger number of women in politics would change those public priorities. In turn, of course, changing those priorities would draw larger numbers of women into political life. But women can't wait. If there is one thing I have learned about the political system, it is that you have to push it. And for women, that means being as pushy now as we were three decades ago when some of us refused to change our names.

During the two decades that followed the introduction of the Canadian Charter of Rights and Freedoms in 1982, the impact of women's voices on the national agenda has diminished and become diffuse. Just staying afloat has become a real challenge for the advocacy and support groups that remain. Where parliamentarians once felt obliged to meet annually with such groups as the National Action Committee, they now ignore them. Worse, for most women, these groups now seem more exotic, less relevant. The vibrant networks of women who have achieved real change have morphed into interest groups, and with that change many of us have slipped away to personal lives and other causes.

My generation of women was very lucky. We had access to education and, gradually, to influence. We were the generation that achieved legal equality for women. We defended legal cases because we believed that equity and equality went hand in hand. Property law in Canada changed because women came together to fight for that reform, and because politicians heard our voices, and saw that it was the right and fair thing to do. We were able to move law and society along to a place that

cream, gel or miracle drug is going to straighten or firm them out ever again.

All of us want to look better, and most women diet, exercise and explore new forms of nutrition and medication. Yet there is a more compelling reason for women to pursue a youthful appearance than vanity or good health. In 2000, almost a quarter of all Canadian women were over the age of fifty-five. Many will outlive their spouse or partner and need to fend for themselves. Ageism is alive and well in our society, and so for many women, our careers and economic independence will be affected by how young we look.

Other issues face women of my generation as we plan for the future. Will we have a private pension and will there be enough money left in public pension funds for all of us? What about our traditional role as caregivers? Some of my friends are already caring for family at both ends of the age spectrum. There is an assumption creeping into our social systems, ravaged by years of cost-cutting by successive governments, that women will take up the slack for home and hospice care in our communities. This attitude extends to child care too, and before we feel too sorry for ourselves, let's remember our daughters and sons who are now starting their families. When Catherine was little, the big issue of my generation was access to quality child care. Twenty-five years later, my child is married and a key issue facing her generation remains child care. What is wrong with this picture? These are tomorrow's priorities for all women, no matter what our current role—mother, spouse or daughter. As we enter this second half of our lives, we are at the height of our power and wisdom, but as we age we become both stronger and more vulnerable. We must still fight to have our priorities heard and addressed by governments so that we may count on a social infrastructure that recognizes the complexity of our lives and human relationships. Catherine's generation is beginning to make its mark on our society in science, the arts, medicine, law, education and journalism, for instance. Society needs their brains and talent to find cures to deadly diseases and to create great artistic masterpieces. We cannot afford to limit or lose their contributions because we offer them little or no support for their many roles as professionals, spouses and mothers. Women of my generation can help. We can be mentors to this new generation—the mothers of the workplace and not just the home; our skills, wisdom and insight can help rebuild a sense of corporate ethics and community that has been devastated by the ugly greed of the past decade. Women of my generation are the glue that binds our nation together; we bridge the generations that have come before and after us, and offer new ideas and approaches to develop co-operation and compassion. To quote from Wallace Stegner's *Wolf Willow*: "History is a pontoon bridge and we are on the building end of it."

When I married in 1973, the first phase of the modern women's movement was gathering force, and for the first time in history, merit mattered more than gender. This was a heady time full of energy, commitment, idealism and hope. Sometimes when Catherine's girlfriends ask me incredulously about the opposition I faced to keeping my own name, I try to explain the depth of the changes that were beginning "way back then" before any of them were even born—and how I represented the unwanted wave of change to many people. My life, and the lives of their own mothers in their early years of middle age, are often too alien for their beautiful and brilliant young minds to absorb, and they prefer to pretend that their lives will never be like ours. The ideal of equality is under siege again, and yet many of our daughters pretend that we are all equal now and that the fight for fair and equal treatment for women has been won. Their mothers and I pray they are right, for we know the price we paid for that ideal and want our daughters to be free of our struggles.

During the past three decades I often hid my frustrations and fears about gender discrimination from Catherine, while working for the better world I wanted to leave her. It was as if I wanted her to absorb by osmosis the many lessons I had learned, and I felt it was a small price to pay to free her from the boundaries and barriers of our sex. Ironically, we want our daughters and granddaughters to know our stories and yet to be free of our struggles. Yet as I age, I see that I cannot ever fully protect Catherine from the vicissitudes of life. Instead, in the years ahead I must be there to help, to share my own wisdom and to give a meaningful context to her life. That is what my mother offered me, and that is ultimately the link that binds us as women across the generations.

Over the years I have enjoyed many opportunities and I have fought for many causes—some popular and some less so—and yet it has taken all these years for people to accept that "the name thing" was not an aberration or a whim but a choice based on my principles and values. As I age I feel free to shed this baggage and to shatter the image that has defined me as a person always out of step with the status quo and courting controversy. At last I feel I can be judged by what I have done in life, and not just by my name. I sometimes wonder what has happened to allow for this change. Maybe this newfound understanding of my choices is simple respect that I not only survived but thrived in a way of life that has torn so many to shreds emotionally and physically. Or it may merely be due to a collective sense of guilt that women of my generation were ever criticized for making such decisions about their own lives.

Time has made my actions and choices acceptable to many. I no longer worry about criticism that I am a dilettante riding on my famous husband's coattails. From where I sit today, I can say that the life I have lived has been worth the pain and the price.

EPILOGUE

JANUARY 6, 2002—EPIPHANY FOR SOME OF US—dawned grey and menacing, a blustery and stormy day in Naples, Florida, where Joe and I were vacationing over the Christmas break with Catherine and Chad. Undaunted by the weather, I had gone for a long walk alone on the beach, which was being pummelled by huge waves that kept others away. As I pushed against the wind, head down, I saw a small compass in the sand and, stooping, I picked it out of its muddy grave and clutched it in my hand. The wind was too strong for me to stop and look at it carefully, but somehow I saw my find as a sign. I had found a compass that had been through a storm that had damaged, if not destroyed, the boat it had guided. It was full of sand, and would never again tell anyone which way was safe to travel. Little shells were wedged so tightly into its crevices that they had become part of its casing. It had weathered gentle breezes and gales so bad that it had been tossed into the sea, washed ashore by the sheer power of the waves that had ended its shift as a sea guide.

This little compass has been beside me on my desk as I have written most of this book. Sometimes I have just sat and held it, staring at its still black needle that points north to 130 degrees. Every time I lift it, fine white sand sifts onto my hand. The compass is as dry now as it is still, yet something about it comforts me. I see it as a talisman, a compass that points one way only—to the future—but with neither comment nor command. I look at it and see a tool made to give direction, but one that can no longer do so. Yet that silence cannot mask its story of past voyages—quite the opposite. In its mute presence, this compass offers me the luxury of deciding where to go, and in that decision, to go anywhere I want without fear that I may be making a mistake in my choice. It reminds me that I have an inner compass too. In its forced silence, it requires me to use my strength and wisdom to find my own way to the future. I know now that I must accept something that I ignored for far too long—that I can really rely only on myself, on my own instincts, my own judgment and my own sense of direction.

Writing this book has been a real challenge for me. I am an intensely private person and do not normally share stories that matter with anyone but my closest friends and family. In these pages, I have moved beyond that private nature to reflect on what mattered during the first half of my very public life. In doing so, I am indulging myself as much as my publishers. Every book I have written has allowed me to move ahead, to close a door on one stage of my life so that I can be free to move on to another. With this book, I was forced to peel back layer after layer to discover what memories and stories lay beneath the surface. That process often revealed sad and bitter memories. But I also found moments of pure joy. Each time I started to write a story I thought I could not share, I experienced the sensation of pain that comes from a fresh wound just beneath the skin. But as I wrote about it, dissected it and laid it bare on the computer screen in front of me, I could feel the pain subsiding and the wound healing. For all of my adult life I have carried the guilt of being absent from my father's deathbed. As I wrote that passage, crying bitter tears in the sheer despair that comes with an emotion of such intensity, I suddenly felt the guilt ebbing away, as if my father had put his hand on my shoulder and said, "Enough."

It is true, as a great philosopher said, that an unexamined life is not worth living. But it takes a supreme act of will to look closely at one's own warts and wrinkles. I have spent almost two years reflecting on many of the moments and events of my fifty years on earth. And one of those years was among the most significant of my life. Catherine married, we moved twice, Joe stepped down as party leader and I took a sabbatical to study and lecture in England. Throughout my months of writing, I have tried to capture among the memories and experiences the larger definition of who I am, and what my purpose is here on earth. I am still looking, of course, but I can do so now from a fresh perspective. The past still matters to me, but as a guide to my future rather than as a burden. I can now store it away as I do my winter clothes with the first true sign of spring. My past has become a backdrop, a term of reference, a starting point for the next phase of my life. Writing these parts of my story has cleared my thoughts and allowed me to tidy up the kitchen of my life so I can move on to something new, demanding and worthwhile. Dreaming of all the adventures that lie ahead has re-energized me and forced me out of the comfort of my favourite chair by the fireplace. Complacency and self-satisfaction are not options for me in this next half of my life. They never were, and they never will be. I see now that I must keep moving forward, living my life fully.

I am proud that I am strong enough to praise what is positive and good, and to condemn what should not be tolerated. That is who I am. Life is not a popularity contest, but a puzzle and a maze. Finding our way through it is as important as our destination. I am halfway through my life's maze and life is still puzzling, but full of promise and adventure. And so I move on. I need no longer feel guilty that I walk along a path that is so different from the path followed by others. Because in the end, it is the path I have been asked to follow, the path laid out for me in all its difficulty, and the one I will follow wherever it leads, living and learning all along the way. I have already walked where I had never thought I would travel, on roads I did not know even existed. I am glad of this journey—that I have survived the losses and celebrated the victories. I have known deep love and experienced the sheer joy of having a child who means more to me than life itself. When my time here is over and my own compass stilled, I want to be remembered as having been brave, of giving guidance and direction, of having left my own mark on the paths I have travelled and the people I have touched.

ACKNOWLEDGEMENTS

MANY PEOPLE STRENGTHEN the spine of a book and mine was no exception. Bruce Westwood, along with Natasha Daneman, started the process; Anne Collins, as my literary mentor at Random House, made it all happen. André Bastien and Carole Levert, who have been my friends and Quebec publishers since 1981, once again made the French text come alive, and Johanne Guay, their new president at Éditions Libre Expression, focused her team on this personal *livre de réflections*. I know how much co-ordination and elbow grease the production of a book takes, and offer Anne's and Johanne's two teams of dedicated staff my sincere thanks.

Catherine and Joe both read the text and diplomatically offered guidance—in part to ensure accuracy, in part to keep me out of the courts. In a life as complex and full as the one I have led, many characters play roles big and small. I thank each of them for the parts they have played, and look forward to the new adventures we might share in the next fifty years. Finally, any and all mistakes in this book (and in my life) are my own responsibility.

INDEX

A

Aboriginal people, and Meech Lake
    Accord, 233–34
Africa, election monitors in, 187
Alexander, Andrea, 140
Anderson, Doris, 146, 147–48
Andre, Coryn, 60, 86
Andre, Harvie, 59–60, 64
Andre, Joan, 60, 86, 143
Andre, Lauren, 86
Andrew, Bob, 61
Arlidge, Bruce, 39
art, Canadian, 81, 143–44
Art Global, 143
Asia Society, Guangdong province
    meeting, 238
Asia, women in, 182
Asselin, Ginette, 138
Asselin, Martial, 138
Athens, Greece, trip to, 98
Atkey, Ron, 98
Axworthy, Lloyd, 147
Aylmer, Quebec
    house in, 165
    move to 1984, 177

B

Baird, Patricia, as chair of
    Royal Commission, 211–16,
    218–20
Balfour, Jim, 82, 111
Band, Sarah, 140
Bangkok, Thailand, slums in, 186
Bassett, Doug, 156
Bastien, André, 142
Batt, Robert, 31
Baxter, David, 189
Baxter, Robert, 62
Baxter, Susan, and Catherine, 155,
    162, 163, 174–75, 189
Beatty, Perrin, 31, 33, 176, 244, 247,
    274
Beaudoin, Denis, 242
Beaudoin, Gérald, 204
Beers, Kurt, 287
Bégin, Monique, 148
Beijing, visit to, 167–68
Beijing World Conference on Women
    (1984), 180–81
Bélanger, Albert, 16
Bennett, Heidi, 118
Bennett, Peter, 62
Berlet, Diane, 83

Berlet, Ron, 83
"Big Blue Machine" (Ontario), 101
bilingualism, 26
    of Joe Clark, 57–58
    importance of, 9
Binks, Ken, 33
Bloc Québécois, 243, 246
    election status 1997, 266
    Official Opposition 1993, 248
Boisselle, Claude, 61
Borins, Sandy, 62–63
Boros, George, 204–5
Bouchard, Benoît, 218
Bouchard, Lucien, 243
Bouchard, Pierre, 61
Bourassa, Robert, 27, 232
Boyle, Rosemarie, 22–24
Bradley, Fred, 59
Brison, Scott, 286, 288
    wins nomination for election
        2000, 286
British Columbia, by-election 2000, 286
Brown, Jan, 262
Bryant, Beth, 63
Bryant, Vic, 63
Budapest, Hungary, and Eastern and
    Central European legal pro-
    grams, 204, 207
Buffler, Patricia, 251
Burlington, Ontario, Clark campaigns
    in, 123

C
Cairo, "Garbage City," 183
Calgary
    move from, 267–68, 298
    move to, 259–60
Calgary, Bishop of, and Gay Pride
    Parade, 293
Calgary Centre riding, 285, 290–94
    gay and lesbian community in,
        292–93

California, move to, 250–52
Calnan, Mike, 192
Cameroon, travel to, 116
Campagnolo, Iona, 175
Campbell, Kim
    election 1993, 246–49
    leadership race 1993, 242–45, 248
    loses seat in election 1993, 248
    wins leadership race, 245
Canada 125 medal, 207
Canada China Health Foundation, 252
Canada Council Art Bank, 81
Canada Funds, 178, 182–83
Canada-U.S. Free Trade Agreement
    (FTA), 194, 257
Canadian Alliance, 290
    leadership race 2000, 285
Canadian Bar Association (CBA)
    Eastern and Central European
        legal programs, 204–7, 216, 245
    Rt. Hon. Louis St. Laurent Award
        1993, 207
Canadian Humanities Institute
    Research Council, 221
Canadian International Development
    Agency (CIDA), 138
    community projects, 178
    and women's lives, 186
Canadian Perspectives Canadiennes,
    143
Caribbean, election monitors in, 187
Carleton-Gloucester riding, McTeer
    runs in 1988, 188–201
Carroll, Marjorie, 61
Carter Center, 237
Carter, Jimmy, 122, 237, 280
Carter, Stephen, 291, 293
Castonguay, Claude, 233
Catley-Carlson, Margaret, 182
Central America
    daycare centre, 184–85
    missionary nuns, 184–85

Centre of Excellence for Women's
  Health, 259, 262–63
Chaing, Theresa, 252
Chambers, Bill, 169–71, 177, 276
Chapman, Katie, 129–30
Charest, Jean, 263–65
  at Catherine's wedding, 1–2
  election 1997, 265–66
  leadership race 1993, 241–45
  and Quebec Liberal Party,
    271–74
  wins seat in election 1993,
    248–49
Charlottetown Accord, 236, 272
Charter of Rights and Freedoms, 144,
  146, 150
Chatelaine magazine
  "Report from Ottawa," 141
  Woman of the Year, 141
Chemla, Claudette, 58, 65
Chengdu, visit to, 167–69
China
  opportunities in, 170
  relations with, 238
  trip to, 167–74
Chrétien government, shelves Royal
  Commission report on reproductive technologies, 211
Chrétien, Jean, 153, 264, 289
Christian Heritage Party, election
  1988, 193–94
Clark, Andrew, 197
Clark, Brendan, 291
Clark, Catherine, 109, 112
  after convention 1983, 160–61
  and Amélie Charest, 245
  by-election 2000, 287–89
  in California, 250–51
  early years, 83–89, 117–18
  education of, 165, 260, 267–68
  election campaign 1979, 107
  election campaign 1980, 129–30

election campaign 1988, 189,
  190–91, 200
  abortion issue, 195–7
  and the media, 291
  at Stornoway, 87–89
  travels with her parents, 186,
    276–77
  water incident in Hawaii, 133–36
  wedding of, 1–3, 295–97
Clark, Charles, 43, 268
Clark, Grace, 43, 152, 267
  death of, 268–69
Clark, Joe, 245, 288–89
  budget of, 122
  campaign financing, 63–64
  consulting practice, 259, 267–68
  early political life, 36–37
  and election 1993, 247
  English Debating Society judge, 38
  leaders' debate 2000, 292
  leadership race 1998, 273–80
  leadership review 1983, 152–54
  and McTeer, 34–36
    marriage to, 39–45
  media coverage, 64–67, 74–75
  move to constitutional affairs,
    232–33
  "name issue," 75–78
  PC Youth President, 36
  and political appointments, 137
  re-election of in Yellowhead, 162
  relationship with daughter, 85
  resignation of as leader, 154, 298
  retirement of from politics, 237
  return to politics 1998–2000,
    282–85, 289
  and the Royal Commission, 217–18
  secretary of state for external
    affairs, 162, 176–77
  spirit of the West in, 284
  swearing-in as Prime Minister,
    111–13

wins by-election 2000, 286–88
wins election 1972, 37
wins leadership 1976, 73–74
wins leadership 1998, 279
wins re-election 1984, 176
Clark, Lee, 61
Clark, Marcia, 70
Clark, Peter, 36, 70, 251, 267–68,
    291
    campaign 1984, 174–75
Clark, Sunny, 291
Clarkson, Pauline, 297
Clinton, Bill, health care, 256
Clinton, Hillary Rodham, 188
    health care, 256
Coates, Bob, 176
Cogger, Michel, 73
Committee of Accreditation of
    Canadian Medical Schools, 270
Commonwealth Conference, Zambia,
    116, 138
Communist Party, 203
Connell, Bruce, 79–80
Constitution
    amending formula, 144–45
    "notwithstanding" clause, 146
    patriation of, 144–51
    and Quebec, 272
Cook, Gay, 86
Cook, Pauline, 96–97
Coolican, Murray, 33
Cooper, George, 61, 82
Cooper, Tia, 82
co-operatives, funding from for
    women, 182
Créditistes, 121, 125
    election status 1980, 131
Crosbie, John, 155–57, 176
Cross, James, 26, 29
Cullen, Mary Jane, 262
Cultural Revolution
    local translators and the, 172

one woman's story of, 170–71
Cumberland, Ontario, family home
    in, 8, 59

D
Dalhousie University, 61
    Health Law Institute, 215, 216
    master's in law, 240
Daubney, David, 199
Daubney, Jennifer, 199
Davis, Bill, 128
    wins Ontario leadership, 30
Day, Stockwell
    by-election 2000, 286, 288
    wins leadership race 2000, 285
de Cotret, Robert René, 156, 176
Desjardins, Adèle, 124, 151
Detroit Red Wings, 6
Diefenbaker, John, 9, 36, 66
Diefenbaker, Olive, 48–49
Dionne, Michèle, 244
Dobbie, Dorothy, 233
Dominican Republic, election moni-
    tors in, 237
Donahoe, Art, 61
Dorrin, Murray, 62
Douglas, Tommy, 28
Dowling, Bob, 61, 109, 159–60
Dowling, Olga, 61, 159–60
Doyle, Donald, 84, 103, 133, 159,
    198
Doyle, Marthe-Andrée, 133
Doyon, Michel, 143
Drapeau, Jean, 27
Drucker, Barbara, 61, 63–64
    birthday party for McTeer, 140
Dubeau, Madame, 10

E
Eagleson, Al, 162
Eagleson, Nancy, 140, 162
Eastern Bloc, tour of, 203

Eastern Hockey League, 6
Easton, Bruck, 60
Ede, Michael, 62
Les Éditions Libre Expression, 142
Edson, Alberta, 109
Eichler, Margrit, 208, 211
election 1972
    Clark wins seat, 37
    Stanfield fails to win, 32–34
election 1974, 55–56
    campaign, 55
    issues
        wage and price controls,
            54–55, 175
    re-election of Clark, 55
election 1979, 109–11
    campaign team, 101
    issues
        Freedom of Information Bill,
            121
        mortgage interest deductibility,
            121
        national energy policy, 121
    parallel campaign of McTeer,
        101–2
    results, 110
    Trudeau calls, 99–100
election 1980
    campaign, 124, 126–30
    issues
        eighteen-cent gas tax, 122,
            127, 175
    results, 130–31
election 1984
    call, 174
    campaign, 174–75
election 1988
    Catherine and, 189, 190–91
    fundraising, 191
    issues
        abortion, 194–97
        free trade, 189, 193–94, 200

GST, 194
    public service cutbacks, 189
    McTeer runs in Carleton-
        Gloucester, 188–201
    nomination meeting Carleton-
        Gloucester, 192
    re-election of Clark in Yellowhead,
        199–200
election 1993, 246–49
    in Ontario, 243, 246
election 1997, 265–66
    results, 266
election 2000, 290–94
election monitors
    Africa, 187
    Caribbean, 187
    Dominican Republic, 237
    Ghana, 237
    Ivory Coast, 237
    Mexico, 237
Elizabeth II, 150–51
Elizabeth, the Queen Mother, Halifax
    visit, 114–15
England, holiday in, 162
English Debating Society, McTeer
    president 1973, 38
Epp, Jake, 154, 176
Ernst & Young accounting, 259
Erola, Judy, 148
Europe, tour of, 82–83
euthanasia, issue of, 228, 230
Everest, Mary Ann, 61, 159–60
Everest, Roy, 61, 109, 159–60

F
feminism
    divorce and property laws, 53
    McTeer's early brush with, 13–15
    See also women
Fenerty Robertson law firm, 58
Ferrabee, Jim, 66–67
Fitzgibbons, Jacqueline Viau, 95

Flagler, Elizabeth, 262
Florida, holiday in, 309
FLQ. *See* Front de libération du
    Québec (FLQ)
foreign affairs
    and McTeer's foreign travel, 179
    role of Canadians in, 179–80
Foster, Jim, 59, 63
Fraser, John, 71, 73, 82, 176
Fraser, Murray, 259
Free Trade Agreement. *See* Canada-
    U.S. Free Trade Agreement
    (FTA)
French Canada
    influence of on McTeer, 11–12
    and relationship with English
        Canada, 26
French-language school, in Royon,
    France, 58
Front de libération du Québec (FLQ),
    26, 27
Frum, Barbara, 75
Fry, Hedy, 253, 255
FTA. *See* Canada-U.S. Free Trade
    Agreement (FTA)
The Fulcrum newspaper, 24
Fulton, Davie, 36

G
G7 summit, Tokyo, 113
Gammon, Mary Alice Beyer, 94
The Gateway newspaper, 60
Gauthier, Paule, 204
gay and lesbian community, Calgary
    Centre riding, 292–93
Gay Pride Parade (Calgary), 293
Gerstein, Gail, 98, 288–89
Gerstein, Irving, 98, 288–90
Ghana, election monitors in, 237
Gillies, Jim, 71
Gilmore, Mary Carol, 22
Gorbachev, Mikhail, 203

Gordon, Joyce, 270
Gordon, Pearl, 117–19
Grafftey, Heward, 71
Grand, Kathy, 262
Gray, Rob, 266
Great Wall of China, 171
Green, Ian, 24–25, 30–31, 98, 100
Greenwood, Hamilton, 62
Guangzhou
    mother and child health confer-
        ence, 253–54
    visit to, 167, 171–73
Guindon, Father Roger, 25

H
Hale, Grete, 86
Halifax, 236
    Meech Lake Accord meeting in,
        234–35
Hancock, David, 62
Harder, Peter, 159
Harper, Elijah, 235
Harrington Lake, 112–14
    book project, 141
    renovations, 115
Harris, Mike, 267
    and Manning, 274–75
Hart, Jim, 286
Harvie, André, defection of to Liberal
    Party, 287
Hatfield, Bruce, 215, 217–22
Hawaii, holiday in, 132–36, 223
Hawkes, Jim, leadership race 1976,
    59–60, 64
Hawkes, Joanne, 60
Hawkesbury, Ontario, McTeer speech
    in, 16
Hayden, Lee, 140
Hayden, Peter, 61
health care
    commercialization, 258
    U.S. and Canadian models, 256–58

Hébert, Martin, 212, 215–22
Hedlin, Ralph, 59
Hees, George, 176
Hehner, Barbara, 165
Hellyer, Paul, 71
Henry, Cory, 118
Herron, Bill, 61
Herron, Carol, 61
Higginbotham, John, 239–40
Higginbotham, Michèle, 239–40
High River Times newspaper, 36
Hill and Knowlton, 291
Hnatyshyn, Ray, 176, 253
Hockey Night in Canada, 13, 65
Hoffman, Abby, 15
Hoffman Cup, 15
Holland, Peter, 129–30
Hong Kong
    surgery in, 238–39
    visit to, 167, 173–74
Horner, Jack, 34, 73
Houlden, Gordon, 167
House of Commons
    Pipeline Debate, 36
    return of Clark to 1998, 289
Hubbard, Dean, 80
Hudon, Jean-Guy, 290
Hughes, Ken, 62
Human Genome Project, 258
Humphreys, Cecilia, 60
    and 24 Sussex Drive, 112, 115
    and Harrington Lake, 115
    New Edinburgh house, 164
    and Stornoway, 80–81, 115, 132,
    139
Humphreys, David, 60
Hungary, 203–4
    Cross of Merit to McTeer, 207
Huskins, Brian, 292–93
Hussein, King (of Jordan), 99

I
illness
    end-of-life control, 228
    living wills, 228–29
India, official trip to, 238
Inniskillin Wines, 116
Israel, trip to, 98–99
Ivory Coast, election monitors in, 237

J
Jamieson, Carol, 61, 65, 67, 74, 279
Jasper Park Lodge, 109
Jasper, PC base in Western Canada,
    111
Jenkins, David, 63, 111
Jenkins, Dreena, 143
Jennett, Penny, 262
Jennings, John, 204
Jewett, Pauline, 146, 148
John Paul II
    papal audience, 82–83, 202
    visit to Ottawa, 186–87
John XXIII, 25
Johnson, Daniel, 265
    resignation of as Quebec Liberal
    leader, 271
Johnston, Dale, 86
Johnston, Howard, 86
Johnstone, George, 21
Jordan, trip to, 98–99
Jutras, Sister Pauline, 19, 22–24

K
Kane, Phyllis, 262
Kashtin rock group, 235
Keddy, Gerald, 288
Kelly, Fran, 193
Kenya, travel to, 116
King, Bill, 291
King, David, 59
King, Mary Claire, 258
Kings-Hants riding, 286–88

KISS system, of political campaigning, 55

Knoppers, Bartha Maria, 220

Kronis, Jules, 60

L

Laakonen, Allan, 61

Laing, Bob, 35, 103

Lalonde, Suzanne, 13

Laporte, Pierre, 26–27, 29

Laschinger, John, 290

Laskin, John, 220

Latimer case, 230

Lau, Shelley, 239

Lawrence, A.B.R. (Bert), leadership race, 29, 31

LeBreton, Marjorie, 35, 213

Lefebvre, Laura, 117–18, 159, 161

Léger, Cardinal Paul-Émile, 116

Lennon, John, "Imagine," 235

Levert, Carole, 142

Lévesque, René, 26, 27

Liberal Party
    election 1988, 193
    election status 1979, 110
    election status 1980, 131
    election status 1997, 266

Liberals for Joe Clark Campaign, 292

Libre Expression, 143

Lindbergh, Anne Morrow, 135

living wills, 228–29, 231

Lloyd, Robert, 63

Lovett, Donn, 292

Lyford Cay, Bahamas, 152

Lynch, Charles, and PC Wives Association, 48

Lynch, Karen, 62

Lyon, Art, 101, 276

Lyons, Jeff, 60, 63, 98

Lyons, Sandy, 98, 140

M

McAleer, Bill, 101, 103

MacAngus, Roseline, 238, 268

McCord, Scott, 192

McCutcheon, Susan, 220

MacDonald, Flora, 63, 72–73, 122–23, 146, 148
    loses election 1988, 198
    re-election of 1984, 176

McDougall, Anne, 193, 239

McDougall, Barbara, 244, 248

McDougall, Elizabeth, 239

McGillis, Kelly, 193

MacKay, Elmer, 176

MacKay, Peter, 286

Mackenzie, Donald, 63

McKinnon, Allan, 49, 59, 63

McKinnon, Elizabeth, 49, 63

McKinnon, Ian, 63

Maclean, Marilyn, 61

McNamara, David, 250–51, 260

McNamara, Kay, 250–51, 260

McTeer, Bea (mother), 109, 112, 129–30, 159
    at Catherine's wedding, 2
    children and marriage, 7–8
    conversion to Roman Catholicism, 6–7
    and election 1988, 199
    ice storms of 1998, 271
    illness of, 224–28
    support of, 84

McTeer, Colleen (sister), 7, 159
    debating tournaments, 19–20
    education, 10–11, 13, 16–20
    election campaign 1988, 199
    on Maureen's marriage to Joe, 41–42
    provincial youth vice-president, 16

McTeer Cup, 15

McTeer family, living wills, 228

McTeer, Jane (sister), 7, 10, 129–30, 159

at Catherine's wedding, 2
election campaign 1979, 105, 107,
    109, 112
election campaign 1988, 193,
    199–200
godmother of Catherine, 87
mother's illness, 225, 227
water incident in Hawaii, 133–36
McTeer, John (brother), 7, 91
election campaign 1979, 109
election campaign 1988, 199
McTeer, John (father), 5, 70
death of, 90–93
and debating tournament, 23–24
early life, 6–7
influence of, 8–9
leadership race 1976, 59–60, 64
on Maureen's marriage to Joe,
    42–43
"name issue," 90–1
Ontario leadership convention,
    29–30
and politics, 13, 15–16
and sports, 6, 13–14
McTeer, Maureen
articling, 79, 94–95, 97–98, 116
call to the Ontario Bar, 138
and Clark, 34–36
    marriage to, 39–45
debating tournaments, 19–20,
    22–24
education, 10–13, 16–20, 24–25
    law schools, 18, 50–53, 80,
    82–85
    master's in law, 203, 215, 216,
    225–26, 240
election campaign 1972, 32
family home in Cumberland, 59
and fear of flying, 67–69, 103–4
fiftieth birthday of, 298, 305–7
foreign travel, 178–87
freedom of expression right, 28

health of, 84, 155, 296–97
    surgery in Hong Kong, 238–40
and her father, 8–9, 21, 89–93,
    104–5
honours and awards, 141, 207
Internet interview program, 287
loses election 1988, 198–99
"name issue," 50, 75–78, 105–6,
    307–8
    and the Queen Mother, 115
Ontario bar admission course,
    116–18, 125–29
PC research office, 31, 32
physical attack on, 128–29
as political spouse, 84–86, 95–96,
    107–8, 140–41, 149–50
pregnancy, 79–80, 82–83
publishing career, 141–43,
    161–62, 165, 229, 282, 298
running for Parliament, 31
wardrobe needs, 49–50
as young political wife, 46–48
See also Royal Commission on
    New Reproductive Technologies
McTeer, Pamela (sister), 7, 43, 93,
    140
mother's illness, 225, 226
McTeer, Patricia (sister), 7, 43
mother's illness, 225
Manitoba, and Meech Lake Accord,
    233–34
Manitoba nurses' association, 208
Manitoban newspaper, 60
Manning, Preston, 248
and Charlottetown Accord, 236
and Harris, 274–75
loses election 1988, 200
loses leadership race 2000, 285
move to Stornoway, 266
runs in Yellowhead 1988, 190
unite-the-right campaign, 283, 284
and the West, 284–85

Manning, Sandra, 285
Marchand, Jean, 150–51
Martin, Paul, 275
Mason, Peggy, 53, 146, 163
Mazankowski, Don, 176
Meech Lake Accord, 232–33, 272
    exclusions from, 235
    regional meetings about, 234
    rejection of, 233
Mexico, election monitors in, 237
Mickey (German shepherd), 196, 217
Middle East, trip to, 98–99
Millar, Suzette, 262
Milner, Fenerty law firm, 259
Miss CFRA contest, 22–23
Montagnais, rock group of, 235
Montreal Canadiens, 13
mother and child health conference,
    Vancouver, 253–56
Mothercraft, nurse for Catherine,
    84–85
Le Moulin des arts, 143
Mulroney, Brian, 64–66, 71–73, 155,
    157, 232
    by-election 1983, 161
    campaign 1984, 175
    Canada-U.S. health care, 256
    leaders' debate 1984, 175
    resignation of from politics, 241
    wins election 1984, 176
Mulroney government, re-election of
    1988, 200
Mulroney, Mila, 157
    campaign 1984, 175
Murdoch, Irene, and provincial prop-
    erty laws, 51–53
Murphy, Gerry, 60
Murray, Colleen, 159
Murray, Lowell, 35, 103, 159
    campaign team, 101

N
Nantucket, holiday in, 224, 285–86
A Nation Too Good to Lose (Clark),
    259
National Action Committee on the
    Status of Women (NAC), 145–46
    and Royal Commission on
    Reproductive Technologies, 221
National Association of Women and
    the Law, 51
National Democratic Institute
    (Washington, D.C.), 237
National Gallery (Ottawa), Clark-
    Schella wedding reception at, 296
NDP. *See* New Democratic Party
    (NDP)
Neville, Bill, 98, 119, 159, 198
Neville, Marilyn, 119, 159, 198–99
New Democratic Party (NDP)
    election 1988, 193
    election status 1979, 110
    election status 1980, 131
    election status 1997, 266
    support for Trudeau's minority
        government, 110, 121, 125
New Edinburgh (Ottawa)
    house in, 161, 164–65, 298
    move from, 174
New York Times, "name issue,"
    75–76
Newfoundland, and Meech Lake
    Accord, 233
NGOs
    in Asia, 187
    and women's lives, 186
NHL, 13–14
Nielsen, Erik, 176
Nixon, Richard, 32
Noor, Queen (of Jordan), 99
North Bay Trappers, 6
Northwest Territories, travel in
    national parks in, 44

Notre Dame Basilica, Clark-Schella
wedding ceremony at, 296
Notre Dame, debating tournament,
19–20
Nova Scotia
by-election 2000, 286–89
defections from PC Party, 287
Nowlan, Pat, 73
nuns
money from Canada for maternity
clinic, 183
and the religious life, 17–18

O
O'Connor, Carroll (Archie Bunker),
and John McTeer, 5
October Crisis, 28–29
Oliver, Linda, 279
Ontario PC Youth Executive, 18
OPEC (Organization of Petroleum
Exporting Countries), energy
prices, 54
Orchard, David, 280
Organization for Economic Co-
operation and Development
(OECD), chemical warfare con-
ference, 202
Orr, Bobby, 103
Orr, Wendy, 62, 86, 112, 129–30
election 1979, 101–4
Osler, Jock, 103, 159, 291
Osteoporosis Society of Canada, 262
Bone China Teas, 270
"Call to Action on Osteoporosis,"
298
O'Sullivan, Sean, 31, 33
Ottawa Journal-University of Ottawa,
debating tournament, 22–24

P
Paproski, Steve, 59, 155
Paris, France

Catherine at American University
in, 261
and discussion of Clark's leader-
ship bid, 275–76, 277
holiday in, 261–62
Paris, Mercier, Sirois, Paris and
Bélanger law firm, 95
Parker, Rob, 98
*Parliament: Canada's Democracy and
How It Works* (McTeer), 165
Parliament, role of Prime Minister,
120
Parti Québécois (PQ), 26
referendum, 138
PC Canada Fund, 154
PC Party. *See* Progressive Conservative
Party (federal)
PC Wives Association, 48
Peckford, Brian, 156
Pell, Brian, 62
Pierre, Helen, 127–28
Piggott, Jean, 149
PLAN, 186–87
Poole, Ed, 61
PQ. *See* Parti Québécois (PQ)
Prentice Hall, 141–42
Prince Edward Island, holidays in, 82
Progressive Conservative Campus
Club, University of Ottawa, 24
Progressive Conservative Party (federal),
66–67, 293
campaign team 1972, 32
Clark government's goals, 278
convention 1976, 59–60
defeat of, 123–25
Diefenbaker's leadership, 36
disarmament policy, 163
election status 1979, 110
election status1980, 130–31
election status 1984, 176
leadership race 1967, 36
leadership race 1976, 58–74

leadership race 1983, 154–57
  post-mortem, 159–60
leadership race 1993, 241–42, 248
leadership race 1998, 1–2, 273–80
leadership review 1983, 152–54
loses official party standing 1993,
  248
maintains party standing 2000,
  293–94
See also entries under election
Progressive Conservative Party
  (Ontario)
  leadership race, 29–30
  and John McTeer, 16
  and unite-the-right campaign,
    283–84
Public Inquiries Act, and Royal
  Commissions, 213–15
Puddister, Kim, 190

Q
Quebec
  conditions for signing constitu-
    tional agreement, 232
  independence, 25–26
    nationalism, 12

R
Rae, Bob, 126
Ralfe, Tim, 27, 193
Rania, Queen (of Jordan), 298
"Rape and the Canadian Legal
  Process" (McTeer), 94
rape laws (federal), 94–95
RCMP, security for Clark's family,
  111, 197
Reagan, Ronald, 169
referendum
  on Charlottetown Accord, 236
  on sovereignty 1995, 263–65
Reform Party, 243, 248, 266–67
  convention 1998, 283

election status 1997, 266
  as regional party, 274
Reid, Judy, 268
religion
  and Ontario school system, 9
  Protestant versus Catholic conflict
    and marriage, 6–7
*Residences: Homes of Canada's
  Leaders* (McTeer), 142–43
Rhinoceros Party, election 1988, 193
Rideau Canoe Club, 6
Rivard, Gaston, 61
Riyadh, Saudi Arabia, 180–81
Robarts, John, 16, 18, 29
Robinson, Richard, 297
Roblin, Duff, 59
Rock, Allan, 262
Rocky Mountain riding
  Clark re-elected election 1974, 55
  Clark wins in election 1972, 37
  travel through, 44
Rodriguez, Sue, 230
Rogers, Loretta, 152
Rogers, Ted, 152
Roman Catholic Church, 211
Rome, visit to 1988, 202
Rotary Club, Adventures in
  Citizenship program, 36
Rounding, Marie, 140
Rousseau, Albert, 143
Roy, Jacques, 10–11
Royal Commission on New
  Reproductive Technologies,
  208–23, 300
  and "family values," 211
  Federal Court of Canada and,
    220–21
  firings from, 221
  members, 210–12
  problems within, 211–17
  pro-choice versus pro-life question,
    210–11

Royon, France, French-language
    school in, 58

S
St. Jacques, Diane, defection of to
    Liberal Party, 288
St. Laurent, Louis, death of, 56
St. Patrick's College, 6
Schella, Chad
    leadership campaign 1998, 276–77
    marriage to Catherine, 1–2
    wedding of, 295–97
Schella, Charmaine, 2
Scorsone, Suzanne, 212
Segal, Hugh, 30–31, 33, 280
seniors, and end-of-life control, 229–30
Shack, Eddie, 13
Shanghai
    translator in, 172–73
    visit to, 167
Shaw's Resort, 82
Sheffield Institute of Biotechnology,
    Law and Ethics, 298
Shenzhen, visit to, 167, 173
Shevardnadze, Eduard, 203
Simpson, Bill, 193
Simpson, Rosemary, 193
Sirois, Jean-Charles, 97–98
Siversky, Alex, 191
Small, David, 193, 198
Smith, Linda, 262
Soros Foundation, 203
Soviet Union, tour of, 203
Speech from the Throne 1979, 120
Speech from the Throne 1989, Royal
    Commission on New
    Reproductive Technologies,
    209–10
Spruce Grove, Alberta, 110
Stanfield, Mary, 48, 142–43
Stanfield, Robert, 27–28, 31, 32,
    48–49, 66, 142

election 1972, 34
election 1974, 55, 57
wins leadership race, 36–37
Stegner, Wallace, 307
Stevens, Noreen, 72
Stevens, Sinclair, 71–72, 98, 176
Stone, Lucy, 75
Storch, Janet, 262
Stornoway, 48–50, 138
    book project, 141–42
    Catherine's first party at, 87–89
    entertaining at, 81–82
    move from 1979, 112
    move from 1983, 161
    move to 1979, 80–82
    move to 1980, 132, 139
    Residences launch at, 142
suicide, 231
    assisted, 228, 230
Sulatycky, Alan, loses election 1972,
    37
Sullivan, Alan, 202
Supreme Court of Canada
    on patriation of the Constitution,
    144–45
    on provincial property laws, 51
    Rodriguez case, 230

T
Taffy (Great Dane), 113
Tannis, Ralph, 60
Tanzania, travel to, 116
Tavender, David, 79
Taylor, Ken, 122
Tellier, Paul, 213, 221
Teresa, Mother, 202
Thurston, Billie, 262
Toronto Maple Leafs, 13
Toronto, Meech Lake Accord meeting
    in, 235
Toronto Star, "Joe Who?" headline,
    74

Torontow, Stella, 191
Tough Choices: Living and Dying in the 21st Century (McTeer), 229, 282
Trudeau, Margaret, 46–48, 281
Trudeau, Michel, death of, 280–81
Trudeau, Pierre, 26, 37, 46–47, 57, 75
  and Charlottetown Accord, 236
  Constitution, 150–51
  election call 1979, 99–100
  and his children, 280–81
  leaves politics, 165
  as Liberal leader, 127
  loses election 1979, 108
  and Quebec sovereignty, 138
  Stornoway staff, 80
Turnbull, Brian, 61
Turner, John, 153
  becomes Prime Minister, 174
  leaders' debate 1984, 175
  Liberal leader, 166
24 Sussex Drive
  book project, 141
  entertaining at, 119, 159
  foods at official functions, 116
  move from 1980, 132
  move to 1979, 112
  renovations, 115
Tze, Wah Jun, 252–55
  death of, 256

U
United Nations
  Clark as Cyprus representative, 238, 250
  Mason as ambassador to, 53
United States
  Canadian-American cultural differences, 256–58
  hostage crisis in Iran, 122–23, 132
  politics in, 32
unite-the-right

campaign, 283
  Reform and PC parties, 266–67, 272–73
University of Alberta, 36
University of British Columbia, reproductive law at, 270
University of Calgary, McTeer's appointment at, 259
University of California at Berkeley
  Canadian Studies department, 238
  Canadian-American cultural differences, 256–58
  School of Public Health, 238, 251–52
    conference on genetic engineering, 251–52, 257–58
  visiting scholars at, 237–8
University of Ottawa, 25–26
  Heart Institute, 256, 270
  law school, 38–39
  scholarship to, 19–20, 24
University of Sheffield, McTeer as research fellow at, 298
Uteck, Barbara, 221

V
Vancouver
  lecturing in, 270–71
  mother and child health conference, 255–56
Vandelac, Louise, 212, 215, 217–22
Vardey, Lucinda, 141
Vatican II, 25
Veale, Hal, 63
Violence in Canada (Gammon, ed.), 94

W
Waddington, Rona, 276
Wagner, Claude, 64–66, 71–73, 82
War Measures Act, 27–28
Ward, Peter, 116

Washington Eagles, 6
Wayne, Elsie, wins seat in election
    1993, 248–49
Wesleyan University, debating tourna-
    ment, 31
White, Jodi, 159, 198, 200, 246–47
White Swan Hotel, Guangzhou,
    253–54
Whitehead, Mary Beth, 209
Wilson, Eileen, 279
Wilson, Mike, 176
Wolf Willow (Stegner), 307
Wolfville, Nova Scotia, 286–89
women
    access of to professional schools,
        39
    Campbell as first Canadian female
        prime minister, 245
    and CIDA-sponsored community
        projects, 178
    in developing world, 185
    and equality, 15, 30–31, 51–53,
        106, 145–50, 303–4
        Saudi Arabia, 180–81
    exclusion of from power, 181–82
    health of, 184
    in law, 97–98
    micro-credit, 182–83
    and politics, 301–4
Women's Connection for Clark cam-
    paign 1983, 279
Wong Kar Mau (surgeon), 239
Woolstencroft, Peter, 61, 63, 70
Woolstencroft, Tim, 62, 70
Wunker, Russ, 129–30

X
Xian, visit to, 167, 169–70

Y
Yad Vashem monument, 99
Yates, Brenda, 169–70, 173–74

Yates, Terry, 154, 174
Yellowhead riding
    campaign 1984, 174–75
    Manning runs in 1988, 190
    re-election of Clark in 1984, 162
    re-election of Clark in 1988,
        199–200
Yugoslavia, ethnic tensions in, 180
Yukon, travel in national parks in, 44

Z
Zambia, Commonwealth Conference
    in, 116, 138
Ziraldo, Donald, 116